zealot

A BOOK ABOUT CULTS

JO THORNELY

hachette
AUSTRALIA

Published in Australia and New Zealand in 2019
by Hachette Australia
(an imprint of Hachette Australia Pty Limited)
Level 17, 207 Kent Street, Sydney NSW 2000
www.hachette.com.au

10 9 8 7 6 5 4 3

A catalogue record for this
book is available from the
National Library of Australia

ISBN: 978 0 7336 4050 6 (paperback)

Cover design by Grace West
Cover photographs courtesy of Alamy
Author photograph courtesy Tristan Lutze
Text design by Bookhouse, Sydney
Typeset in 12.5/18.6 pt Adobe Garamond Pro by Bookhouse, Sydney
Printed and bound in Great Britain by Clays Ltd, Elcograf S.p.A.

The paper this book is printed on is certified against the Forest Stewardship Council® Standards. McPherson's Printing Group holds FSC® chain of custody certification SA-COC-005379. FSC® promotes environmentally responsible, socially beneficial and economically viable management of the world's forests.

For all of the Messiahs past, present and future,
in the hope that you find a better hobby.

CONTENTS

INTRODUCTION

or

HEY, COME TO OUR BIBLE STUDY GROUP, THERE'S SNACKS

ARGUMENTS RAGE ABOUT what the definition of a cult is and what its essential characteristics are. The number of cults in existence pretty much depends on where your personal slider is positioned on the scale – a loose definition with few criteria would sit Catholicism square on the cult couch, whereas a tighter definition with numerous strict criteria would eliminate all but the crazy and dangerous.

There might be good cults out there. There might. Even in this book, there's a group that doesn't really do anything much worse than lie about a few things in the hope that someone in the room might get their boobs out. And there's no denying that – in their early stages at the very least – cults help people. Cults scoop up people who are looking for something, and they try to help them find it. Cults often imagine a utopia and then provide it. They show people unconditional love. For a little while. Right before they heap a whole bunch of conditions on it. Cults are exactly what people who join cults are looking for. But those people are not joining a cult; they're joining something that feels right.

For the purposes of this book, a 'cult' fulfils most or all of the following criteria:

- It has a leader whose instructions must be followed. The leader often has a vital part in the cult's story — he or she is a messenger for God, or is God, or will save the world from certain destruction.
- It has a prescribed way of life peculiar to the group, including some loss of free will, autonomy, and independent decision-making. For its members, anyway. The leader can usually do whatever the hell they like.
- It has a definite and succinct separation — physically, culturally, or philosophically — from the outside world. A sense of 'us' versus 'them', where the 'us' is on the side of righteousness, and the 'them' is a bunch of losers who are either going to die or end up in Hell, and they're almost certainly out to destroy 'us'.
- There are negative consequences — real or perceived — for those who leave the group. If you leave, you might just be told that your soul will writhe in fiery damnation for the rest of eternity, or something else benign and imaginary like that, or you might be the target of an uncomfortable hate campaign. Or, on the severe end of the scale, you might get straight-out murdered. It's a real lucky dip out there.

- It has its own beliefs that are different from those of other groups. Mind you, most cults pinch the beliefs of other religions, shake them up in a bag, tip them onto a plate and add a garnish. Across Eastern mysticism, the Christian Bible, the imminent apocalypse, aliens in UFOs and rampant, unbridled horniness, there's not a whole lot of genuine innovation when it comes to what cults believe, just a lot of rearrangement and recycling, with a cute twist. And an almost unbelievable amount of meditation and yoga.

People are drawn to cults for a number of reasons, but commonly they attract people whose current religion or lifestyle is lacking – it's too restrictive, it's not restrictive or pious enough, it doesn't seem to offer solutions for a chaotic and dangerous world, it doesn't let them have enough sex with aliens.

Whatever the drawcard, once people are in, it's usually very difficult for them to leave. Imagine someone telling you that you couldn't use your phone anymore. You'd definitely survive, and there would even be some benefits, but you'd feel lost and disconnected. Your phone is what makes you feel like you're part of society – it gives you the information you want and keeps you in touch with the people you like. If you didn't have your phone, you'd feel a lot less like a participant in the world.

If, in order to keep your phone, you were told you'd have to give up chocolate and endure a single punch in the guts once a week, you might seriously consider it. After a couple of months, you could still keep your phone, but you'd only be allowed to look at it five times a day, and there'd be a punch in the guts and a slap across the face.

Or you might say screw it, and decide to go without your phone – it's not worth this.

But then you start to miss your phone. You realise that having a phone, despite the punches, slaps, and carob, was the thing that made you feel whole. Like part of something.

You beg to have your phone back. You get it back, but now you can only check it twice a week, and it's a punch and a slap every day. Fine. You're back. It feels like home.

People undergo a lot of loopy and dangerous stuff to maintain their lifeline to their cult, which makes them feel secure, or at the very least terrified of the outside world. While there's a lot of debate among psychologists and theorists about whether or not brainwashing is a real thing, most people agree that social influence, the hive mind and straight-out coercion can have powerful effects on people in particular situations, and cults are definitely some of those situations. If you're around people who all believe the same stories, those stories are reinforced daily, and you have almost no access to any dissenting voices, then those stories become your life.

You probably think you're too intelligent to be taken in by a charismatic leader, but a lot of people who join cults are smart, educated, and switched on. They just want something more, and it's likely they're a lot like you. Normal, good people.

Cult leaders are usually bastards though.

This book looks at some of the world's most interesting and well-known cults – how they started, their beliefs, their practices, their leaders, and their downfall. There have been thousands of cults, and there's probably a cult member within walking distance of wherever you are right now. They're all different, and in some ways, they're all similar.

Cults can provide answers – at least temporarily – for people who need answers to be happy. Cults help people find their 'tribe' and give them a sense of belonging deeper than any they might have experienced before. Cults offer people the things they think they're missing, in exchange for what, at the time, doesn't feel like that much of a sacrifice.

That said, cults also do some deeply, astoundingly messed-up shit.

You probably shouldn't join one.

JIM JONES AND THE PEOPLES TEMPLE

Congressman Leo Ryan, a Democrat with a reputation for full-contact, grass-roots level interaction with his constituents, stood up to leave the Peoples Temple Agricultural Project in Guyana. It was mid-November 1978, and he'd just done one last sweep of the compound's residents to see if any of them wanted to leave with him.

Some of them did, some of them didn't. But rather than just nodding the Congressman away with a 'no thanks, bye', one of the residents who didn't want to leave the compound also didn't want Leo Ryan to leave the compound. So Peoples Temple member Don Sly tried to stab Congressman Ryan in the throat. Two of the people accompanying Ryan saw Sly lunging at him and thwarted the attack, and Ryan walked away with just a few spatters of his attacker's blood on his shirt.

Ryan realised that perhaps his welcome at the commune had worn a bit thin, so he took his old and new buddies and hoofed it for the airstrip where his plane was waiting.

Less than two hours later, Congressman Ryan lay dead on the airstrip from multiple bullet wounds, and just over 900 people lay dead in the temple compound from cyanide poisoning. It was a very, very bad day.

In anyone's language, and by many reports, Jim Jones, who would grow up to create and lead the Peoples Temple, was a weird little kid. The writing was probably on the wall in 1931 when his mother Lynetta gave birth to him and immediately suggested that she might have just squeezed out the Messiah. You have to figure that any kid growing up in that environment can reasonably be expected to have an unconventional development arc. Jim's parents were two of only a handful of people in Lynne, Indiana, who didn't attend church on Sundays, a trait that probably exacerbated their surprise when their son became a student pastor in his early twenties after practising his preaching skills as a child

And preach, little Jimmy Jones did. While other kids were riding their scooters or playing tiddlywinks, Jones was presiding over sermons in the barn near his house, or holding funerals for dead animals. There are rumours that Jim himself was responsible for facilitating the deaths of his funeral subjects – such as, say, stabbing a cat to death – but these haven't been proven. Spreading rumours about someone who murders cats is a risky thing to do.

When he wasn't holding death rituals in the backyard, Jim also enjoyed a spot of childhood reading, ensconcing himself in kiddy favourites such as the collected works of Karl Marx, Joseph Stalin's back catalogue, and Adolf Hitler's juvenile romp *Mein Kampf*. He became utterly obsessed with socialism, a theme that would continue throughout his life. His interest in the tenets of socialism relating to the equal treatment of all citizens and the dismantling of power structures was particularly spiked when he observed the different ways black people and white people were treated in his neck of the woods. In the 1940s and 1950s, racial segregation, whether official or de facto, was practised with gusto in residential areas, schools, and churches in Indiana. Jim Jones particularly noted the segregation in churches, and fixated particularly on the fact that white people and black people worshipped the same god separately. He started to think about how stupid that was.

Jones grew up, married young, and started work on his so-called 'rainbow family' with his wife, Marceline. The couple had one biological child and adopted six others, some of African-American, Korean and Native American heritage, in keeping with Jim's developing love for getting people of different races to squish together under the same roof. In his early twenties he started preaching to small congregations from a shopfront in the low-rent end of Indianapolis, attracting a largely African-American group and focusing less on hymns and Bible tracts and more on listening to the woes of his attendees and problem-solving. Moving to larger and larger church premises during the fifties, he'd help his followers with their domestic worries, employment troubles, getting back on their feet after conviction or addiction, and ensuring they were treated fairly by the white community. Comparing his set-up to the other places of worship in Indiana at the time, Jones wanted his church to have a reputation as the church that got shit done. And, to make sure he himself could make ends meet, he supplemented his meagre collection-plate earnings by selling spider monkeys door-to-door. That's not even a lie. Jim Jones sold monkeys. It's the greatest.

Jones and his church set up a soup kitchen, established an unemployment assistance service, clothed jobseekers in interview-appropriate attire, helped people get sober, and helped retirees get comfortable – he did so many good things for so many people that in 1961 he was appointed head of the Human Rights Commission in Indianapolis by the mayor. His job was to focus on racial inequality in the city, and he continued to convince businesses to open their doors to both black and white customers. Jones was unequivocally one of the pioneers of racial integration in Indiana, and it's a desperate, horrifying shame that he didn't just leave it at that. He started out a really good guy. A really good guy who became completely addicted to being thought of as a really good guy.

Two things marked Jim Jones's twenties: his involvement in local politics – especially racial politics – and his involvement in preaching to whoever would listen, of whatever background or colour. By visiting sparsely populated local meetings of the Communist party in addition to accompanying his wife to a Methodist church on Sundays, he realised a major common theme of commies and the churchies was helping the downtrodden. In

Indiana in the early 1950s, 'the downtrodden' were the poor, the black community, and women, and while churches claimed to believe that everyone was equal and that the less fortunate and less dominant members of society should be looked after, Jim saw precious little evidence of this actually occurring. He twigged. If he dressed socialism and Communism up as religion, he could palatably sell it to locals, like pushing dog medicine into a lump of steak, or calling very, very bad music 'Nu Metal'.

Jim Jones had an intensely engaging oratory style, coupled with a borderline rockabilly, Brylcreem, early-Elvis-slash-late-Roy-Orbison, transition-lenses look that he stuck to from pulpit to grave, making him a formidably popular and dynamic preacher. Mix into that his steely, pious fervour for social justice, his inclusion of people of all races and denominations into his sermons, and his development of what he called 'apostolic socialism' – a cocktail of Christianity and Marxism – and Jones actually presents at this stage as a deadset cool guy. During this time, Jim was absolutely a champion of the disenfranchised. If you accidentally dropped a biography of Jim Jones in the bath at this point, you might forever think he would just go on to greater and greater advances in equality, justice, and the well-being of humankind. You idiot.

Jones was one hell of a preacher, particularly once he really started marching to the beat of his own drum. He strayed further and further from the literal Christian Bible, claiming that the words in it – rather than the way it was interpreted, as is usually the accusation – were responsible for keeping the downtrodden down, and for reinforcing the power of the dominant white man. During more than one sermon he would chuck the Bible he had at his pulpit clear across the room, or throw it to the ground and jump up and down on it like a theological trampoline. The congregation gasped, but Jim pointed out to them that nobody had been struck by lightning. Nobody had been smitten by God for disrespecting the actual physical written words of the Bible, therefore perhaps the words in it were not the true word of God. Jones wrote a booklet called 'The Word Killeth', in which he waxed lyrical about all the bits of the Bible he thought were incorrect, lies, or just flat-out stupid. Jones claimed that the Bible wasn't an ancient text, but a book written by the oppressive, drunk King James with the aim of keeping slaves slaves. An ostensibly Christian preacher telling his congregation that the Bible's a piece of shit – now that's unusual and weirdly refreshing.

Not everyone in Indiana loved this racial-integration-loving, Bible-flinging preacher with his flamboyantly socialist hooey. Jones reported a number of different attacks by detractors designed to quieten and intimidate him, although it's suspected that some of the claims were lies, and some of the attacks were actually staged by Jim. Strangers would spit on his wife, Marceline, especially when they saw her in the street with their adopted African-American son. Swastikas were found painted on the church door, and a church official reportedly found dynamite in the building's coal feeder, ready to blow once it hit the furnace. Jones told his followers that there had been murder attempts by people who put glass in his food, but that the shards miraculously passed from mouth to anus without piercing any useful organs, hallelujah. Jim Jones knew that perceptions of persecution – that people were out to get ya – were a great way of making people believe you were preaching something revolutionary and worthwhile. If the establishment hates it, it must be because the establishment is afraid of it, which is confirmation that it must be the streetlight over the just and progressive path.

But if Jones was right and the Bible was to be taken with a grain of salt – if not an entire pillar – then who *did* represent the true word of God? Why, good old Jimmy Jones, of course! According to Jones, he was the living embodiment of reincarnated mates Jesus, Buddha, Lenin, Allah, and an Egyptian pharaoh or two. It was very, very crowded inside Jim Jones, but luckily he had voluminous reams of satin robes to accommodate everybody. Because of this unprecedented and exclusive influence on Jones by the greatest spiritual and ideological minds in history, he alone had the vision. He alone could achieve true equality between black and white, rich and poor.

That said, for all Jones's banging on about racial equality, even though the overwhelming majority of his followers were African-American, the overwhelming majority of his 'management team' – those closest to him who helped him run things – were white women. Under his thrall, and in some cases under his bedsheets, Jones was always selective about his executive elite, and just like many other men who like power, adoration, and shallow bolsters to their fragile self-esteem, he surrounded himself with women he found non-threatening and easy to control.

Eventually Indiana felt a bit too small-town for Jones, and he realised that his radical approach to socialism-laced Christianity and inclusion needed a more open-minded audience. He'd also read an *Esquire* article that discussed the best places to avoid fallout from a nuclear attack – just some light reading to pass the time – and it mentioned both California and a couple of choice spots in South America, so he earmarked those as possible destinations. For the time being, California won the cult-destination lottery. He couldn't think of anywhere more ready for a funky charismatic preacher with social justice on his mind than California, so in 1965 he and around 150 members of his congregation got themselves into a couple of buses, headed to the West Coast and settled in. His predicted appeal was spot-on, and the popularity of the Peoples Temple grew so rapidly that it had several branches, with the main headquarters in San Francisco. Hippies in the 1960s, man. *So* ready for a bit of cult action.

A few things set the Peoples Temple apart from regular churches. The inclusiveness, the charismatic buzz as soon as you walked in the door, the warmth with which newcomers were welcomed, and the relentless promotion and advertising. Thirty thousand copies of a newsletter spruiking the temple's deeds and dogma were distributed monthly, and Jones dabbled in a spot of radio broadcasting, knowing his oratory skills were the bomb. And then Jim Jones realised that his skills weren't just limited to booming, inspirational public speaking, a keen sense of fashion, and a great Bible-flinging arm. He was going to start faith healing, and he was going to start faith healing HUGE.

There are a handful of well-known tricks involved with faith healing.

The first trick is research. Jim had learned in his early years that a few minutes' worth of eavesdropping on conversations in the church vestibule before the service could really come in handy for pretending you were a little bit psychic later on down the track. Someone mentioning their arthritis or broken marriage to a friend as an aside on their way from porch to pew is guaranteed to be utterly amazed an hour later when a preacher points at them and directly mentions their arthritis or broken marriage.

The second trick is to find some trusted co-conspirators with acting skills. It's way, way easier to get someone who can walk to sit in a wheelchair for a bit than it is to actually heal a paraplegic, so work smarter not harder, and get one of your mates to pretend they can't walk. Lay some hands on them, say a bit of a prayer and bish bosh bash, Gary from down the pub's walking again and it only cost you a few whiskies. On more than one occasion Jones got one of his secretaries to dress as an older woman, rock up in a wheelchair for healing, then when Jim had done his thing she'd take a few shaky, unsure steps before getting up and sprinting around the room.

The third trick is props, and Jim Jones had a doozy. He'd stash a handful of chicken gizzards in his pulpit or somewhere in his vast satin-robe situation, and whenever he was 'healing' someone with a 'tumour' – and for the record, he was not healing anyone and nobody in the story actually has a tumour – he would make grand sweeping statements and sweeping grand gestures and WHAM! It looks for all the world like Jim Jones has pulled a suspiciously chicken-gizzard-looking cancerous tumour clear through your skin and is holding it up in the air like a gold medal at the bullshit Olympics while everyone cheers.

The main justification faith healers give for all the deceit that is necessarily an essential part of faith healing is that the end justifies the means. If it takes a little bit of lying and sleight-of-hand to start people on the right godly path, then it's worth it, right? God and Jim Jones can totally and definitely perform miracles, but we'll fake the first couple just to get you in, yeah? Kind of a try-before-you-buy dealio, like the fake plastic food outside a Japanese restaurant. The showroom model.

As Jones amassed followers who were willing to do his bidding, he realised that having the backing of influential political power-slingers was a super-good idea. In the late fifties he had befriended, and learned a lot from, Father Divine, the African-American head of a let's-call-it-a-cult religious group called the International Peace Mission. Jones also fostered connections with Harvey Milk, Rosalynn Carter, Walter Mondale and Dianne Feinstein, and courted many more to fatten his address book and offer his services. With hundreds of temple people ready to shout whatever slogans were required of them available at the drop of a hat, Jim was able to provide mobile protest and rally fodder to the highest bidder, delivered by temple-owned buses, with a guaranteed six-hour turnaround. That's some impressive turnarounding. Jones and his rent-a-crowd were a pivotal part of San Francisco mayor hopeful George Moscone's 1975 election win – partly through feet-on-the-street campaigning, and partly through turning up to election booths more than once to vote illegally. The following year Jim Jones was made chairman of the San Francisco Housing Authority, an appointment rumoured to be connected to Jones having some juicy gossip that he wasn't afraid to use as blackmail. Who even knew that cults and politics could be corrupt?

Some of the techniques Jim Jones used when he was preaching have been seen across multiple religions and denominations – shouted sermons, faith healing, claims of divinity, really cool sunglasses – but some were a little more unique. The big unique one, and one that was the harbinger of very bad things indeed, was something Jimmy called 'white night', or 'revolutionary suicide'. Jim Jones, wacky, nutty fun guy that he was, liked to make his followers practise poisoning themselves.

More than once, Jim and his assistants would instruct his followers to line up and receive a paper cup containing brightly coloured liquid. Early on, followers would be told to drink the liquid, and afterwards informed that the cup contained poison and that they were all about to die. Later, as a progressive development of increasing loopiness, followers were informed *before* drinking that the cups contained poison, and that they were to drink it and die within the hour. Either way, two things would happen. First, almost all of the congregation would drink the liquid. Second, at some point and usually after the predicted dying time had just passed, the congregation would be told that there was no poison in the cups.

This ingenious and unquestionably fucked-up routine was clever and diabolical in two ways. It not only tested which of Jones's followers would be willing to neck poison at his casual bidding, it also meant that his followers became extremely accustomed to lining up for a big ol' cup o' maybe-poison. If there's one way to make something less shocking and problematic, it's to expose people to it all the time. And if there's one way to see which of the people around you are likely to stay loyal to you and do whatever you ask them to, you can bet it's by seeing which ones are willing to swallow a cupful of cyanide for you.

The ingredients in church-sponsored refreshments were not the only things Jim's followers couldn't always be sure of – sex was also confusing in the Peoples Temple. Jones believed in both marriage *and* infidelity. He was in favour of both sexual liberation *and* celibacy. He preached to his followers that sex diluted their spirit and focus *and* had sex with many, many people who weren't his wife, Marceline. He encouraged all his followers to speak openly about their sex lives, asking them what they had and hadn't done, and how inadequate their husbands or wives were.

Jim's extra-marital affairs were relatively well known within his inner circle – it's not unusual for someone with Jim's personality and need to be seen as the big man at all times to be happy for those around to acknowledge them as a massive stud. A large number of the women in the temple elite considered it their duty to tend to the whims of their leader's penis, and Jim considered it a gift to them. In his mind, he was literally God's gift to women. And he was also God. His Facebook relationship status was almost certainly 'it's complicated'.

In 1973, Jim Jones was arrested for soliciting sex from a man in the toilets of a Macarthur Park cinema, or rather soliciting sex from an undercover police officer in the toilets of a Macarthur Park cinema, back when lots and lots of money and resources were wasted by making that sort of thing against the law. There are also stories of Jones having sex with male members of his congregation and offering to pop his holy wang into their anus for a bit. But you see, Jim Jones wasn't gay, or even bisexual. To the contrary, he consistently insisted that he was in fact the only true heterosexual in the world, and that all others had the potential to show homosexual tendencies. By having sex with other men, Jim Jones was just proving that the *other men* were gay. This guy. This guy who offered to blow a dude in a cinema toilet claims he's the only heterosexual in the world. Jimmy, mate, do whatever feels good, but make your lies believable.

So how does a socialist cult masquerading as a proper churchy religion fund itself? When the temple first started, collection-plate donations were voluntary. From each according to his ability thank you very much, Karl Marx. But as is a cult's modus operandi, as soon as you've established a particular level of faith and sacrifice among your followers, it's time to turn the screws a little bit more to see who *really* believes. Particularly as the temple moved from Indiana to significantly-higher-disposable-income California and Jim got popular with more and more high-profile movers and shakers, a higher level of financial commitment was required of its members. Eventually a minimum of twenty-five per cent of each congregant's income was required and, where possible, all of their property and savings thank you very much.

Mind you, the temple gave back a bit, in the tricky way cults do. See, a normal person not in a cult would pay for their own food and electricity and medical care from the money they earn. But when you're in a particular kind of cult, the cult provides all of that – all you have to do is hand over all your money. So it's the same money, it's just that you don't get to decide what's done with it, and you don't get to keep the leftovers. Sure, you also sacrifice most of your power to make any decisions whatsoever about your life, but hey – FREE DENTAL.

In return for being relieved of their savings, temple members were required to show more and more loyalty. In a kind of 'if you're not with us, you're against us' campaign, anyone showing less-than-ideal levels of commitment and belief in apostolic socialism would be punished. If you didn't conform and obey, that was a sign that you were short on faith, and history has shown that faith is easily topped up by physical violence. Punishments graduated from just verbal humiliation to actual beatings at the front of the church, and from a light spanking to upwards of fifty whacks from a paddle Jones dubbed 'the board of education'. Followers were absolutely convinced that the punishments were exactly what they needed to correct themselves and get back on the right track, so they actually thanked him for them afterwards. Additionally, Jones could enlist those who were fearful of punishment to help him punish others. If nothing else, Jim Jones understood irony. And it's an irony peculiar to cults that, provided the pacing of the indoctrination is right, the worse you treat your followers, the more they'll believe that the outside world will treat them badly. Peoples Temple members lost their trust for the government and any institutions that were not the temple. The outside world wouldn't help them improve, but the temple would. The only person they had left to trust was Jim Jones.

The more Jim got used to receiving people's money, belongings and social security cheques in exchange for basic services, the more he started really gagging for a commune-type scenario, with him as its benevolent, all-knowing overlord. Everybody contributing (except him). Everybody living in communal quarters (except him). Everybody according to their ability (except him). It was the socialist ideal (for him, for others not so much). Life is easier with fewer possessions and fewer choices to make, so Jones was pleased to grant his followers the favour of relieving them of those inconveniences. He'd make all the decisions – you guys just relax by working really, really hard doing whatever he tells you, and everything will be fine.

It's hard to know if Jim Jones truly believed that the Peoples Temple, and to a lesser extent the world, was really at imminent risk of being destroyed by a nuclear apocalypse, although he certainly talked about it to his followers enough. Due to the Cold War between the US and Russia, there was a lot of talk in the media about the possibility of a holocaust, and Jim had already identified South America as a place that he considered safest from nuclear fallout. It may just be coincidence that, to run a socialist cult according to your own rules and without too much outside interference, it's a great idea to isolate yourself and head out into a remote part of the South American jungle. It may just be coincidence that around the time Jones was considering putting some geographical distance between his church and the rest of the world, the Peoples Temple was attracting more and more negative attention from investigative reporters and damning articles and angsty questions from family members of followers. Coincidence or no, Jones and his easily influenced congregation were ready to turn on their heels and stomp off into isolation, like a teenager slamming the door to their room because their parents just don't understand.

Jones decided on Guyana, next to Venezuela on the northern part of the South American mainland, for the next destination for Peoples Temple headquarters. He liked the fact that the Guyanese government had some pretty solid socialist beliefs, and the Guyanese government liked the fact that Jim Jones had money and influence.

One of the advantages of ingratiating yourself with the government of a country your commune is in is that you might occasionally need their customs department to turn a blind eye to some of the things you bring across the border. And Jim Jones, it's a desperate understatement to say, liked the drugs and the poison. He'd long been obsessed with poison, and definitely kept some of his control by feeding drugs to his followers, but he was also a massive fan of drugs for his own personal use. Amphetamines to get him riled up, barbiturates to bring him back down, Jones had a bloodstream like the plumbing in jail on cell inspection day. Eventually his slurred speech started to give him away, and his signature ever-present sunglasses could well have been to hide his enthusiastically dilated pupils. Jim Jones didn't do many things by halves. Jim Jones was a drug addict.

In 1976 Jones leased just over fifteen square kilometres of land from the Guyanese government and sent his hardest working and most able followers over to start construction on what he hoped would be a utopian agricultural commune, or as anybody who has ever heard a single thing about cults calls it: a gigantic red flag.

Jim Jones just needed to name the place. Let's see . . . Narcissism Village? Who's the Man, I'm the Man City? Nah. JONESTOWN.

Make no mistake – Jonestown was impressive. Land was cleared, buildings went up, the absolutely rubbish soil was cultivated to make it more or less arable – this was a place that could comfortably accommodate at *most* three-quarters of the number of people who were uncomfortably accommodated there. By the time Jones encouraged his followers to make the mass move in mid-1977, the facilities built for around 600 people were swamped by closer to a thousand people, and everyone who's ever lived in a university share house knows how much that blows. Nobody knows whose pubes are whose in the shower drain, and Lorraine keeps using your moisturiser.

The compound consisted of a large undercover pavilion, cottages, dormitories, communal bathroom blocks, medical buildings, school tents, a kitchen and bakery, and fields and orchards for growing food. There were plenty of temple animals, used for both food and companionship – cattle, pigs, chickens, dogs, cats, macaws, and everybody's favourite, a chimpanzee called Mr Muggs. It was a decent set-up, albeit on iffy soil prone to getting muddy under any of the frequent downpours, but, compared to the jungle that was cleared to accommodate it, acceptably liveable.

Unfortunately for the people in Jonestown who hoped to enjoy the paradise they were promised, there was no time to. Due to the many mouths to feed, the heat, the shitty soil and the unpredictable weather, there was a crapload of work to do, approximately all of the time. Common for people in a cult-based utopia, every single person (except the leader, obviously) worked all of the time, for no pay, with little sleep, and with little food. Nothing makes people more loyal than isolating them far, far from any external influences and making them so exhausted they can't be bothered to do anything but follow instructions and eat bananas.

Following instructions is even easier when those instructions are blared from loudspeakers up to twenty-four hours per day. Jim recorded sermons – hours and hours and hours of them – and had them playing throughout the compound. It might have been annoying if the people listening weren't exhausted and, as it turns out, on heeeeaps of drugs. Delicious, intoxicating, stupefying, will-diminishing drugs. Thorazine, Valium, Quaaludes and morphine were all used liberally to shave the spiky parts off any likely troublemakers or people with their own strong opinions. There were stacks of the things at Jonestown, just waiting to dull the demands of dissidents.

You'd think that with that level of exhaustion and occasional soakings with pharmaceuticals, one of the very hardest things to do would be to learn a new language. But *nyet*. Jim Jones had the residents of Jonestown learn Russian, because Jim Jones had a whatever-the-Russian-word-for-boner-is for the Soviet Union. Not only was Russia the giant pot that socialism and Communism had been stewing away in for years, Russia also hated the US government, so Jones considered them the perfect society. He insisted that followers learn the language, made vague, sweeping plans to move the entire Jonestown shebang to the Soviet Union, and entertained Soviet ambassadors in Guyana on more than one occasion. Jim was a complex guy.

When you combine isolation, drugs, and a leader with increasing levels of obvious psychosis, at some point you're going to get a big visit from the paranoia pixie. Jim Jones, and therefore by default the Peoples Temple, was convinced that outside enemies were hovering and ever-present, waiting for an opportunity to persecute, murder, and undermine. Jones was particularly suspicious of the US government, knowing that historically they weren't huge fans of socialist or Communist ideals. They were jealous of his successful Marxist set-up, see. He figured the government would worry that if regular people saw that a socialist state could live so purely, so cleanly, and so perfectly, surely the entire capitalist system that was lining their pockets would crumble and fall. The government would want to destroy an outpost of outcasts to protect its thriving economy.

Some temple members noticed that Jim was spiralling into a pit of drug use, paranoia, and psychosis. The relentlessness of the slurred rants against capitalism and the temple's vague and ever-changing enemies, the talk of betrayal by and punishment for anyone who dared consider leaving or even questioning temple doctrine – they were all ominous harbingers of things to come. A church that once performed community outreach, charity, and the goodest of deeds had become an isolated, jumpy, self-serving commune, the residents of which often preferred it when their leader wasn't there.

An unimaginatively titled group called the Concerned Relatives had been gathering, organising and harrumphing in opposition to the Peoples Temple for many months, led by ex-temple members, including a bloke called Tim Stoen. Tim had been extremely high up in the temple's organisation, and his defection must have really hurt Jimmy Jones's feelings. Admittedly Jones had been schtupping Tim's wife and claimed to have fathered her son, so Tim had fair reason to hold a hefty grudge, but others in the group also had good reason to rally against the cult. Unsurprisingly, Jim Jones considered the Concerned Relatives his enemies. Mind you, by this round of the game, Jim Jones likely considered moths and dust his enemies.

The Concerned Relatives contacted numerous congressmen and US government departments, warning them that American citizens were currently at the mercy of a megalomaniac in Guyana. Members of the lobby group had been surveilled and threatened by temple members, and the good terms Jim Jones was on with Guyanese immigration officials meant that the Concerned Relatives had a lot of trouble getting anywhere physically near the Jonestown compound to contact their family members within its walls. They needed official help from people with influence. Fatefully, one of those people was Leo Ryan.

In 1977, Congressman Leo Ryan was chatting with his friend Sam Houston. Sam was the father of Bob Houston, a young man who had been killed under a train the year before, the day after leaving the Peoples Temple. Sam wasn't sure that Bob leaving the temple and Bob dying were completely unrelated, and the coincidence piqued Ryan's interest in the cult. Gradually he collected more and more information from articles, letters written to him from interested lobbyists, and meetings with the Concerned Relatives. He was starting to hear about suicide rehearsals, people being held as prisoners, threats to those trying to leave, and an assortment of other iffy practices.

Congressman Ryan was a guy who liked to go on 'fact-finding missions', seeing the benefits as twofold: firstly, he was able to get out into the neighbourhoods of his constituents and really see what life was like from their level, and secondly, it looked really, really good for him from a publicity point of view. After the Watts riots in Los Angeles he did a stint as a substitute teacher in a local school, and spent time anonymously in Folsom Prison to find out how death row prisoners were treated. Publicity stunts or not, the fact-finding missions seemed like the calling card of a better-than-average politician and a reasonably cool guy. When he started hearing that people in Jonestown might be being held against their will, he was pretty sure pretty quickly that he had to go to Guyana and have a squiz for himself. In November 1978, he gathered a small entourage of congressional staffers, a bunch of journalists who were excited at the prospect of finally having access to Jonestown, and a handful of concerned relatives of temple members, packed his most breathable fabrics, and got on a plane. Whether he was too trusting, too naïve, or too confident of his untouchable congressman bubble, Ryan didn't take any of his own security. As far as decisions about taking your own security to potentially dangerous cult compounds go, that turned out to be not a good one.

It took Jim Jones a couple of days to agree to give Congressman Ryan and his homies access to his utopia, but when his wife, Marceline, insisted that they should proudly show them what they'd built, and Ryan indicated civilly but stridently that he'd be dropping in regardless of whether he was welcome or not, Jones relented, and he and Ryan both painted smiles on their faces and met. The compound's residents had worked furiously to prepare everything to appear in its best light, and Jonestown had never looked neater or crisper in its year and a half of operation. Ryan's crew was given a relatively superficial tour and then treated to an evening meal with singing and dancing. Exactly the kind of treatment you get at a reasonably priced tropical holiday resort, but with a bit of despotic leadership and intense feelings of persecution mixed in.

Residents of Jonestown had been thoroughly briefed-slash-threatened, and knew that they had to present their dusty Disneyland as the happiest place on Earth. They put on a grand show, hiding the fact that they were tired, trapped and frightened, pulling together to present a united, harmonious front that really wanted to avoid punishment. After dinner on the first day of his inspection, Congressman Ryan got on the microphone. 'I think that all of you know that I'm here to find out more about questions that have been raised about your operation here,' he announced to the assembled temple members. 'I can tell you right now that from the few conversations I've had with some of the folks here already this evening that whatever the comments are, there are some people here who believe that this is the best thing that ever happened to them in their whole life.' The crowd broke into cheers and rapturous applause. The announcement was likely only about three-quarters sincere. It's easy to believe that Ryan was pleasantly surprised by and highly impressed at the community and its achievements and pleasantries. By the same token though, he could easily see that some members were not happy. Partly because some of the members had approached him and said cryptic things like 'I'm not happy.'

The illusion of an idyllic utopia that was presented to Congressman Ryan showed its first robust crack when temple member Vernon Gosney secretly passed a note to Don Harris, an NBC News reporter who had gone along for the trip. The note said, 'Please help us get out of Jonestown.' That's a bad thing to read in a note that's been passed to you. When you're secretly passed a note it should read 'Geography class sucks balls', or 'I like you. Do you like me? Y/N', it should not contain a desperate plea from a virtual prisoner in fear for their life. People should be able to enter and leave their homes as they please, they shouldn't have to surreptitiously pass notes to visiting reporters.

The passing of the note was reported to Jim Jones. Guys. GUYS. When someone passes you a note in class, you do NOT take it up front and show the teacher. Jones was predictably upset, concerned that his extended, exhausted family was falling apart, and worried that any defectors might spread lies and ruin his hard-won community. He didn't think that the drugs or the borderline slavery or the beatings or the poor living conditions would bring them down, see. The *lies* would bring them down.

The note nudged the topsoil off a minor landslide, as around fifteen temple members spilled that they wanted to leave. They saw this opportunity – in the care of a government representative, accompanied by journalists – as the safest way to leave the commune without being violently stopped. If they'd tried to leave before Ryan's arrival, they would have done so with no money, passport, official papers or help from authorities, as all of these things had been surrendered to Jim Jones. The plane on the nearby airstrip that was waiting to take Ryan's original group back to the US was starting to look inadequate for the needs of the growing group, so departure was delayed until a second plane could be arranged. In addition to the temple members Ryan was personally accompanying out of the compound, another nine took his visit as an opportunity to escape of their own accord, and quietly took themselves off into the surrounding jungle.

Jim Jones was exactly as calm and comfortable as you might expect with the idea that a chunk of his loyal subordinates was rebelling and abandoning him, and that a congressman and some reporters were about to head back to the US and spread the idea that his magical village was flawed, or that he was a madman, or even that he was in any way not the coolest guy around. Jim Jones was not calm, and Jim Jones was not comfortable.

One of the Jonestown residents that got onto a plane was Larry Layton, which aroused the suspicion of some of the other escapees. Layton had never expressed a desire to leave and was well known as one of Jim Jones's besties, but he managed to convince Ryan's entourage that he was good to go, and took a seat in one of the aeroplanes.

As other departing temple members filed onto the planes ready to leave, Layton pulled a gun from under his rain poncho and started shooting at them. A tractor-trailer emerged from the road out of the jungle and drove onto the airstrip with a handful of men in the back, brandishing guns. They aimed their guns at the politician and his staff, the journalists, and the departing temple members, and shot. They shot a lot. They killed five people: Congressman Ryan, note-receiving journalist Don Harris, journalists Bob Brown and Greg Robinson, and temple defector Patricia Parks. They badly injured ten others, and the airstrip was littered with crumpled men and women.

At roughly the same time, back at the compound under the pavilion the sound of shit hitting the fan was deafening. The knife attack on Congressman Ryan, believed to have been ordered by Jim Jones, had failed. The cult leader had sent gunmen to finish the job. Jones knew that the very specific group of people who get pissed when you kill a congressman was basically everybody, and that things were going to get pretty uncomfortable from here on in, extremely quickly. This was it.

Jim Jones called his last white night. It was time for revolutionary suicide.

A big metal vat in the pavilion was filled with cyanide, Valium, and grape Flavor Aid, peculiarly not improving the taste of the grape Flavor Aid.

Jim Jones got on the microphone, danged if he was going to let this hugely momentous occasion and undertaking occur without every last scrap of attention being on him.

'How very much I've tried my best to give you the good life,' began Jim Jones in his final sermon.

'In spite of all that I've tried, a handful of people, with their lies, have made our lives impossible. There's no way to distract ourselves from what's happened today.'

This was a speech by a man who did not consider letting his followers walk away as an option. He told the gathered group that they were sitting on a powder keg, which was no way to have their babies die. It didn't occur to them that their babies didn't have to die at all. Nobody did. But they thought they were under siege, because that's what an egomaniacal psychopath, their trusted leader, had told them.

'If we can't live in peace, then let us die in peace,' he said. 'What's going to happen in a few minutes is that one of the people on that plane is going to shoot the pilot. I know that. I didn't plan it but I know it's going to happen. They're going to shoot that pilot, and down comes that plane into the jungle, and we had better not have any of our children left when it's over, because they'll parachute in here on us.'

Some temple members argued and implored Jim and the rest of the congregation to think of alternatives, such as going to Russia, or sparing the children. But nope. Jim Jones had not spent his life letting other people change his mind, and he wasn't about to start now, so close to the end of it. He assured the gathered crowd in the pavilion that the Guyanese army and the CIA were definitely on their way to kill them all. There were absolutely no members of the military or CIA anywhere near the place, but the truth wasn't important to Jim Jones.

He'd built up and spread paranoia about outside enemies for so long that it didn't take much to convince people that they were about to be brutally massacred. Whether or not he believed his own hype about imminent slaughter, Jim was certain he wasn't going to let anyone embarrass him. Nothing was important to Jim Jones except Jim Jones and everyone thinking Jim Jones was the greatest. In his mind, his reputation would be more damaged by a handful of people leaving, or by Jonestown gently folding, than by what was about to happen. There was nothing else for it.

'So my opinion is that you be kind to children and be kind to seniors and take the potion like they used to take in ancient Greece, and step over quietly. Because we are not committing suicide. It's a revolutionary act. We can't go back. They won't leave us alone. They're now going back to tell more lies, which means more congressmen. And there's no way we can survive,' said Jim Jones.

Peoples Temple guards surrounded the pavilion, holding weapons. Poisoned Flavor Aid was distributed in paper cups for the adults and plastic syringes for squirting into children's mouths.

'Please get us some medication. It's simple. It's simple. There's no convulsions with it. It's just simple,' said Jim Jones.

Parents gave their children poison first, and the children cried because of the bitter taste. The parents comforted them and held them in their arms while they died.

'Lay down your life with dignity. Don't lay down with tears and agony. There's nothing to death. It's just stepping over to another plane. Don't be this way. Stop these hysterics. This is not the way for people who are socialists or Communists to die. No way for us to die. We must die with some dignity,' said Jim Jones.

With the children dead or dying, the adults drank, and poisoned themselves. They lay down with their family members – all over the compound, in the pavilion, on surrounding pathways and open areas, wherever they could find room – and died.

'Take our life from us. We laid it down. We got tired. We didn't commit suicide, we committed an act of revolutionary suicide protesting the conditions of an inhumane world,' said Jim Jones.

The people of Jonestown died because they believed that they would be killed anyway, or that their socialist ideal was worth dying to preserve, or that they had nothing else. They died because they believed that nobody else would take them in or care for them in their old age or treat their beliefs with dignity. They died because they believed they had no other choice. But even though they believed they had good reasons to die, it still feels very, very strongly like they died for no good reason.

The people of Jonestown died because Jim Jones – a monumentally power-crazed fuckwit in a safari suit – decided they should die.

Aerial photographs of the compound after the mass poisoning are devastating to look at. At first it looks like the laundry of an entire suburb has been blown by a gust of wind and scattered across the grounds. But then you look closer, and you realise the scattered splotches of shapes and colour are people. Investigators and the Guyanese military were greeted with the sight – and smell – of hundreds of corpses, including those of the animals in the temple menagerie. Someone had shot all the dogs and Mr Muggs the chimpanzee. Someone shot the goddamn chimpanzee.

When Jim Jones's body was found, it had a single gunshot wound in it, located ironically near his own temple. After watching almost his entire congregation – the people who trusted him, put their faith in him, and relied on him for everything – die pointless deaths that took five long minutes, over and over again more than 900 times, Jim Jones took the coward's way out. In his early life and career, Jim Jones did a lot of good things and helped hundreds of people. But sometimes bad things people do override and overshadow any good things they do. This is one of those times. What an asshole.

In a bizarre footnote, one of the survivors of the mass suicide, Mike Prokes – he was absent because Jim Jones had sent him to deliver a suitcase of money to the Russian embassy in Georgetown – called a press conference in his California hotel room four months after the massacre. He read a statement to the assembled clutch of journalists, politely excused himself to go to the toilet, and shot himself in the bathroom. In notes he left, he claimed he wanted to draw attention to the fact that the people of Jonestown were outcasts who had been subjected to marginalisation and oppression, and that the government was out to get them. Indirectly, Mike Prokes drew attention to the fact that the influence of a cult leader can last for a fair while after his death. And that killing yourself in the middle of a press conference is a really good way to get people to read your suicide note.

Until 9/11, Jonestown was the biggest ever killing of US civilians. It's the cult by which so many other cults are measured. When cults were investigated at any time after 1978, it was so often because people 'didn't want another Jonestown on their hands'. Jim Jones's failed socialist project is one of the best-known cults of all time, and generated the phrase 'drinking the Kool-Aid', which must have really pissed off the marketing team at Kool-Aid. Jonestown cyanide was mixed into Flavor Aid, a competing brand, which perhaps due to it just being not as phonetically punchy, weirdly didn't become a globally known brand associated with blind obedience to an apocalyptic dickhead.

More appropriately: don't drink the poison served to you by a cult leader.

Or anyone, really. Yes. Don't drink poison, and have a nice day.

THE MOONIES

July 1982, Madison Square Garden. An arena filled with people from twelve different countries. Pair up the ones in the middle and you've got 2075 couples. The men are all dressed in tuxedos with red neckties concealing their nervous swallowing, and the women are all draped in white wedding dresses with identical, cheap synthetic veils and identical, cheap synthetic white gloves. Some of the couples have only met for the first time in the last few days, some have been communicating via letters or phonecalls for months or years but have only just seen each other for the first time physically during this week. Some of the couples can barely make themselves understood to their partners, being from different countries and cultures with different languages. Almost all of them are virgins. All of them are getting married today.

Well, sort of married. According to the laws of the countries or states they travelled here from, today's ceremony will not represent an official marriage. Rather, to the rest of the world, this is a blessing ceremony, where the dude up the front in the fancy robes and crown, asking the crowd questions about commitment to God and each other while they respond with shouts of 'NAY!' – or 'ne', the Korean word for 'yes', confusingly – bestows his blessing upon the unions of these disparate, as-yet-unconsummated hook-ups. But to the Unification Church, or as they're more commonly known, 'The Moonies', this is a wedding for reals, and they're stuck with this person they didn't choose for themselves for life.

The dude in the crown is Sun Myung Moon, and he's accompanied on stage by his wife, Hak Ja Han Moon. Within The Moonies, these two middle-to-late-aged, borderline pudgy, five-foot-something humans are known as The Perfect Parents or True Parents. From the looks of Mr and Mrs Moon, despite lists and lists of high standards elsewhere within the church, it would seem that 'perfection' is at least very achievable. You just always expected the couple chosen by God to represent the pinnacle of human coupledom to look less likely to offer you a cup of tea and a biscuit.

Be careful when you call Moonies 'Moonies', though. Most Moonies don't like being called Moonies. The problem is, the full name of the original church is 'Holy Spirit Association for the Unification of World Christianity', a mouthful in anyone's language, and there are a *lot* of different languages in this massive room full of wedding folk. Saying 'Moonies' is just so much easier.

Sun Myung Moon, or 'Reverend' Moon as he would eventually insist on being addressed, grew up in a simple North Korean family that converted from Confucianism to Christianity while he was still a little kid. After studying electrical engineering

for a bit but finding it unacceptably lacking in glory and attention, he looked around for something better. Reasonably pious,
reasonably cross with Communists, and reasonably fond of
the sound of his own voice, at twenty-five Moon moved to
Pyongyang and started preaching, which in 1945 irritated the
occupying Communist authorities a great deal. Look, being an
anti-Communist preacher of any influence was not a good idea in
North Korea in the late forties, or arguably any time since then,
and Moon was also rumoured to be partly preaching with his
penis. Moon was a bit of a fan of the process of 'pikareum', in
which someone of pure blood – a Messiah, for example – has sex
with someone to cleanse that person's blood. They in turn have
sex with their partner (but no gays please, we're homophobic),
until everybody's spent and pure, and free of sin, like the world's
most holy and uplifting venereal disease. Unfortunately, adul-
tery was illegal in Korea at the time, so for either that reason,
or for being an anti-Communist upstart, Moon was chucked
in jail in 1948 for a bit to have a good hard look at himself.
Well, 'jail' if we're being generous. 'Communist prison camp'
if we're calling a spade a tool of the proletariat.

According to some records, Moon was released when United
Nations forces raided the prison camp, but according to others
Moon escaped, because Messiahs are brave and crafty and wily,
you know. Church believers are also under the impression that
Moon underwent horrible ordeals in the camp, being subjected
to beatings and torture at levels befitting a martyr that must
undergo severe trials before emerging triumphant, phoenix-like,
and a bit jowly. Whatever the truth, Moon correctly assumed

that South Korea would have a more lax attitude towards his beliefs, so he set up shop in the South and began writing down some pretty big ideas.

In 1954 he took these ideas and started the snappily named Holy Spirit Association for the Unification of World Christianity. With all those good-sounding words and his very big ideas, Moon capitalised on the rapid growth of Christianity and Christian-seeming new religious movements in post-war Korea and easily raked in followers.

Beyond the first couple of big principles, it's difficult to get too excited about the actual beliefs of the Unification Church. While the rituals and practices that the beliefs give rise to can be bizarre, hilarious, and at times unbelievably gross, the beliefs themselves range limply from classic Christianity to old-fashioned family values to garden-variety sexism to a spot of disappointing (but not surprising considering their other beliefs) homophobia. Like so many quirky new religious movements, it's Christianity with a twist.

The Moonies' belief system is based primarily on a book written by Sun Myung Moon called *The Exposition of the Divine Principle*. Considering its title, it doesn't really do a whole lot of exposing, and the lengthy, repetitive theories forming the fundamental bases of *The Divine Principle* itself are all pretty dense, tentative, and blurry around the edges. Still, we can give it a red-hot go, and some of the lighter, clearer bits can be explained thus:

Eve was a very terrible lady, and responsible for pretty much most of the bad things in the world. Certainly the original Christian Bible says more or less the same thing, but Moon really likes to labour the point. In theory, Adam represents Heaven and Eve represents the Earth – when they get married and love each other very much and have sex, Heaven and Earth are united as one. In theory. Adam and Eve were perfect humans united in God's love and totally ready to start a family. In theory. But Adam and Eve stuffed up. They loved each other more than they loved God, and acted on their sexy feelings before they were spiritually mature, the daft nude idiots.

But in case there's any doubt, the reverend wants you to be quite sure that the premature sex with Adam was way more Eve's fault than Adam's, because chicks, right? To add insult to injury, it's suggested that Eve had sex with Satan first – the minx. You can't really blame her though – have you even seen Satan's buff abs? So, Eve had a bit of a fling with Satan and then turned right around and had sex with Adam, probably giving him Satanic chlamydia and certainly stuffing up humanity's bloodline with Satan's diabolical DNA. Either way, by dooming all future humans to failure and making Satan their daddy, Eve fell out of favour and she and Adam lost their chance to become the perfect couple who were supposed to have perfect babies and then become the perfect family. Honestly, some deities are just *so* fussy about what people do with their genitals.

Happily enough, a couple of millennia later, along came Sun Myung Moon and his second wife. When the reverend was forty years old he married Hak Ja Han, the seventeen-year-old daughter of his cook. His new wife was born the year Moon had married his previous wife, Sun-kil Choi, who he had a son with. Sun Myung's marriage to Sun-kil was arranged by his parents and ended in divorce ten years later, an indicator that arranged marriages aren't always the hunky-doriest idea, ironic considering Sun Myung's later policies on the subject. Learning from the experience of a first wife who was unconvinced of the fact that he was a deity incarnate, Sun Myung chose a young thing with hardly anything in the way of her own meaningful life direction.

Before marrying Hak Ja Han and knocking her up with fourteen perfect children, Sun Myung made sure that he'd found a lady with none of those pesky, weak qualities that demon-screwing Eve had. He checked all the qualities off on his Big Man's Perfect Wife checklist: strong enough hips to keep pushing out babies, a pretty face, chastity for days, no inconvenient emotional attachments to other blokes such as her father, and the ability to completely and utterly surrender her own needs in favour of those of her husband's. Jackpot, mate. Moon knew that the younger his wife was, the less likely she'd have developed any independence. So now, where Adam and Eve had failed, Sun Myung and Hak Ja Han had succeeded – two towering pillars of perfection, shooting out perfect child after perfect child with a pure, Satan-free bloodline. Suck it Adam and Eve, ya failures.

In case they doubted his birthright destiny as the Messiah, Moon told his followers that Jesus visited him when he was sixteen years old, to have a bit of a chat and ask him to take over where he'd left off as God's representative on Earth, that kind of thing. Moon never really explained why it took him twenty-odd years to finally get around to actually starting work, but as anyone with a sixteen-year-old with a messy bedroom will tell you, you can't rush them, and they'll get around to it eventually, and why do you have to RUIN their LIFE, oh my GOD. In the interim, Moon claims he was also visited by Mohammed, Buddha, Abraham, and Moses, most likely looking at him with raised eyebrows, tapping impatiently at their wrist-watches. Moon quizzed them about the nature of God to better understand his future vocation as his personal representative, and they were only too glad to help him with his homework.

See, according to *The Divine Principle*, Jesus failed in his mission on Earth. He was inconveniently murdered before he got around to uniting Heaven and Earth by getting married, having children, and making everyone perfect, so it was now up to Reverend Moon to finish the job. Honestly, if you want something done properly, you have to do it yourself, and where Adam and Jesus had failed, Moon was absolutely determined to succeed. Creating the Kingdom of Heaven on Earth was now Sun Myung's job, so he got busy letting everybody know how to rid themselves of sin and get a wristband to enter the VIP section in Heaven.

First of all, you definitely have to be married to go to Heaven. But equally importantly, people must make up for all the shitty things they've done that might have contributed to the fall of humanity to its imperfect state in the first place, which is fun. What *The Divine Principle* calls 'the providence of restoration through indemnity', which we can all agree is too many words, is really just 'making up for bad stuff'. The lengthy, unbeliev-ably boring explanation of indemnity in *The Divine Principle* can more or less be summed up as 'karma, plus thesaurus'.

In theory, indemnity means being nice to people and doing good deeds to cancel out any sins that have been committed in the past. In one of the unnecessarily bitchy examples given in his writings however, Moon explained that the Holocaust, in which millions of Jews were slaughtered, was simply indemnity to make up for the fact that they killed Jesus. See how that works? The decision to crucify Jesus Christ 2000 years ago, that may or may not have been heavily fictionalised, and that may or may not have been made by Jews or Romans or have happened at all, can be made up for by deporting, shooting, doing experiments on and gassing a few million Jews. Mr Moon, that is not a very nice theory. After some very prominent Jewish leaders in the US kicked up a considerable stink about the references to Jews being punished for the crucifixion, the Moonie back-pedalling began in earnest. Realising that the theories would probably make them unpopular, and having a relentless semi-erection for popularity, Moon later glossed over his previous anti-Semitic statements in *The Divine Principle* with some slick PR, press conferences, and a full-page ad in the *New York Times*. He might have been a bastard, but he was a smart bastard.

In *The Divine Principle*, it's made clear that one of the things that pisses God off most of all is when people don't make everything about him, which is also known to piss off most cult leaders and Kardashians. Moon stressed that it was very, very important to focus on and include God in all your daily activities. Conveniently, Moon himself was more or less God, so it was advised to think about him while you're doing the washing, handing over your money, or trying to make babies with your wife, regardless of how difficult that might make it to get an erection. It was also considered very inconvenient to God, and Moon, if you kept in touch with non-church family or friends, thank you very much. You haven't spent all this time and money and effort making yourself pure just to have your thinking dirtied and soiled by people you *love*, have you? You love your True Parents now. That's it, end of list.

Moreover, making things all about God-slash-Reverend Moon meant not making anything about yourself. Thinking of your own money as yours is selfish, so you might as well give it to the church. Making your own decisions is the height of conceit, so you might as well let Sun Myung and Hak Ja Han, your True Parents, make those for you. Picking your own girlfriend? Nope. Stopping your fundraising before you've reached your quota? Nope. Have sex? Oh my GOD, you BEAST, no.

In 1965 Reverend Moon, having decided to take his let's-get-married show on the Western road, first visited the United States, wandering around plonking chunks of Korean soil in different places and declaring them holy. Satan would not interrupt your prayers in these places, he claimed, making Korean dirt the equivalent of citronella to nefarious Hell-mosquitoes.

By 1971 the Perfect Family — at that stage consisting of two parents and seven children — had decided to move to the United States, settling in New York State. Moon had given all his children both Korean and Western names, presumably to make their message and example more palatable to a wider variety of Westerners who, certainly in the early 1970s, sometimes baulked a little at the difficulty of unfamiliar words and cultures. Western society's taste for Eastern mysticism peaked in the 1970s and 1980s, so the Unification Church perhaps represented an easy sell for the less adventurous enlightenment-seeker who was already familiar with the well-known bits of the Christian Bible frequently referenced in *The Divine Principle*. It saved a lot of time rather than learning a whole new religion.

Moon quickly made his presence in the US well and truly felt, organising well-attended public speeches about the future of America according to God at significant sites like Madison Square Garden, Yankee Stadium and the Washington Monument. His disguise as an earnest holy man with a vision for humanity fit very snugly over his crafty businessman narcissist underwear, and thousands of people bought it. Not just in the States, either – throughout its history the Unification Church has had active branches in over 100 countries including the UK, Australia, Japan, and extensively across Europe and South America. The Reverend Moon started up a bewildering array of organisations, foundations, and conferences to give the impression of a bene-volent, politically interested, peace-loving dynamo, and it bloody worked a treat.

Recruiting started in earnest in the US in the seventies, with family values, clean living free of drugs, alcohol, and pre-marital sex appealing to young Christian college students who were looking for the path to a better world. It's easy to imagine that, to a reasonably devout Christian college freshman, being plunged suddenly into the sex-soaked collegiate environment where everybody's underpants seemed to dissolve as soon as they walked into a dorm party might have been overwhelming and confronting. If you were a cool-ish-looking young Moonie recruiter hanging out on campus talking about making pure, honest human partnerships for life, convincing these freshmen to attend a Bible study group or sociological lecture or creative retreat would have been pretty easy if you picked the right virginal nerds as your targets. And let's face it, virginal nerds are pretty easy to spot on university campuses.

Recruiters would invite potential Moonies to chilled-out Bible discussion or community groups, and when they got there, treat them like they were the best human on Earth. It was known as 'love-bombing'. By the time participants had finished the meeting, full of ideas for making the world better and unifying all the races, they would feel so high on their own self-esteem that they'd be mildly bummed at the thought of returning to their families where they were just regarded as normal, mid-level human beings who had to take the bins out. Craving the kick of the love-bomb, a lot of people would return to the scene of the high, without even having heard a word about the Unification Church or Reverend Moon yet. They might be invited to a camp, or a workshop, or a retreat, or a commune with messages from *The Divine Principle* being slowly merged into the relentless love-bombing. It would often be weeks until recruits realised that this was a church, but by that time they didn't care. They were already in.

That's the thing, see. If you're in a place and with people who make you feel good, and as if you have a purpose, and that provides you with things to do and food to eat and books to read and new ideas to consider, and the only payment asked is that you reject the people and society and habits that *don't* make you feel that good, like your friends and family and education and future – and a fair bit of money, let's be honest – the temptation to stay would be huge. People don't join cults because they're stupid or bad people. They join cults because cults make them feel better. It's a bugger of a thing.

Daily life as a Moonie can look different depending on where you are, how devout you are, and at which point in the cult's history you were a member. Most Moonies work normal jobs, live with their partner, and offer up their daily prayer to God and Reverend Moon. They attend Moonie church every Sunday, where they genuflect towards a portrait of Moon and listen to sermons – some given live by elders, some recorded – in Korean and their native language. They volunteer to do work for the church, and generally only socialise with other Moonies, where the babysitting circle is no doubt thriving. There has been no shortage of missionary and other often-unpaid work available in the past, although in the early 1990s Moon decided full-time membership of the church was no longer required of its adherents. Just, y'know, keep the donations coming.

In the early days though, full-time membership was definitely a thing, and church members often lived in Unification Church centres, learning, listening to lectures, selling flowers and candles and being indoctrinated with Moon's theories from *The Divine Principle*. Classic cult tropes like believing they were the chosen ones, considering outside meddlers to be oppressive and dangerous, and instilling a fear that leaving the cult would mean a massive roasting in Hell were handed out with gleeful abandon. Classic techniques like providing a low-calorie diet, limiting sleeping hours and working members for up to seventeen hours a day helped with compliance and a disinterest in sex. But, of course, people stayed because they felt loved and understood. They felt that they were contributing to the unification of the world, and that they were the marrying, child-producing future. They felt that they were right, and the rest of the world was wrong. And they felt like they didn't want to go back to live with their parents, who were complete squares, man.

With recruiting skill, which the Moonies definitely had in spades, generally comes income. New members would not only hand over their existing cash, they were also full of enough God-loving, new-friend-impressing energy to get out and fundraise, selling salvation souvenirs out on the streets, and providing their own labour for free. And with income, if you're as canny with investment and expansion as Sun Myung Moon was, comes more income. From the very beginning in 1954, a lot of the money he made from religion was invested into business, and a lot of the money he made from business was invested into expanding his religion, albeit with quite an impressive chunk set aside for making its leader comfortable. Holding both spiritual and financial power can be a heady mix, and it perfectly suited Reverend Moon to be a complete champion at both.

Over the cult's history, from its inception to Moon's death, the Unification Church owned or part-owned hotels, ship-building companies, car factories, a recording studio, print media (including the ultra-conservative favourite newspaper of Ronald Reagan *The Washington Times*), a cable TV network, a pharmaceuticals company, a tea producer, a titanium mine, a construction firm and a ballet company, for starters. At one time, the church owned more sushi restaurants across America than any other organisation. Moon wasn't just the fisher of men, he was the fisher of fish restaurants. He became a billionaire, and mentioned once or twice that he wouldn't mind being the ruler of the entire world, should he find the time and resources. If all countries were united, and all religions unified into one, then *someone* has to be the boss, right? I mean, Sun Myung's already wearing a crown, it would just be silly to look elsewhere.

But fundraising and world domination were just two of the three big pillars of the Moonie Empire. The third was definitely, almost ostentatiously, marriage. When it comes time as a Unification Church member to settle down and get married, like most things, Reverend Moon has the whole thing figured out on your behalf. Like a blessed, holy dating app, Moon will pick a partner for you from a great big stack of photographs, or by pointing at you and then at your future, totally-not-picked-at-random partner in a purpose-built hall, and that's it. His word is reasonably final. Love is all you need, and what better chance at love than with a complete stranger who may not even speak your language. That's your life partner, off you go, best of luck.

The cool thing is, Sun Myung Moon had a vision of a caramel world. When you believe that everyone has the same parents, you pretty much by default have to believe that all races are equal, so the Reverend Moon intentionally mixed races when he made marriage matches. This was one of the main principles that signified the 'unification' part of the Unification

Church – by uniting all the races in marriage, world peace is a shoo-in. Reverend Moon was super-cool with everyone. Except women were obviously secondary to men. And as long as you weren't a Communist. Or Jewish. Or gay. That's the less cool thing. Moon was an *unbelievable* bigot. He was all for bringing people together, as long as they were the *right* people.

I mean, you wouldn't expect a guy whose main bag is heterosexual marriage and constant baby-making to be completely in favour of same-sex relationships, but Moon went a smidge over the top. He called homosexuality a perversion, implied that God would wipe gay folk out, and he used the word 'dung' a lot whenever he was talking about homosexuality. Moon's inability to accept that some people, good people, with 100 per cent consent, are going to stick it wherever they want to stick it really took the shine off his other messages of inclusion, unification, and peace. It's almost like all those other messages were just thinly veiled manifestations of Sun Myung Moon's narrow and bigoted world view. It's almost like that.

Suffice to say, in the world of the Unification Church, marriage is *everything*. It's the path to sinless perfection, the reversal of original sin, the gate through which people can become the new Adam and Eve, and the gimmick by which the Moonies can reach a worldwide audience via very predictable news reports every single time. Nothing puts eyes on a telly screen like rows and rows of identically dressed couples in wedding garb, where black tuxedos alternating with white wedding dresses ad nauseam make a pleasing repetitive pattern in a massive, well-known sports stadium. Black, white, black, white, ultra-right, no sex for forty nights.

To participate in a Moonie Holy Marriage Blessing Ceremony, held every few years, you will have already had your partner picked for you, traditionally by Reverend Moon himself, or more recently your parents, a Unification Church pastor, online matching sites, or a qualified 'matching advisor'. While you should love your chosen partner, actual romantic love isn't necessary or encouraged, as that's the kind of nasty business that leads to promiscuity and bad marriages. Think with your god, not your gonads.

Once you've become probably at-best-acquaintances with your betrothed, head to your local or international blessing ceremony. Mind you, if you haven't found a match well before the ceremony, you can often be matched a few days before from among the other losers who can't even find an arranged partner – a bit like scalping tickets to your virginity outside a rock concert twenty minutes before the support band comes on. The first of these blessing ceremonies was held in 1960 in Seoul with thirty-six couples, and ceremonies involving thousands of couples have been conducted around the world, from Madison Square Garden to Seoul's Olympic Stadium. Some marriage aspirants travel internationally to attend the ceremonies in massive sporting stadiums, and some even participate via a video link, which is only as weird as the ceremonies occurring at all.

Unless you're very lucky to get a post-dawn appointment, your hair and make-up appointment on the big day will be at some ungodly hour in the middle of the night, crammed between literally hundreds of other hair and make-up appointments. Hours afterwards, once you've picked up your standard veil, gloves, and scarf, you'll hoist yourself and your partner into a bus heading to the great big blessing barn, take a plastic seat, and get ready for some very, very long speeches from the reverend and/or his missus. Lucky for you, you've got someone next to you to fall asleep on for the rest of your life, provided you even live in the same country. Then it's your turn for action: chasten and purify your partner by striking them gently three times, symbolically banishing the last of their sin out. Next, have a little sip of holy wine or grape cordial with your significant stranger, symbolically digesting little bits of Adam and Eve. Finally, after being sprinkled with holy water by the reverend himself, who would probably do better with a firehose on the mist setting at this scale, get symbolically-but-not-legally hitched by reciting some vows and exchanging rings. It's as romantic as a football field full of battery hens, and considering the amount of polyester, a lot more flammable.

Your primary commitment to God and the church is appreciated, your secondary commitment to each other is acknowledged, and all going well you'll learn to tolerate each other for many decades to come.

But what of consummation? By far the most interesting and least hygienic of the Unification Church's rituals is the three-day sex ritual, performed by newly married couples no sooner than forty days after their crowded nuptials. See, to prove how devoted you are to God, you have to abstain from sex for forty days after marriage. Considering nearly everyone in the church is a virgin when they're married, that's some pretty hardcore celibacy – a lifetime plus forty days. But in the Unification Church, nothing proves you love God more than an intense case of blue balls. There are even couples who wait for much, much longer than the forty days, some due to logistical issues, like living in different countries waiting for visas, and some because they don't want to make the same mistake Adam and Eve made, by fornicating before they were spiritually ready. Either way, by the time everybody gets to the three-day sex ritual, suffice to say everybody is pretty ready for a three-day sex ritual.

And the three-day sex ritual goes like this:

First, pick a holy place, or for want of a less euphemistically juvenile term, select a sacred room. Somewhere with a spiritual vibe. Somewhere goddy, but still *sexy*.

Bring with you some ordinary household items with the word 'holy' in front of them. A holy handkerchief. Holy salt. Holy clothes. Bring some bowls to hold water, and a picture of Sun Myung and Hak Ja Han, your True Parents, because there's nothing quite like losing your virginity with your parents watching.

Before you start, say a prayer that blesses the room, because you do NOT want Satan walking in on you in the middle of this. Then sprinkle some of the salt around the room and the bathroom – go north, south, east, west, and bless your sheets and pillows. They deserve it, they're about to get a workout.

Have a bath or a shower, fill up one of your bowls with water, and wet your hanky in it. Sure, you've just had a shower, but go ahead and wipe holy water all over your body with your holy hanky. Hell, do it three times, God loves things that come in threes. Bow to the picture of your True Parents three times, pray, bow, pray more, bow more, then when all that praying and bowing has made you super-horny: STRIP OFF AND DO IT. Woman on top, please. Go nuts, mates, you've waited long enough.

For the second day, just repeat the whole thing, again with the praying and the bowing and the hankies and the salt and the woman on top. Virginity is just a distant memory now, you sexy badasses.

For the third day though, the prayers are a bit different, because you're about to be reborn as Adam and Eve and you'll be husband and wife forever. Celebrate by having the man on top, and then when you're done, get ready to really get those hankies good and gross. Each of you take your holy handkerchief and give your genitals a good wipe with them. Don't you dare ever wash that hanky, and make sure you store it for the rest of time, your crusty sexual residue drying and caking up on it in the same box you keep your Christmas cards in.

There! You're done. You're proper man and wife now, with some truly disgusting jizz accessories in storage.

With all the odd mass rituals and slowly drying handkerchiefs, it is easy to forget that Sun Myung Moon was a clever operator. Despite his golden robes and ostentatious crown, he was no idiot. Even though the Unification Church thrived successfully in a number of Asian countries, Moon was obsessed with being big and staying big in America. If you want to operate your cult with as few problems or investigative probes as possible, it makes sense to befriend as many potentially simpatico politicians as you can. And, let's see, for a cult that regards money and power as priorities over the needs of the individual, which politicians are most likely to be simpatico? Republicans! Good ol' Republicans. The Unification Church's ownership of the super right-wing *Washington Times* meant that friends in conservative politics could be easily made via vicious journalistic attacks on the centre and left of politics. Moon made donations to and rallied for Richard Nixon, particularly backing him throughout the Watergate scandal, and helped both found and fund conservative organisations, movements, and campaigns in both the US and Korea. Presidents Ford, Reagan, and Bush Snr were all happy to accept Moon's help. Anywhere where extreme conservatism, anti-Communist sentiment and the canonisation of heterosexual marriage were found, Moon was willing to throw spare change and shoe-leather at it.

Reverend Moon was also in strong cahoots with the South Korean government, helping start the aggressively titled 'International Federation for the Extermination of Communism', which is just about as cute a name as you can get. He gained a lot of favour with Western governments for his strong stance against Communism, partly because they didn't see him as a cult leader, however there was a teensy bit of suspicion that Moon was trying to strongly influence US Congress with pro–South Korean propaganda. Some suggested that the Unification Church was a front for the South Korean version of the CIA, but most politicians had a more favourable opinion, at least as far as they could use him. They saw Moon as a charismatic religious minister with a lot of followers, who unless you counted mass weddings and thinking you're the actual Messiah, believed in a lot of the same things, and had the same kind of fears and concerns about the future of humanity as their voters did.

Unfortunately for Reverend Moon, lining the pockets of politicians can draw a lot of attention to your organisation, particularly from the opponents of the politicians you're greasing up who'd like to throw trip-wires in front of your attempts to keep funding them. In 1984 Moon was tried and convicted for tax fraud, because he'd failed to declare quite a chunk of income and investment. Moon's defence team argued that the money was church money, not personal money, but the difficult thing about cults run by people who like to earn a lot of money by exploiting its members for cash is that the line between personal money and church money is just so damn blurry.

Moon had done such a good job of ingratiating himself to conservative US powerbrokers before his arrest that prominent American religious leaders and politicians campaigned heavily for his release while he was incarcerated, claiming the conviction was politically and racially motivated, sprinkled with religious-persecution polka-dots. Say what you like about rich and powerful people, they're sure good at keeping other rich and powerful people out of jail. Moon was released after thirteen months.

By the early 2000s, Moon had redeemed himself somewhat in the US, although it's likely he wasn't taken as seriously as he was previously. It was a considerable risk to his credibility then to invite a bunch of congressmen to the Dirksen Senate Office Building in Washington to watch him be crowned as humanity's saviour and the second coming of Christ, but that didn't stop him. He invited some very high ranking politicos to attend a vaguely described award ceremony, only to throw himself an I'm-the-Messiah surprise party. Moon could have stopped there, but added whimsically in his acceptance speech that he'd already convinced both Stalin and Hitler to overcome their wickedness in the afterlife and be born again, fresh and sinless. Reverend Moon, everybody knows that as soon as you bring up Hitler, you've lost the argument.

The audience listening to the grandiose, unhinged speech shifted uncomfortably, because the audience was made up of normal human beings. Mind you, most of the dignitaries and bigwigs attending thought they were there to see a ceremony honouring folks who had contributed to world peace and whatnot, not the coronation of a kooky nut. Moon had used the same technique he usually employed for recruiting college students – inviting them to something they'd feel they'd like to attend, without mentioning who's behind it or what its true agenda is – on distinguished, experienced statesmen. How embarrassing.

The Moonies have drawn a lot of attention from cult special-ists and 'deprogrammers' in the past, making it onto television reports as parents and siblings plead for their kin to come on home, or as the subject of raging, winnerless arguments about whether or not brainwashing is real, or as a slick PR represen-tative from the church dressed in a natty eighties suit calmly and warmly refutes an interviewer's cult claims as jealousy, persecution, and nonsense. In reports that focus on kidnapping people to get them out of cults, the Moonies are really over-represented, par-ticularly in the 1970s when cult-panic was at its peak. Family members would turn up at church centre gates and front doors, sons and daughters were stuffed into vans or ambushed with interventions on rare home visits. Parents, understandably at their wits' end with worry, were literally kidnapping their own kids.

For deprogrammers – who have never really been overly successful, despite charging large fees and being incredibly earnest – the advantage of focusing on a cult that has a lot of members like the Unification Church is that it is also likely to have a lot of ex-members. Ex-members are fantastic at understanding the mental and emotional processes that current members are going through, so they're a great resource for deprogrammers to use to try and get people to leave. In the usual scenario, a de-programmer would question, cajole and harangue a kidnapped cult member, and rope in the sympathetic ex-cult member to talk about their experience in a good-cop/bad-cop set-up. Often though, the subject of the deprogramming sessions would just fake improvement and acceptance and then simply trot back to the cult once the heat was off. Sometimes to someone who believes that outsiders are on the way to Hell, the presence of 'fallen' ex-members just serves to reinforce the idea that if you leave, you're stuffed.

By anyone's account, Moon's family, the 'Perfect Family', was almost comically far from perfect. By the time they'd been settled in the United States for a decade and a half, the cracks had been showing for some time. Brought up as incredibly spoiled rich brats with little parental involvement, Sun Myung and Hak Ja Han's children were a mess of unfettered entitlement, an utter lack of discipline, and blatant imperfection. Because they were busy doing cult stuff, avoiding tax, and shopping, the Moons insisted that their followers take care of all the child-rearing duties, but understandably none of the followers were game to discipline the Perfect Family's children. Disciplining the children of someone you believed to be God would be like one of the three shepherds of the nativity spanking Jesus over his knee – unimaginable.

The children lived in a massive mansion – one of those grotesque jobs with a bowling alley and waterfall in it, for the kind of people who can't stand bowling or looking at waterfalls with riffraff off the street. For all the problems that their father claimed America had, and that he could help solve, the children of Sun Myung Moon were constantly and enthusiastically suckling at its debauched teat.

In the late seventies Steve Moon, the Reverend's eldest son, shot some of his fellow high-school students with a BB gun and was expelled, which just left him with more free time to drink heavily and do drugs. Despite his father's faith in the curative powers of a good wedding, marriage didn't tame Steve, and he continued on his diet of eighty per cent cocaine. When his wife suggested that he was doing perhaps a smidge too many drugs a touch too often, he punched her in the face. She divorced him, and he died of a heart attack at age forty-five.

Heung Jin Moon didn't take enough care driving his Jeep on an icy road and died when he crashed it at the age of seventeen. He was unmarried at the time, which caused a problem as his father had always preached that unmarried people wouldn't be admitted into Heaven. There ain't a problem that the Korean

Messiah can't fix though, and that was easily solved – Sun Myung married his dead son off to the daughter of one of his mates, and she walked up the aisle carrying a photograph of him, thankfully taken pre-crash. It is important to note that there was no honeymoon.

Daughter Un Jin Moon, having submitted obediently to her own husband according to her father's guidelines, left him after claims of physical abuse.

In 1999 the True Parents' eleventh child, Phillip Moon, committed suicide rather than continue in his unhappy, arranged marriage, dying in Las Vegas after chucking himself off a casino balcony.

Everything was a bit of a mess, and it was all downhill from there. Reverend Moon wasn't as sprightly as he used to be, and news of his errant children kept slipping out. It was time for a change.

In 2008 Reverend Moon appointed his youngest son, Hyung Jin Sean, as the new leader of the Unification Church worldwide, and in 2009, his daughter and fourth child, In Jin, assumed public control of the Unification Church in America. In Jin initiated a period of intense modernisation in the relatively progressive US. Well, as modern as a church that espouses traditional marriage between two virgins can get, and even then not actually super-modern in the textbook sense. The church was renamed 'Lovin' Life Ministries' with the aim of attracting younger, cooler recruits who really appreciate the hip power of apostrophes. One of the biggest and most significant changes In Jin made was allowing church members to choose their own spouses, which admittedly is a gigantic leap forward for a church in say, the 1800s, but in 2009 seems just a bit on the tardy side. She also encouraged a lighter attitude to divorce, which may have had something to do with her own unhappy marriage and multiple lovers. Church gatherings became less formal and more like teenage hang-out sessions, including table tennis, video games, concerts, and rock music. You know that unbelievably edgy, vaguely Christian, highly religious rock band you like? No. Nobody does.

Unsurprisingly, In Jin's changes weren't popular with every-body in the church. Many saw her as a pretentious upstart with a bogus British accent who was trampling all over tradition, but realistically that was only because she was a pretentious upstart with a bogus British accent who was trampling all over tra-dition. Membership dwindled dramatically and then – almost as dramatically – In Jin disappeared from public life. It turned out she had a pregnancy to hide, and she lay low in Cape Cod to gestate a baby that wasn't her husband's.

Sun Myung Moon, father of ostensibly one of the least perfect families ever known in public life, died of pneumonia compli-cations in September 2012, leaving his wife to lead his church and businesses, and reclaim her children's carved-out chunks of them as her own. Sun Myung also left at least one illegitimate child behind, leaving the values he had preached for most of his life in a big, steaming, farcical heap.

Moon's legacy is a confused tangle at best. His body lay in state for visitors to come and genuflect to in a room in his South Korean mansion, a rambling house built to intentionally resemble the US Capitol Building. His church lay around the world with new and various names and a blurry succession plan. In Jin was head of the Unification Church in America, Hyung Jin Sean was the head of the worldwide organisation, known as (shakes up pious words in a bag, empties bag) Family Federation for World Peace and Unification, and then when his mother kicked him out of power, he started the (shakes, empties) World Peace and Unification Sanctuary. Hak Ja Han took over as Messiah, leaving an empty chair beside her during blessing ceremonies to signify Sun Myung's absence, while another son, Hyun Jin Preston, runs the (shakes, empties) Family Peace Association and the Global Peace Foundation. Put simply, it's a bloody shambles, and nothing a three-hour committee meeting and some good marketing couldn't sort out.

Still, even though the Unification Church's power and influence has dwindled to a whisper, it and its oddly mutated offshoots still make the news occasionally.

In March 2018, Hyung Jin Sean presided over a blessing ceremony conducted by his World Peace and Unification Sanctuary church in Pennsylvania, a gun-obsessed cluster of nuts with only loose ideological ties to the Moonies. He'd started the offshoot when his mother ousted him from the original church, claiming he was the true heir of the True Parents. A massive fan of automatic firearms and really long names for things, Sean intentionally uses and misuses some of his father's terminology in his own church, including at this ceremony, the 'Cosmic True Parents of Heaven, Earth and Humanity Book of Life Registration Blessing'. Ties are made to the original Moonies manifesto with phrases like 'true parents', although while the original Reverend Moon occasionally referred to the Bible's 'rods of iron' as being the truth or word of God, Sean decided that rods of iron are definitely, totally guns. The faithful were invited to pop along and renew their wedding vows with rods of iron as accessories, giving rise to the bizarre sight of couples in formal wear standing reverently in rows, wielding automatic weapons. Conveniently another Moon son, Justin, runs a gun-manufacturing business and provided equipment for attendees, who were each told to bring an AR15 automatic rifle along for show. Partly because you don't usually see mass wedding vow renewals attended by gun-toting couples bedecked with crowns made from bullets, and partly because the ceremony occurred just two weeks after a school shooting by a gunman with an AR15 at Stoneman Douglas High School in Florida, the story made the news with horrified gusto.

Depending on who you read or believe, the Unification Church has had up to three million members, making it one of the most successful cults of all time if you consider membership an indication of success. If you consider whether or not the cult leader's professed goal was reached as an indication of success, you'd be disappointed. In his lifetime – at least on Earth; jury's out on how he's going in Heaven – Sun Myung Moon was no more successful than Adam or Jesus at finishing the mission of getting everyone married and establishing the Kingdom of Heaven on Earth.

Mind you, Jesus never owned a newspaper.

THE FAMILY

IN THE EARLY hours of 14 August 1987, a Friday, state and federal police barged their way into a secluded house near the edge of Lake Eildon in regional Victoria, Australia. Officers held a handful of the adults there back while they searched the whole house, picking up and removing any of the nervous, crying children they found. The children were skinny and hungry, some with bleached-blond hair, all believing they were brothers and sisters with the same parents, and not a collection of fraudulently adopted, unrelated children, which was the truth.

This was a house owned by a cult called The Family, led by Anne Hamilton-Byrne. Despite the fact she'd only ever given birth to one child, all of the children at the house at Lake Eildon believed Anne was their mother. Anne was a glamorous woman with a commanding presence and a fondness for hallucinogenic drugs, and the 1987 raid on one of her properties was the beginning of the end of the most scandalous phase of her cult – the phase in which Anne and her faithful followers acquired children by questionable means, severely disciplined them, and dressed them in adorable clothes.

There are so many stories about Anne and The Family, and most of them are difficult to prove. In the time since the events in the stories are supposed to have occurred, Hamilton-Byrne has, thanks to the ravages of dementia, stopped making sense. By the time you read this sentence, she may have even died. Long after the time when Hamilton-Byrne stopped having the kind of brain that the law would consider reliable, an incredible amount of research has been undertaken on Anne and her cult. Members past and present have been interviewed, police files and videos pored over, and now-adult cult children gently asked to share their stories. Two of the prime gatherers of this information have been Australian journalist Chris Johnston and film maker Rosie Jones, who between them have generated a book, a documentary, and countless articles comprised of and based on those stories. But even true stories don't get doddering, nonsensical old ladies into court. If it wasn't both unlikely and unkind, you could entertain a fanciful notion that getting dementia is a crafty way to avoid getting in trouble.

Now. The stories.

Despite a ravenous taste for a chic life of affluence and a desperate need to have people believe she was born with a silver spoon in every orifice, Anne Hamilton-Byrne was originally Evelyn Edwards, born to a semi-present, itinerant father and a paranoid schizophrenic mother. Her mother, Florence, was mentally ill at a time in Australia where mental illness was absolutely not efficiently or sensitively treated, and she spent great chunks of her life in mental health institutions – the kind cutely called 'asylums' at the time, with all of the progressive treatment methods and uplifting environs the word 'asylum' evokes. Florence suffered partly from extreme paranoia and delusions, including believing she could speak to the dead as a medium. It would not be fully outrageous to suggest that her daughter inherited some of her delusional, paranoid behaviour, at least as far as believing she could talk to those on another plane, and being considered a teensy bit bonkers by objective observers at the time.

With Anne's mother in care and her father disinterested in parental or other responsibilities, Anne spent a lot of time in an orphanage in Melbourne. Despite being able to find evidence of thousands of people who spent time in orphanages not growing up to be obsessive and illegal adopters of other people's children, the orphanage part of Anne Hamilton-Byrne's early life is still the kind of thing that makes you raise your eyebrows and say 'Well, no wonder' under your breath. Many theories circulate about Hamilton-Byrne that suggest her attitude towards, and treatment of, children and motherhood were seeded directly from her own relatively neglected, lonely, and intensely lower-class upbringing. Still, not everyone from that kind of background grows up to be accused of cruelty by a medium-sized group of people, so the jury's still out.

Anne married her first husband, Lionel, in 1941 and began adopting the airs and graces of the elegant socialite she aspired to be, and badly wanted others to believe she was. The Evelyn of her modest childhood was gone, and now 'Anne' wanted all the fixings – expensive clothes, flashy cars, impressive jewellery, facelift after facelift after facelift, and children. Lots and lots of children.

Anne and Lionel had one biological daughter, Judith, but whether via reproductive problems or a sense that reproduction was an undignified, mucky business, she was Anne's first and last biological child. Anne and Lionel set out to adopt a boy from Dr Barnardo's Homes, an organisation that fostered and adopted out children from disadvantaged backgrounds. She no doubt considered herself the saviour of disadvantaged children, but with a bit of a narcissistic twist: she believed that there was no way a disadvantaged child could be better off with their real parents than they would be with her. Ironically, over the next few decades, she very successfully proved the opposite.

Unfortunately, Lionel died in a car accident before he and Anne had a chance to adopt their first baby. She married a second time, to a man who was helpful as a usable contact for academic patsies at the University of Melbourne, and a third time to Bill Byrne, her partner in crime and main cameraman when she wanted her idyllic frolics in her gardens with pets and flowers captured for posterity.

In the 1950s and 1960s, suburban Australia was settling very comfortably into its relaxing post-war semi-affluence, and in the more well-to-do areas – those that Anne Hamilton-Byrne loved the absolute Pucci pantsuits out of – affluent toffs and their well-meaning but quite-bored-indeed wives were looking for something more than their tolerably comfortable existence offered. Just as it was the Petri dish for so many other new religious movements in the same period, an intense interest in Eastern mysticism, new age philosophies and the occult flourished in neighbourhoods with too much time on their hands and the privileged luxury of wondering what life was all about. You simply couldn't *move* at a 1960s Australian fancy cocktail party without a prawn vol-au-vent and a lengthy discussion about your guru. The upper classes didn't want anything too weird, though. Maybe just a bit of homemade satay sauce on the hors d'oeuvres at the next cocktail party, some Japanese lanterns around the jacuzzi, and lots and lots of yoga.

This time in suburban Australia's history was truly Anne Hamilton-Byrne's time to shine. She had an open, arresting face, particularly after her cosmetic surgery, with eyes that pierced directly through your soul until they hit your wallet. In her calm, confident voice, which she'd trained to almost be completely rid of her background working-class Australian twang, she could spout gently mutated streams of vague Hinduism, Buddhist theosophical yarns and enlightened Christian claptrap, all dressed up in yoga classes for primarily well-to-do ladies. In her reconstructed theological macramé, Anne was offering believers a restart, a cleansing of any of the karmic detritus her listeners and yoga students had accumulated in their lives, past and present. She was offering a way to ensure life after earthly death in a higher realm, not the same old, same old terrestrial life that stuffy, boring reincarnation offered. Here was a way to kick the repetitive cycle of reincarnation and get past the velvet rope to the good afterlife.

Anne was a bit fond of the odd white lie here and there along the way to make herself sound more sparkly and mystical. In addition to the everyday acceptable visual fibs about hair colour – she was a natural redhead, but a public blonde – and the natural shape of her facial features, Anne scattered little lies like biscuit crumbs at a lisp clinic. On different days her children were descendants of King David, or she herself was descended from French aristocracy. She used to be a celebrated opera singer, or she was trained in psychiatry and physiotherapy. Her father was mates with millionaires, and her mother hung out with Tibetan gurus. Sometimes she signed her name Anne Hamilton, sometimes Fiona McDonald, sometimes Michelle Sutherland. Whatever, her penmanship was gorgeous. Her array of blonde wigs, perched atop her increasingly surprised-looking head, were a lot less convincing than her falsified signatures, but wigs aren't lying or forgery, per se. They're more *styling*.

It wasn't enough for Anne Hamilton-Byrne to pretend she was of high-society lineage, though. Possibly after an LSD-inspired revelation, or possibly after a quick decision to just lie to people from that point onwards, she decided to take her aspirational bullshit one giant step further and claim that she was Jesus Christ in lady form. A steady stream of cult leaders throughout history have also claimed they were the living embodiment of the Messiah, but few of them have done so just to impress their upper-class suburban friends. While the neighbours are just renovating a second-floor parents' retreat or putting in a swimming pool, this sheila thinks she's Jesus. Surrounding house values must have skyrocketed.

By the early 1960s, Anne had amassed a loyal cluster of yoga students, drawn to her self-assured manner, inspirational monologues, and no doubt impressive bendiness. Initially injecting more and more spiritual and occult patter into her yoga classes and then moving to increasingly well-attended, less yoga-centric meetings in church halls and members' houses, Anne was becoming an absolutely natural leader, utterly convinced of her own appeal and easily able to inspire devotion. She had introduced long speeches about loyalty and started asking her devotees to undergo initiation rituals. It was time to get serious.

Hamilton-Byrne's human ticket into the circle she wanted to not only be included in, but to be the leader of, was scrawny British intellectual Dr Raynor Johnson, head of Queen's College at the University of Melbourne at the time, who had influence, rich friends, and looked for all the world like Colonel Sanders after many hours in a tumble dryer, but without the benefit of always being around fried chicken. Dr Johnson was keenly, uncomfortably interested in the supernatural and the nature of God, and liked to do things like visit mystics in India for a good old spiritual chinwag. Somehow, ostensibly via incredible intuition and psychic powers – but probably by asking around and thanks to the fact that her husband at the time was his gardener – Anne knew the doctor was looking for mystical guidance. She had her timing just right in late 1962 when she knocked on Raynor's door, and he let her in and listened to her theories, sought her guidance, and stared at her comparatively youthful perkiness. Anne also knew that Dr Johnson was dripping with exactly the kind of social cachet and intellectual credibility that would get her in good with a ritzy crowd, one that was also looking for something a little bit glamorous and out there. It was a symbiotic relationship with naïvety and curiosity on one side, and a desperate thirst for social climbing and power on the other.

There's no specific evidence available that proves Raynor was in love with Anne, but he behaved exactly like the kind of smart guy who thinks he deserves the attention of a hot babe, finds one, and then lets her boss him around and treat him like garbage for decades. In his diary he wrote – presumably with his free hand – that Anne was 'supernaturally beautiful', so it's reasonable to project that he was a bit into her in a wishful, not-strictly-professional way.

As a professor of physics, Dr Johnson should probably have known better than to become involved in a group that spread grossly unscientific rumours about the nature of life, death and existence. With the later revelations of the cult's practices, university officials have considered revoking his honours and renaming a wing that bears his name. But sometimes good physicists turn bad, get interested in metaphysics, meet a Svengali-like glamour with high ideas and higher hairlines, and boom, suddenly they're the co-founder of a cult. It's a tale as old as time.

In Anne Hamilton-Byrne's world, you're nothing without a guru. Throughout her religious life, Anne claimed that her mother had had an Indian guru that, obviously, she used to astral travel to go and visit, and that Anne herself had several gurus, including a couple that had been dead for decades, but came and gave her a visit anyway. Death and plane fares were just not a problem for Hamilton-Byrne. When she turned up at Raynor's door, she insisted that she was his guru. She did not meet with much argument.

Around the time Raynor joined, Anne's group was called The Great White Brotherhood of Initiates and Masters, a name that could not sound more like an offshoot of the Ku Klux Klan if you put it in a pillowcase and set it on fire. She introduced Raynor to the group via its standard method of initiation or 'going through', which was to take lots and lots of LSD, and he knew he'd found his Messiah. He knew loads of rich members of elite society – intellectuals who quite liked a cocktail party with a touch of the occult, the kind of party that holds only slightly more potential danger than everyone throwing the keys to their fancy cars in a bowl at the front door.

Anne was a massive, devoted fan of LSD, and from around 1960, she found an easy way to get it. As she fancied herself a nurse, and very much liked associating with people like the head matron and administrator of private hospitals, Anne found herself tightly associated with the Newhaven Psychiatric Hospital in Kew, a relatively well-to-do suburb of Melbourne. A number of the shakers and decision-makers at Newhaven were under Anne's thrall, convinced by her spirituality and uncanny intuition and drawn to her group of sophisticated theological dabblers. The hospital, now closed, was putting itself at the cutting edge of LSD and electro-convulsive therapy, and Anne sourced LSD – still legal at the time – from her willing contacts there.

From the 1950s through to the 1970s, LSD was experimentally and then legitimately used to treat a number of conditions, including anxiety, alcoholism, and depression. This was because it was considered to foster feelings of interconnection and really sidle up to a body's serotonin producers on the dance floor and give them a vigorous shimmy. Research in the 1960s showed that LSD users were more likely than others to have what they called 'spiritual experiences' and feel closer to those around them during their acid session, even imagining their 'therapists' as parental figures. All the better then, for self-proclaimed Messiah Anne Hamilton-Byrne to hang out around 'patients' while they were undergoing 'therapy', asserting a gentle influence, manipulating a spiritual experience, and whispering strong suggestions in their ears about being their only logical choice as life coach and leader.

At Newhaven Hospital, LSD 'subjects' would sit in a darkened room, sometimes listening to music, while therapists observed them and Anne wafted in and out, making sure her ethereal presence was an integral part of each tripper's intensely spiritual experience. The therapists were fine with it. They were professionals, they weren't going to let a little thing like a female Messiah putting thoughts into drug-addled patients' heads stop them from getting their work done.

As Anne's association with Newhaven became more entrenched, the hospital also came in handy as a tool for threatening cult members whose loyalty was in question, or who didn't know how to stay quiet. According to a previous member, followers were reminded that for a cult with strong connections to a psychiatric hospital, getting someone committed would be easy. The fact that Newhaven was also very heavily into treatment by electro-convulsive therapy sweetened the threat considerably – it was either shut up and behave, or have electrodes stuck on your head and try not to bite your own tongue.

Newhaven was also where Anne had met her third husband, Bill, who had taken his son there for treatment for depression and addiction. Anne did her neat trick of burning into his very essence with her super-sexy eyes and, boom, he left his wife and took up his rightful place just behind Anne for the rest of his life.

But Newhaven Hospital was good for more than just picking up dapper, adoring husbands, it was also a primo place from which to recruit followers – vulnerable people, suggestible people, people who were looking for a solution to their problems or someone to just take care of their lives from that point on. How kind of Anne then, to focus for her own purposes on people seeking psychiatric help. Having inside information about their therapy and problems before meeting her recruit victims, thanks to so many of those conducting the therapy already being cult members, would have made it easy to pretend to have incredible psychic insight into each individual on a deeply personal level, should a cult leader wish to do so. Patients were both impressed and convinced, and honoured that this god-like creature had deigned to include them in her plane. They didn't need much more encouragement than that.

The growing group started meeting at Raynor's house, and as it approached a couple of hundred members, at a freshly built Dandenong Ranges building called 'Santiniketan Lodge', paid for by the spiritually besotted Raynor. Exactly like those rich neighbourhoods you didn't grow up in, Anne, Raynor, and later her third husband Bill's simpatico mates all liked to live near each other, forming a kind of creepy reverse ghetto with unbelievably lush carpeting. It's easy to generate the standard us-and-them cult mentality when you already consider yourselves intellectually separate by virtue of education, spiritually separate by way of superior enlightenment, and geographically separate by way of a posh enclave out in the sticks.

One of the things that The Family did well was to hang out in fancy houses in out-of-the-way rural areas, a skill more often displayed by people who haven't swindled money out of followers who believe they're the living embodiment of Christ, but not always. There was the aforementioned Santiniketan Lodge – named after an Indian town that was home to an experimental school run by Indian mystic Rabindranath Tagore, quite appropriate for a mission-brown bungalow in downtown Ferny Creek, where weekly meetings were held. Well, 'meetings'. Casual meetings at Dr Raynor's house with a handful of followers evolved into far more structured events with over a hundred attending regularly. Sometimes focusing on meditation, sometimes yoga, often sermons by Anne Hamilton-Byrne, assisted greatly by a light-show specifically designed to make her seem extra Jesus-spooky. Anne wanted everyone to know that she was the focus of their attention, thank you very much, and you may gaze on her downward dog with reverence, awe, and incredibly flattering lighting.

There was also Broom Farm in Kent, England, and more than one house on an expanse of property near the Catskill Mountains in New York State, both purchased thanks to generous donations from The Family cult members so that Anne herself never had to reach into her breezy, brushed-linen pockets. The international properties easily facilitated Anne's and Bill's love of travel, giving them places to stay any time they wanted to visit non-Australian spiritual gurus who were too lazy to appear in visions to them locally, or whenever they wanted to abandon the children they proclaimed love for into the care of others for weeks on end, or whenever they were on the run from investigation, prosecution, and extradition. Handy.

And then there was Kai Lama at Lake Eildon, where fourteen children who were not Anne Hamilton-Byrne's were kept. Some may say that Kai Lama, nicknamed 'Uptop' because every kiddy prison needs a catchy pseudonym, was where the children were 'raised'. Others, including the actual children, are just as likely to call it the place they were 'kept as prisoners for their entire formative years'. Pota[y]to/pota[h]to. Up to twenty-eight children were housed at Kai Lama over two decades, fewer than one-twenty-eighth of that figure happily or voluntarily. Some were children of willing cult members who handed them over, and some were – depending on how much faith you're willing to put into signed paperwork – Anne and Bill's adopted children.

One of the most disturbing features of The Family was how thoroughly its nefarious tendrils permeated the institutions it relied on for its survival. The number of adopted children Anne Hamilton-Byrne was able to secure for her own manufactured brood would have been much smaller were it not for sneaky helping hands at all stages of the baby-introduction process. Anne sought out recruitable cult members who were already working in health services, or ensured existing members were placed in useful positions of employment in relevant hospitals and institutions.

That said, the fact that Hamilton-Byrne was looking to adopt Australian and New Zealand children before adoptions were subject to strict regulations also worked in her favour. From the 1950s to the 1980s in Australia, it was relatively easy to adopt a baby from a young, unmarried mother, and unbelievably difficult as a young, unmarried mother to access counselling, be aware of your legal rights, or object to your baby being whisked out and away from you and adopted off before you'd even sat up for a sip of orange juice. Not only did impressionable pregnant ladies have to deal with the considerable and grossly unfair stigma attached to being pregnant without a husband, a great number of them simply weren't properly consulted regarding whether or not they actually wanted to keep their biological child. Women with mental health problems or substance abuse problems had virtually no chance of keeping their babies once they were labelled 'unfit', and it was handy that cult members at Newhaven had ready access to a number of substances people could happily be invited to abuse. So-called 'forced adoptions' were already happening all over the place, but The Family had the added advantage of containing people in high medical places. Say what you like about Anne, but she was one hell of a networker.

When a mother of acceptable stock – white, attractive, and vulnerable – presented at the Maternity Ward for Single Girls Who Should Be Ashamed of Themselves, word would get around via the midwife grapevine and – after quickly patting herself on the back for having the foresight to recruit a whole mess of nurses into her baby-stealing cult – Anne would prepare the house for another new addition. In some cases, Anne would adopt them, in others some of Anne's followers would adopt them and then 'gift' them to her. Anne adopted fourteen children. *Fourteen.* That is a LOT of children for somebody who already has an intensive daily moisturising and wig-maintenance schedule.

Hamilton-Byrne went to even more bizarre lengths to make people believe that she was popping out at least some of these babies herself, commissioning roomy smocks to wear during her mock incubations, and then suddenly appearing with babies. In one instance she even managed to convince – although in this case 'convince' is an uncommonly strong word – people that she'd just squeezed out triplets. She and Bill doctored adoption documents and even went as far as to register the triplets with the authorities in order to claim that all three babies were hers, when they were not even from the same mother. It's such a fine line between 'serene, sudden mother of three' and 'severe and dangerous mental illness gone untreated' sometimes, isn't it? With the other children, she would bunch them together roughly according to height and declare them twins or triplets, re-assigning their birthdays to fit. What the hell, there's no actual evidence that children develop emotional and behavioural problems if they're brought up without love and stability and a sense of identity. Well, not *much.*

According to her so-called children, Anne's plan was to have them continue her work after some kind of unspecified holocausty, apocalypsey event. They'd inherit the leftover Earth with the power of vegetables, hair dye, and isolation from the rest of society. Divine orders, it was claimed. No choice. They were the chosen ones, and if you're into things like calling blond-haired children a 'master race' – something that historically has not ended well – the children were definitely under the impression that they were a pivotal part of a master race. There's chatter about the traps that when Anne regularly went and stayed in her US property, she was also investigating the possibility of starting another adoption-scam-based family in the Northern Hemisphere as well, although no evidence. Spares, perhaps, just in case Armageddon happened in an unexpected spot of the globe. A kind of Master Race 2: Apocalyptic Boogaloo.

Partly due to her dream of being an effortless mother to an idyllic, *Sound of Music* pack of saccharine brats, and partly due to her need to make them truly believe that they were all part of the same family, Anne and her followers did their best to make all her adopted children look the same. And make no mistake – 'the same' was very much at the racial purity end of the spectrum that some of the world's worst people hang out near. The girls were dressed in identical demure, almost turn-of-the-century frocks, with their long hair tied back with ribbons. The boys were also dressed in exactly the same outfits as each other, with horrifying identical triangular bowl cuts that were bleached white, looking in much the same way that children who are not in horror movies don't. In fact, due to the white, bobbed hair and because his stepfather had ties to The Family, rumours abound that Julian Assange is one of the children in the family photographs. He isn't, but he has spent at least a decade unintentionally copying their look.

The children's surnames were changed to Hamilton-Byrne to further extend the bizarre Brady Bunch fantasy, and a fanciful flexibility was displayed with their first names. Possibly helped by Bill Byrne's British birth, many of the children had more than one passport, and due to documents within the cult generally being treated as useful tools, reportedly many of the children had more than one birth certificate as well. Almost every news story and magazine article about The Family includes haunting pictures of the children lined up for photographs, their hair glinting in the regional Victorian sun, looking like their instant mind-control of you is a mere chanted nursery rhyme away, and yet getting through customs was a breeze.

In addition to the so-posed-it-hurts photographs of the children neatly lined up according to actual height and non-factual age, there's also a load of videos of them playing outdoors – exercising, soaking up regulation sunshine, running gleefully towards the camera in their play uniforms. Anne *loved* a home video – of herself, mostly – and would often appear alongside the children in the videos, drawing them into awkward embraces and exclaiming to camera how beautiful they were. In later life, the children said they were rewarded with sweets if they played up to the camera pretending they loved the shit out of being the plaything of a possible non-diagnosed psychopath, an easy win for children who were used to eating just two small serves of vegetables per day. The videos of happy munchkins waxing carefree and digging life are, like so many of their adoption circumstances, bullshit. These children had an absolute bugger of a horrible life, and there was little they could do to change it.

See, while Anne banged on and on endlessly about loving children, and how being a mother was the absolute ultimate shizz, she was utterly, utterly garbage at motherhood. Great at hamming it up for the camera, but completely terrible at anything even remotely resembling parenting skills. She lived in a separate house to her so-called children most of the time, and often in a different country, so child-rearing was primarily left to cult members willing to take on the job. Considering most members of The Great White Brotherhood would gladly do anything Hamilton-Byrne commanded, many were extremely willing to take on the job, and they were nicknamed 'aunties'. The children were home-schooled by the aunties, fed by the aunties, dressed by them, and most certainly disciplined by them.

Kai Lama was even registered as a school in 1984, passing yearly inspections by the education department so that it could keep operating undisturbed. The children were well versed in acting like everything was hunky-dory when inspectors, authorities and visitors were around, upon threat of – as with all of their activities – punishment and discipline. At times they were even encouraged to act 'retarded' to convince tradesmen that Kai Lama was a school for special needs children so that they wouldn't think anything dodgy was going on. You know. Nothing dodgy in this remote house full of skinny kids with bleached-blond hair. All normal.

Discipline was a strong, constantly applied theme in The Family, particularly at Kai Lama. Because The Family had co-opted loose interpretations of karma and reincarnation into its generally messed-up religious manifesto muesli, childhood suffering was considered to be an essential part of the process of clearing the sins of a past life. The delivery of punishments at Kai Lama was a task delegated to the aunties, who by some reports from the children took that responsibility extremely seriously. There are many reports of beatings – for tiny crimes, like a child speaking when they weren't supposed to, or for wetting the bed, or for accidentally breaking a recently imposed rule that they were completely unaware of. Stories of being hit around the legs and face with sticks and wooden rulers, doused with cold water, being denied food, and made to sleep outdoors all make regular fairy-tale stereotypes of evil stepmothers and strict governesses seem like a walk in the park.

But, as might be expected among miserable, hungry children with zero contact with the outside world, who don't know who their real parents are and are beaten regularly, physical discipline could only subdue them to a certain degree. As Hamilton-Byrne was already a robust fan of the controlling qualities of pharmaceuticals, the children in her remote care were dosed regularly and heavily with well-behaved-cherub-inducing drugs by the aunties. Mogadon, Serepax, Valium – no drug loosely intended for anxiety sufferers or bored, frustrated housewives was too good for the captive little darlings. Unsurprisingly, many of the surviving adopted children now report severe emotional problems and poor memories – the first being one of the reasons they have a right to legal justice, and the second being one of the reasons their testimony is often considered unreliable. Those kids never had a real chance of developing and maintaining normal serotonin levels, and even those who are still alive and living as respectable adults are likely at least partly broken. In addition to the actual medicines, as Anne also considered herself an expert in homeopathy, the aunties regularly gave homeopathic 'remedies' to their charges to help with vague physical or behavioural complaints, real or imagined. But, as everybody knows that both the benefits and the side-effects of homeopathic medicines are entirely imaginary, it seems a far sight less cruel than the other administered pharmaceuticals.

By the time the children reached the age of fourteen, it was time for their initiation, which unsurprisingly by this point involved a big ol' kiss from the LSD fairy. Still one of the cornerstones of The Family's messed-up suite of practices for both children and adults alike was the enthusiastic and almost indiscriminately applied use of LSD. More and more, the drug was regarded as the clearer of souls, able to erase bad karma from both the present and several previous lives, and the elevator to another plane of existence. It also allowed Anne to hint very gently to people in a highly suggestible state that she was definitely and totally Jesus. For Anne, LSD was like WD40 and gaffer tape combined – just throw it at any problem that arises and it'll probably solve it.

While Anne Hamilton-Byrne represented originality in that she was one of very few female cult leaders, few of the beliefs that she inflicted on her devout followers were original. She borrowed heavily from existing religions; even her claims that she was the resurrected Jesus Christ followed a narrative path well worn by multiple cranks before her. She claimed that when Jesus Christ was on Earth, the world was not ready for his message so he upped sticks and decided to pop back when it was a better time and place. And where better than Melbourne in the seventies, right? If it was good enough for Skyhooks, it was definitely good enough for Anne Hamilton-Byrne-slash-Jesus. She decided Raynor was her John the Baptist, and others close to her, such as her lawyer Peter Kibby, were her apostles. Just your normal, run-of-the-mill suburban book club, really.

The group hiked a familiar cult trail when the faithful, and especially the children, were given the idea that outsiders were dangerous and they were to keep to themselves and shut up. The children's motto was 'Unseen, Unheard, Unknown', and they were encouraged to keep themselves secret from anybody outside the walls of Kai Lama. Whenever any strangers approached the house, even distantly, the children all had well-rehearsed hiding places to run to in the basement and cupboards of the house, like a super-paranoid game of hide and seek. The children properly believed that unauthorised visitors to the house were there to kill them, just another sweet thought to pop into a child's head as they drift off to nightmare sleepytown before waking up for another day with a lack of food and a light beating.

To keep her adult followers in line, and remind them that their beliefs and practices were strictly not for outsiders, Anne loved to bang on about Judas and betrayal in between downward dogs. 'For neither have I betrayed any secrets to thine enemies, nor have I given thee a kiss of Judas' she would recite and make her followers repeat, really lifting the mood in the room to unprecedented levels of upbeat. Loyalty was almost as important to Anne as lipstick.

Sacrifice was also important to Anne Hamilton-Byrne, provided it was made by others and preferably directly into either her bank account or property portfolio. So effective were her methods of convincing her faithful to shove all their assets her way that Hamilton-Byrne's net worth is estimated at around $50 million. Aside from regular tithing, followers would pay for yoga classes and meditation guidance, and pitch in whenever Anne and Bill felt like a new house somewhere. When Jesus says she wants renovations on her country property and you suspect she might have the contacts to have you committed, you open your wallet.

Not content with a life filled with imprisoned children, being the Messiah, and getting facelifts, Anne Hamilton-Byrne also liked to spend her time telling people who they should and shouldn't marry, make babies with, or break up with. With what looked for all the world like arbitrary selection methods, she'd tell some Family-initiated couples they were no longer married to their partners, pair them off with other recently forcibly separated people, and tell them to get pregnant. Or she'd tell people their baby-making days were done and they should shut up reproductive shop. Or she'd tell people they didn't live in their old house anymore, but now lived in a different house. And the thing is, cult members would do what she said. They'd uproot the lives they were used to and switch into the lives they were told to get used to, because Anne had told them to.

It was easy for Anne to convince people that she knew more than them – even without the drugs, lightshows or threats of punishment – because Anne Hamilton-Byrne had what is known in the scientific literature as One of Those Faces. Or more realistically, due to her love of cosmetic surgery, Four or Five of

Those Faces. People reported that her eyes breaststroked instantly through your soul, and her calm, deep, reassuring voice was the kind that could convince you your bottom was on fire when you were sitting in the bath. You'd do whatever you could to avoid disappointing her, and not just because she had a kind of menacing, omniscient edge. For the people she'd specifically chosen, she was exactly the kind of person they'd happily obey, and once you were in her thrall you were probably there for life.

One of the most common questions asked about cults is – why? Why do people do all of these bizarre things simply because a cult leader tells them to? The answer is both simple and complex: it's because God is telling them to. When you're a child and your parent gives you instructions, there is no higher authority, and if you've ever believed in a god, imagine him or her arriving on Earth and giving you instructions. You would just obey. The one and only thing that a cult leader has to do is convince their followers that they're either God, or that they have an exclusive and personal friendship with God. After that, convincing them to do anything – from wearing a teapot on their head to disciplining stolen children in a house by a lake – is a piece of cake. Nasty, stale, bad cake with a couple of weevils in it.

Thus, in line with Anne's orders, daily life at Kai Lama for the children progressed along very particular lines. Meals were carefully apportioned, with frequent incidences of a child missing out here or there because of a punishment or penance that had to be performed during mealtimes. Because of its general scarcity and its frequent use as both a dangled carrot and a withdrawn privilege, most of the children at Kai Lama became obsessed with food. The kitchen was a no-go area with locks on all the food storage cabinets and the refrigerator, just to add to the general practice of relaxed, happy childhoods developing in a normal, developmentally advantageous way. Weekly weigh-ins were the norm, presumably as part of Anne's obsession with appearance – it just wouldn't do for anyone to accuse her of having overweight children. Far preferable, if you're a big-haired, image-obsessed lady, to be accused of causing malnutrition, as a disciplined and svelte second coming of Jesus is an admirable second coming of Jesus.

Exercise usually took the form of daily yoga sessions, resulting in some of the world's most flexible blond cult foster children, although admittedly it's not a crowded field. Then it was meditation, then school, then enforced organised playtime, then more school, cleaning, meditation, homework, listening to Anne's taped mantras, a brief, highly regulated bath or shower, then bed. Again. And again. And again. And again.

Routine was strictly adhered to unless it was detected that there were strangers snooping around outside, anywhere in the wide, normally deserted wooded regional area. In those circumstances, any outdoor activity was cancelled, with children and aunties confined indoors for weeks at a time. Often the perceived snoopers were nothing of the sort, but paranoia runs white-hot in secluded cult compounds, and you can't be too careful. The non-intruder routine was clearly spelt out in 'Mummy's Book', a long list of instructions written by Anne that the aunties and the children were expected to follow unquestioningly every single day. Having been led to believe that 'Mummy' had psychic powers and could see them even when she was very frequently away in one of her other houses, rules would likely have been followed even without the overbearing and brutal enforcement of the aunties.

Completely and utterly bloody sick of it all, in 1987 at the traditionally rebellious age of seventeen, Anne's adopted daughter Sarah was so prone to argument and disobedience that she was expelled from The Family and asked to leave Kai Lama. Another 'daughter', Leeanne, showing a normal sixteen-year-old's indignance and will, but with the fact that she'd been beaten and starved acting as icing on her standard teen-angst cake, escaped out of her bedroom window and ran away.

Encouraged by neighbours and the social workers they alerted, Sarah and Leeanne notified the police of the situation at Kai Lama, and the police figured – correctly – that it was beyond time they stepped in. Of prime importance to the police was the safety and wellbeing of the children, and with the help of Sarah in particular, they gathered enough information to justify a raid.

In August 1987, federal police officers and community services representatives pounced on Kai Lama in the very early morning, ignored the protests of the resident aunties, who were in turn terrified that they'd be punished as soon as Anne Hamilton-Byrne found out, and removed six of the children that they found there. The children found out that their surnames were not real, and that other children did not live like they did, and that almost everything they knew about their lives and parents and the world was a lie. It was not a fun day.

Police later formed a task force called Operation Forest – presumably because the name Operation Get the Kids Away from the Cult was too long – with the intention of investigating all of the iffy bits it thought had taken place out at The Family's Lake Eildon compound. They settled in for six years, gathering information, interviewing people who lived there, or had lived there, and building as much of a case as they could. They interviewed the children who were old enough, any aunties they could get to talk, and ex-cult lawyer Peter Kibby, who had decided to leave after realising that being in a cult is a dumb thing to do.

During Operation Forest's investigation, Anne and Bill did the opposite of what people who have nothing to hide and nothing to be ashamed of do: they fled overseas and hid from authorities. To appease their followers and keep them supportive and faithful, Anne fed them the heavy line that she had been rescuing the children – who she claimed had birth defects and other problems – from a far worse fate than being mothered by her. You have to admit, when you're using fictional brain damage as a justification for your terrible mothering skills, maybe parenthood was never really your thing.

Anne and Bill were finally tracked down in 1993 in the Catskills in New York State after the FBI had traced calls they made to Australia, and a long process to extradite the pair back to Australia and actually get them to turn up for trial began. There are reports that Anne and Bill had been living with up to a hundred cats and dogs in their Catskills house, because that nutty pair just couldn't stop surrounding themselves with so many dependants that appropriate care of them becomes impossible. As she had her entire life, when the feds turned up to arrest her at her front door, Anne prioritised her own appearance over the safety of her children and asked if she could pop a wig and some lippy on. For whatever reason, the agent refused to let her tidy herself up, and she suffered what she considered the ultimate indignity of appearing in public looking dishevelled. Sometimes you just feel like buying an FBI agent a beer.

With most of Anne's child victims either unwilling to testify, unable to testify because of the crappy fact-recall skills they had after a lifetime on drugs, or regarded as too fragile to testify considering the intense emotional trauma she'd subjected them to, a prosecution case based on the abuses the children reported to authorities would have been small and weak like the children themselves. They couldn't prove kidnapping. They couldn't prove the administration of drugs to children. They couldn't prove child abuse. But they could prove fraud. It's very difficult to find material evidence more than a decade after the fact of forced LSD use and child abuse, but a forged document is a forged document forever.

The prosecution was helped in no small part by ex-Family-member Peter Kibby, the cult's former lawyer who suffered from Obsessive Compulsive Disorder. Kibby says that Anne had lured him into the cult with promises of effective treatment for his OCD, no doubt drawing on her complete lack of expertise in treating it or anything remotely like it. Instead of being cured, he was married off to someone he didn't choose, lied to, and encouraged to do not-strictly-legal things with legal paperwork. By the time he left, Kibby was only too pleased to fess up to falsifying adoption documents and dobbing Anne in for a light spot of forgery. Ironically, if Anne had succeeded in treating Peter's OCD, he might not have kept such fastidious records or thought that sitting in a dirty jail would be unbearable. Sucks to be bad at curing people, Anne.

While Anne and Bill were investigated for multiple suspected offences, police made the decision to only press charges on those that didn't involve further traumatising children by forcing them through the court process. After a frustrating trial, Anne and Bill were found guilty of fraud. Originally they were tried for defrauding the New Zealand registry of births, as that's where they'd claimed that their 'triplets' were their own biological multiple birth, but it's difficult to try a New Zealand crime in a Victorian court, so Anne and Bill were given a wrist-slap and each fined five thousand dollars. Five thousand dollars would not pay the therapy bills for a single year for an adult who was kept in a violent rural prison without parents as a child. But when you only have the testimony of emotionally damaged adults that you choose not to use, and no actual proof of imprisonment, involuntary drug use, cruel punishment, deep corruption and frequent, broad sprays of loose, liquid bullshit, that's what you get.

A couple of the aunties fared much worse and, accused and convicted of welfare fraud to the value of just under $200,000, received short prison sentences. The fact that it wouldn't have even occurred to them to commit any crimes without the direct influence of their membership in a cult was a mere inconvenience.

In her late nineties at the time of writing, Hamilton-Byrne sits mush-brained and useless in palliative care in suburban

Melbourne. There's not enough of her oddly balanced brain left to make any sense, so there's definitely not enough left for her to answer any charges, make any reparations, or express any understanding of or remorse for the shitty lives people say she dealt to them.

She fuzzily receives a dwindling number of visitors in the nursing home – a drizzle of people who still believe in her, or possibly believe that their visits might increase their chances of being left some of her property fortune. They're definitely not there for a yoga class, though – the old woman would probably snap under the strain of even a light asana. It's likely that she has absolutely no idea who or where she is, which, even though she'll never own up to it, seems a fitting circumstance for someone who, according to them, made a whole bunch of children feel exactly the same way. A small handful of those children have managed to wangle out-of-court settlements out of Anne, as much as her well-paid lawyers would allow, but the settlements were most definitely not accompanied by anything approaching a confession or admission of culpability, or even an apology.

Mothers like Anne Hamilton-Byrne do most other mothers a favour by making them look spectacular by comparison.

Go tell your mother you love her.

CHILDREN OF GOD

CHILDREN OF GOD is only one of the names given to a cult originally led by David Berg, a man who looked like a thinner, less jolly, more randy Santa. The group started as the relatively denim-clad, happy-clappy-sounding Teens for Christ, and now exists feebly under the boringly ambiguous name of The Family International.

Until you get to the darker side of Children of God – and there definitely is one – the group appears gleefully like a late sixties or early seventies hippie stereotype, with good-looking, pious hedonists in flared jeans playing acoustic guitars and growing large quantities of organic vegetables and unfettered sideburns. The kind of people you just *know* would say things like 'Jesus was a real groovy cat' while they braid your hair in a meadow. The kind of people who want to be good Christians, but also want to have an almost unbelievable amount of sex.

The timing and sexy doctrine suited Jeremy Spencer, one of the founding members of Fleetwood Mac, so well that he became a long-term member, and the cult is hardly ever mentioned without making reference to its other celebrity alumni. Early followers also included actress Rose McGowan's parents and the parents of River, Joaquin, and Rain Phoenix, all three of whom sang on the streets for donations to help fund the cult's communal lifestyle. It's important – although admittedly not narratively necessary – to note that River, Joaquin, and Rain's real surname at the time was 'Bottom', changed to 'Phoenix' after splitting with the cult in the late seventies. Certainly the phoenix imagery was incredibly symbolic to the family in the circumstances they found themselves in – rising from the controlling and deeply problematic flames of a cult. The name-change was also no doubt a considerable relief for Rain Bottom.

Born to Christian evangelists in 1919, it's unsurprising that David Berg was a fan of Jesus. As a young man he helped his parents with their missionary work, and by the time he was in his thirties in the 1950s he was pretty sure he wanted to take on preaching himself, on his own terms. He started to think more and more that other Christians weren't interpreting the Bible properly or following Christ's teachings accurately. Berg believed that too much time was spent in fancy churches performing rituals, and not enough out in the world, doing and saying good things to the unconverted instead of within the echo chamber of the parish. As he worked odd jobs and searched for direction, Berg crystallised his philosophy and perfected his schtick. Church was for squares, man. He was more for spreading the word through good-looking missionaries and evangelists, living poor like old mate Jesus did, and reaching out. He called the kind of outreach evangelism he dug 'witnessing' and decided what the path forward should be.

Starting in 1968 in Huntington Beach, California, Berg successfully targeted the disillusioned, free-love-seeking hippie counterculture. Running a coffee shop and slinging an acoustic guitar across his torso like that guy you hate at a party, Berg found it easy to catch the ear of the young and the restless, and he gathered enough attention to come to the notice of Fred Jordan, a 1950s television evangelist, who offered him use of a ranch of his in Texas to base his group from, should he need it. Soon Berg had enough followers to up sticks and haul their holies westward, and with just over a hundred missionary wannabes he settled at the ranch, which Jordan had whimsically called the Texas Soul Clinic, near Thurber.

Fred was only too pleased to become a kind of evangelical mentor to David, as he was fixing to expand his niche – wholesome Christian families – to crack the youth Christian market. Jordan was a pioneer of televised preaching with his show *Church in the Home*, and he and his wife opened a number of missions in the US, Africa and South America with the aim of providing aid to the homeless. David Berg learned a lot about evangelising from Fred Jordan, and Jordan made use of Berg's natural promotional abilities and his knack for youth outreach. Members of Teens for Christ appeared regularly on *Church in the Home*, so it was a happy-clappy symbiotic relationship for some time, each holy dude successfully using the other to expand their message to a broader group.

In 1970 around 120 of Berg's followers, having renamed themselves the marginally more adult 'Children of God', moved in to the Texas Soul Clinic ranch and started transforming the place. The sudden overnight presence of a bunch of barefoot hippies upset the local cowboys and rattlesnakes in equal measure, but nothing gets yard work done like blind faith, and Berg had soon organised the disused ranch from a backwater to a relatively high functioning community. The early commune relied heavily on donations, so members spent most of their extensive waking hours working in the commune – cleaning, cooking, planting, fixing up old school buses – and attending classes to hear the word of God, or heading in all directions, witnessing to strangers with their hands out.

Berg considered the compound a 'training ground', pioneering a brand-new communal Christian society and preparing its members to go out into the world changing people's minds and glorifying Jesus. In Berg's mind, this was the first anthill of what he hoped would become a thriving colony, and its ants were being coached to branch out, seeding similar colonies all over the place. Much of his message to followers consisted of claims that the society they were building was superior to anything a church ever could or ever had attempted, so his followers laboured cheerfully, convinced that they were the start of something world-changing.

Members were expected to give up their possessions and income for the cause, change their names to something more appropriately biblical, and be pretty suspicious of 'the System', being any organisation that wasn't the Children of God. Government, higher education, churches, hospitals, the media – these were all 'the System' and spiritually funded by Satan, which no doubt kept him busy. As a result, Children of God became typically cult-insular, and kept things in-house whenever they weren't witnessing. Children were born in the commune, schooled in the commune, worked in the commune, and only sent out as cherub-faced separators of System people and their money. Numbers swelled to a couple of thousand in the early seventies, and small colonies began their infancy in California, Ohio, Georgia, and Kentucky.

The more followers you have, the more the families and friends of those followers start taking an interest in the group that has taken their loved ones away from them. Parents really hate it when their children leave home to become Christian hippies wandering the streets asking for money and handing out pamphlets, as weird as that sounds. Early in the seventies, groups of parents joined together and started hassling the Children of God for their children back, and this struck Fred Jordan with a case of the willies. Fred was a family man, respected across the country for his conservative godliness, and he couldn't risk the damage that negative parents throwing the words 'sect' and 'cult' around might have on his broad and profitable ministry. David Berg was also becoming more and more demanding of Fred's generosity, insisting that they had the right to fully occupy properties Fred owned in exchange for their contributions to both maintenance of the properties and support of Fred's religious empire. Unable to solve their fiscal and ideological disagreements, Jordan and Berg parted ways in 1971. The Children of God had established enough additional colonies during their time staying on Fred Jordan's couch that they had plenty of places to go.

The group was no longer confining itself to the United States, either. David and some of his more industrious disciples travelled further afield on missionary-style vacations to Europe where they witnessed their little hearts out and soon established small colonies in England, Germany, the Netherlands, Italy, Switzerland, Spain, and France. The group's heady mix of Christianity and the potential for loads of sex was irresistible to new territories full of horny yet devout Europeans. It was like the Children of God world tour, with the same kind of reach and fashion sense as the Eurovision Song Contest. Eventually the cult also expanded into areas of South America, India, Asia, and Australia, establishing communes and spreading the word.

But anyone can go out on the street, talk about Jesus, and ask for money. In the late sixties and early seventies, Berg became less interested in preaching directly to people and decided that handing out pamphlets – or 'litnessing', as he called it – was a much more effective and profitable exercise. Photocopies cost less than shoe-leather and bus repairs, and pamphlets would allow Berg the opportunity to spread his message equally to followers while being under less public scrutiny himself. Attractive prospects all round.

Berg started to spread his own wisdom and instruction via illustrated newsletters known as 'The Mo Letters'. The 'Mo' came from Berg's cult nickname 'Moses David' – because one of the advantages of being a cult leader is that you can give your-self whatever cool name you want. He was also called 'Daddy' by first-generation cult members and 'Grandpa' by their chil-dren, which should successfully prepare you for just how creepy this is about to get.

In 1970 one of the first Mo letters, entitled 'I Gotta Split!', notified Children of God members that Mo had decided to pop himself into seclusion, heralding Berg's decision to live separately from most members and keep his location a secret. He split up from his scarcely mentioned first wife, Jane, in the same year, further signalling a new phase in his life. According to Dad, he wasn't in hiding because he was getting bad press and pressure from disgruntled System parents of Children of God members, but because God told him to isolate himself. Just as Jesus had chosen to go away one Easter to spread his word more widely and effectively, so must Mo, under visionary orders from God. God's timing was extremely convenient, and his use of Jesus to set precedents for David Berg was genius. No wonder people are so fond of God.

Figuring that his young counterculture followers needed their Christian information delivered via a medium less stuffy and more hip than the Bible, the Mo Letters became more and more prescriptive, outlining how many pieces of toilet paper followers should use for a number two, and what weight their letters should ideally be to save on postage. As the Children of God established communes, called 'homes', in more and more countries – partly as the result of avoiding pesky investigations by those uptight

Systemites – Mo Letters were a great way to maintain control over members from a distance.

Via the Mo Letters, Berg was able to give his followers instructions regarding where they should live, which commune would best suit them, which members of their family they could and couldn't live with, what they should and shouldn't eat, and who they should sleep with. Often the movements of followers from commune to commune and from country to country, all decreed by Berg, were said to be the result of dreams and visions Berg had, instead of by the fugitive necessity and suspicious persecution that was more likely to blame. Mo Letters also allowed David Berg to live in relative luxury, financed by the tithes members were required to pay, without his commune-bound, living-poor followers getting too irritated by it. He surrounded himself with an elite group that would work for him and give him access to their genitals. And access to their genitals, David Berg definitely had. There's no other way to put it: he was a randy old bugger.

Separation and seclusion also allowed Berg to be relatively anonymous, at least once-removed from any bad behaviour, and difficult to find – handy when you're being investigated for a crime or two here or there, which he eventually was – and to maintain an air of authoritative mystery to his followers. Whenever images of Berg appeared in the Mo Letters, the photograph was usually altered so a lion's head was sketched in over his head, in exactly the same way that photographs of normal people who don't control thousands of people to feed their own narcissism aren't altered.

It was a two-way street, too, as members would return information and statistics – about how many people they'd witnessed to and donations they'd collected, mostly – via post. They also sent a lot of videos – about boobs, mostly. As one of Berg's repeated lessons was that God gave us flesh so flesh should be exposed and celebrated, and that followers – or at least female followers – should glorify God via dancing, he instructed that videos of women dancing should be sent back to him. In true Mo style, in 1981 he first sent a detailed list of instructions for the dance videos, dictating that dancers should wear veils that they gradually removed, describing how he liked the dancers to fondle themselves, instructing dancers to start slow and then get faster, and insisting that anyone too pregnant or with sagging breasts should cover up.

Reading the list of instructions, it's obvious that 62-year-old Berg was essentially directing porn for himself. Unsettlingly, videos of both adult women and girls were made, as children were encouraged to learn as much about sex as possible, as early as possible. According to Children of God, sex was one part of God's love, so sharing love was good and pure, and withholding love was selfish, proud, and often punishable.

The Children of God 'law of love' dictates that free expression of love – and therefore sex – is holy. Berg figured that since the only sex act God specifically seemed to find distasteful in the Bible was sodomy, then everything else glorified God. There's only one hole that ain't holy, according to Mo. Berg, who was totally fine with being sent a videotape of a child performing a striptease just for him, called male homosexuality a disgusting perversion, most likely caused by female demons. Berg was at least efficient in packaging his sexism and homophobia, combining them both into one neat, succinct accusation. Gay guys are gross, and it's because of chicks!

It would be a terrific relief if that were where it stopped with David Berg and his uncanny talent for perviness, but we haven't even *started* on wanking yet. Followers were encouraged to imagine that Jesus was always present when they were having sex, including when they were masturbating. A Mo Letter was even distributed containing a list of suggested sexy things you could say to Jesus while you're pretending you're making love to him, just in case you run out of ideas when you're dirty-talking with the Messiah. At the less-erotic end of the list are suggestions like telling Jesus you're in love with him, and that you're open for him, and an only mildly ambiguous request that Jesus 'fill you', if he's not too busy with other things. Things get way more freaky at the more erotic end of the list, with increasingly urgent ejaculations such as 'I receive your love, Lord, with open arms and open legs!', 'Flood me with your seeds!', and the utterly non-ambiguous 'My pussy is excited for you, Jesus!'. Apparently, despite a busy schedule, Jesus always has time for imaginary commune quickies with multiple partners. Truly a miracle.

Men indulging in the wank arts were politely requested to adopt a female persona for themselves in their sex-with-Jesus fantasies so as not to make it a gay thing. See, in David Berg's mind, men pretending they're women while they gratify themselves and imagine they're having sex with Jesus is way, way more normal behaviour than just being gay. Female homosexuality was a-okay with Berg though, because hypocrisy has no place in an old man's inconsistent erections. It's a shame the internet hadn't been invented when David Berg was just getting his start, otherwise he might have been too busy looking at porn to even think about starting a cult.

Because of the almost-anything-goes attitude of Berg and his followers (except gay sex between blokes, obviously), some fairly uncomfortable practices emerged inside and outside the communes, and it's these practices that have brought Children of God the most notoriety and media coverage. The first and easily most upsetting of these practices was the involvement of children in sexual activity. To be fair, the belief that children have sexual organs and should therefore learn about and experience sex didn't result in acts of paedophilia across the board, and many, many Children of God children report confidently that they did not suffer any sexual abuse. Tarring all cult members with the same brush is unfair, but it *is* fair to say that all children in the group were taught about sex – often via demonstration – from a broadly unacceptable age and often from as young as three or four. Sex education is important, anybody with a brain and a functioning conscience knows that. But knowing the difference between teaching children about sex and showing children some fucking is vitally essential if you don't want to fling them into therapy or dangerous behaviour later in life.

The communal life, populated as it primarily was with hippies in their early twenties, involved communal living – eating, sleeping, parties and sex, with children present to observe everything. A five-year-old in the Children of God was more likely to have seen his or her parents having sex – with each other or with other temporary partners – than to have seen a television. A Mo Letter by David Berg entitled 'My Childhood Sex!' is full of excited claims that 'It just stands to reason that if it feels good at that age, then the Lord intended for kids to get used to feeling good with sex. If they can have an orgasm at that age, He intended for them to have an orgasm and enjoy it! Why not? What's evil about an orgasm?' Berg tells a story in the same missive about a nanny of his fellating him to sleep each afternoon as a three-year-old, which, if true, goes some way to explaining his own broken and repugnant mores. Children are not Mount Everest, Mr Berg. You do not climb them merely because they are there.

If this attitude to early sex education had been purely just that, perhaps far less damage might have been done, although undoubtedly still some damage. However, two factors turned this generally questionable attitude into actual illegal activity. Firstly, a religious group that preaches an early introduction to sex will inevitably pique the interest of abusers and create an environment where paedophiles are more or less camouflaged. Secondly, and nauseatingly, David Berg was super-into incest. He called 'System' laws against incest crazy, and believed that neither age nor familial ties mattered if you acted in pure love. Berg claimed that there was nothing wrong with, for example, parents helping their children discover themselves sexually by participating in sexual acts with them. Oh sure, he admitted that there were *System* laws about it, but nothing in the Bible said it was wrong, so it must be okay with God. Conveniently,

Berg just ignored the parts of the Bible that specifically say not to sleep with your relatives, but then religious spokespeople have been cherry-picking bits of the Bible for their own agendas for a very, very long time. Berg did advise against speaking openly about incest and the sexual activity of the commune's children outside of the communes though because, weirdly, the System just wouldn't understand their specific brand of sex education. Crazy!

Children were also deemed to be communal – although there's no evidence to suggest this was sexual – sometimes removed from their parents and moved from commune to commune on a different schedule to their parents, and instructed to call any non-parental members 'auntie' or 'uncle'. It was not unheard of for Children of God children to forget what their parents looked like or to have never met their fathers.

The second icky practice that generated a lot of attention – barely any supportive – for the Children of God seems relatively benign when compared to the condoning of paedophilia and incest, but it's still undeniably gross. Women – whether they felt like it or not – were required to share themselves sexually with other men in the Children of God homes. It was considered a duty, and a duty that was only required of women. Within the Children of God, adult men only had sex when they wanted to, but, very frequently, adult women had sex when they didn't want to, with people they did not want to have sex with. 'Sharing' was so commonplace that the word became a euphemism for sex, and some homes drew up 'sharing schedules' to really get organised about coercing people into a swinger lifestyle. A passionate Mo Letter entitled 'One Wife!' claimed that, to become stronger, sometimes selfish little exclusionary twosomes should be abandoned for the greater good of the larger communal family. It was a fancy way of saying, 'Can the rest of us sleep with your wife, please?'

Thanks to his love of sexism and exploitation, David Berg taught his followers that women were made for men. They're God's way of saying, 'Here, I love you so I made you a thing with boobs on it.' Furthermore, he both believed and taught that the best way to celebrate that God loves you is to have sex with his gift to you. The cool thing is, gifts aren't supposed to say no. Any gift that does say no is selfish, self-righteous, and possibly affected by demons. Those demons are *such* cockblockers sometimes.

By now it should be unsurprising, but no less egregious, to learn that David Berg had a pretty laissez-faire attitude towards rape. His views that a lot of women who are raped provoke it by doing things like walking alone at night, and that most cases of rape are reported by women who simply changed their minds after having sex and decided to cause trouble, are in line with the thinking of the worst humans, a category of people Berg seemingly aspired to be king of. Not one to rest on his laurels, Grandpa Mo also felt strongly that once a man is past a certain point of arousal there's just no point stopping him, so you might as well just go along with it so you don't get hurt.

Just to be clear: David Berg was not a good person.

If you're not convinced yet: David Berg sent women out to lure men into the cult with their vaginas.

Children of God's most notorious and well-known practice was 'Flirty Fishing', referred to casually as 'FFing' in the Mo

Letters, and as 'Prostitution in the name of Jesus' by any reasonable person. Fond of carefully selecting parts of the Bible out of their intended context for authoritative manipulation, David Berg decided that Jesus's statement in Matthew 4:19 to 'Follow me, and I will make you fishers of men' meant that using sex to spread the word of God was a super-cool thing to do. Most of the adult women in Children of God were encouraged to have sex with as many strangers as they could find. They were sent out as bait to 'fish' for men in bars and on the streets, and where possible they were encouraged to get paid for it to help raise funds for the communes. Women were required to identify men out in the world who they thought might listen to some stories about Jesus with a little encouragement and befriend them, using all their womanly tools from mild flirtation through to actual sex to keep them listening. It makes sense, when your leader considers that women's bodies are instruments for enjoyment and that men outside in the System are simpletons so utterly ruled by their penises that you could effectively fuck the word of God into them. After 'witnessing' and 'litnessing', it's a wonder Flirty Fishing wasn't called 'clitnessing' – a rare missed opportunity for Berg, colloquially speaking.

The Mo Letters on the subject of Flirty Fishing referred to FFers as 'Hookers for Jesus!' and 'God's Whores?' which are as interesting for their random approach to punctuation as they are for their celebration of physical exploitation. In one Mo Letter from 1974, Berg writes that 'if you've already got a reputation of being quite free with your sex you might as well expect to get raped once in a while or run across a situation where you may be forced somewhat against your will'. Just letting women in the Children of God know that, every once in a while, they might get raped as a general work hazard. Not to worry though because being raped provides an excellent opportunity to tell your rapist about Jesus. Don't fight, show 'em the light!

In addition to the Mo Letters, their covers resplendent with nubile young pieces of bait with their tits out, there were publications called 'True Komix', more liberally saturated with illustrations than standard Mo Letters in order to appeal to younger members of the Children of God. There was an issue of True Komix entitled 'The Little Flirty Fishy', which was intended to explain to children why Mummy sometimes comes home late and crying.

Women not willing to sell their bodies for the cause were considered proud and selfish, while at the other end of the spectrum, women who not only fished but snatched a donation in the process were sanctified, celebrated, and seen to be selflessly doing the Lord's work. Successful fishers were lauded in Mo Letters, unsuccessful or unwilling ones scorned and ostracised. Instructions were soon distributed via Mo Letters regarding how to 'ES', or 'Escort Service', making sex work for donations a legitimate Children of God policy. If there was one thing David Berg loved more than using women for sex, it was using acronyms for phrases that described using women for sex.

Each communal home was required to send detailed monthly reports to leaders listing how many times FFers had sex, how heavily they witnessed at the time, what the occupation of their 'fish' was, and who their top three 'fishers' were. Of course, men were discouraged from fishing, partly because the ladies could be more successful and profitable without a bloke hanging around, but mostly because of Berg's general philosophical stance of 'no homo'.

This whole mess becomes even more grotesquely horrifying when you consider David Berg's stance on birth control. At this point there should be no shock at all to learn that he was dead against it, and even more vehemently opposed to abortion. In the Children of God, the greatest gift the Lord could give you was a child, and methods of birth control – or Satan's own contraptions – were incredibly offensive to God. It's a woman's duty to have children, along with all of her other duties, and the more children there were, the more members of the Children of God there were. Berg claimed that the boys would grow up to be kings, and the girls would grow up to be their queens. It would appear that either David Berg didn't realise, when he was busy sending women out to have unprotected sex with strangers in the name of God, that most birth control has a secondary purpose in the field of disease prevention, or he considered STDs to also be a precious gift from God. Either way, what a dumb bastard.

These upsetting practices – those of the involvement of children in sexual practice and the exploitation of women to lure followers – are both embodied in the example of Ricky Rodriguez. David Berg had five children himself – four biological and one 'adopted'. The officialness of the adoption is questionable considering the flexible approach to parenting within the cult, where children were more or less brought up by whoever was nearby rather than his or her biological parents, but Ricky

Rodriguez was the son of Berg's second wife, Karen Zerby, and considered part of the 'royal family'. According to the story told in Children of God publications, Karen became pregnant with Ricky after 'Flirty Fishing' his father, a hotel employee in Tenerife. It's not clear whether or not Karen was able to successfully indoctrinate the hotel employee with the word of Jesus, but the hotel employee definitely indoctrinated Karen with a growing fetus.

When Ricky was born, in a textbook display of narcissism, Berg renamed him 'Davidito'. He also named the daughter of Ricky's nanny Sara and her husband, Alfred, 'Davida'. Davida was also considered a member of the 'royal family', and permitted to live in the same house as David and whoever else was considered devout and sexy enough at the time. The day-to-day activities and development of Davidito and Davida were used in a number of Mo Letters and a book called *The Story of Davidito* as examples of good and godly child-rearing. The two were relentlessly photographed for the letters as the perfect children of the perfect father, despite Berg being the biological father of neither of them. Children who become famous at a young age are often messed up by the experience, and there was no child more famous within the cult than Ricky as Davidito. Unfortunately, *The Story of Davidito* proves to be more of a warning than a book of instructions.

While some of the instructional narratives in *The Story of Davidito* were about playtime, education, and religious instruction, a horribly large part of it was about Davidito's interaction with his nanny, Sara. Many of their interactions could quite feasibly be understood, by normal people, as sexual grooming. Looking through the pages of the book is not recommended. The book implies strongly that, even at two years old, Davidito was interested in sex, and loved having his penis washed, kissed and played with. It refers to Davidito as 'flirty' and 'sexy', and includes photographs of him in bed with Sara, both naked, in utterly inappropriate scenarios. In later years, when the cult had morphed into The Family International, *The Story of Davidito* was one of many documents cult leaders ordered destroyed or heavily censored due to unwelcome investigation by outsiders in the System. The extremely watered down *Dito: His Early Years* is seen as the previous book's more appropriate replacement, but the idea that the censorship occurred to protect the group from investigation and prosecution – and not to protect children from paedophilia and damage – remains heinous.

And damage it certainly did. Ricky left the cult in 2001 at the age of twenty-six with his partner, finally breaking from what he had long considered to be an abusive and manipulative organisation. Like so many other ex-cult members, he found it impossible to adjust to life on the outside. His marriage broke down, and Ricky became obsessed with revenge against his mother and nannies, and justice for all those harmed by the group's practices. In 2005, Rodriguez made a video of himself calmly loading a gun and preparing other weapons, praising the Republicans for their lax gun laws and explaining to the camera that he was abused as a child, had contemplated suicide ever since, and that his mother must pay for the things she'd done. He'd had difficulty tracking her down, as due to her position first as David Berg's wife and then as the cult leader after his death, it was in her best interests to maintain her husband's fondness for seclusion.

Soon after making the video, Rodriguez arranged to meet Angela Smith, one of his former nannies in the Children of God. He stabbed Angela to death in her apartment in Arizona, drove to California, sat in his car, and committed suicide. The number of alleged crimes committed within the cult is high. The number of prosecutions of adult members of the cult is low. The number of prosecutions of David Berg is – astoundingly – zero. While Rodriguez's actions brought some attention to the cult for a short time, no one was put in jail and the cult continues to this day.

After the legitimately abhorrent policies that David Berg inflicted upon his followers, and particularly after the horror of Ricky's story – two things that are inextricably linked – it seems petty and ineffectual to ridicule the cult leader. That said, few people deserve ridicule more than those who exert their power for their own needs without a single thought for those they wield power over. To offset the feeling of despair and wretchedness experienced by others, it's extremely important to make fun of cult leaders for the things they were terrible at. But where to start?

As good a place to start as any is Berg's complete and utter ineptitude at prophecy. Dude could not predict his way out of a paper bag. For someone who claimed to be a messenger of God, Berg had his wires almost comically crossed, particularly when it came to telling people about the end of the world.

See, the Children of God wasn't just a sex-and-commune cult. It was also, in its own way, a doomsday cult full of people preparing for the end of the world. Throw that into the mix and it's easier to understand why sex featured so prominently in their doctrine – if we're all going to die, we might as well go out bonking. Berg called the apocalyptic end of everything 'Endtime', and was entirely unoriginal in that he based some of his theories on the Book of Revelation in the Bible.

Okay now – the Book of Revelation. If it's been a while since you've spent a balmy, be-hammocked evening flipping the Bible's pages over a gin and tonic, here's a refresher: a dude called John ate some cheese before bed, had an intensely screwy dream, then woke up and wrote it all down, pretty sure it was an exact description of how the world was going to end. The problem is, the dream was so incredibly trippy and vaguely transcribed that it's been open to guesswork, interpretation, and conjecture ever since. The second problem is that due to its high interpretability and general Armageddony flavour, cult leaders *love* it. There's all *sorts* of imagery and fire and swords and earthquakes and creatures, ready to have their storylines twisted to the whim of any megalomaniac who comes along. You can pick one of many absolutely bonkers characters in it and claim that you're that guy, incarnate, and other people are hard-pressed to argue. It's just borderline impossible to come up with a counter position to someone who's claiming to be an olive branch, or a Schrodinger's-cat-styled lamb that's slaughtered but somehow also alive, or a vaguely recognisable farmyard animal except 100 per cent covered in eyes. David Berg, like a lot of other Book of Revelation devotees, was especially enamoured with the two witnesses mentioned in its pages, a pair pivotal to the end times.

The always-imminent end times meant that investment and property ownership were seen as unnecessary, so available funds – being basically all of the money cult members had – were encouraged into leadership pockets. Children weren't given much of a traditional education, as it was assumed that it would be of little or no use after Armageddon. So, while they weren't learning much about history, science, politics, and literature, they were learning camping and survival skills so they'd fare better in a dystopian after-future. Little post-apocalyptic urchins. Cute.

The thing is, if you're going to predict the end of the world you're supposed to get it right, which is a rule that every single person who has predicted the end of the world has broken so far. David Berg has a more astounding record than most for being really, just stupidly wrong, though. Here, have a laundry list of things he said would happen but didn't:

- That the Comet Kohoutek, which was predicted to be brighter than the moon but turned out to be a monumental fizzer, would kickstart a world-ending cataclysm in 1973. It didn't.
- That Halley's Comet would signal the rise of the Anti-Christ in 1986, information which was distributed to the public via a Children of God newsletter called *The Endtime News*, which could win a Walkley Award for Newspaper Containing the Most Spoilers in its Title. As you've probably gathered already, Halley's Comet did not signal the rise of the Anti-Christ in

1986. Sure, the Olsen twins were born in 1986, but anybody partially responsible for *Full House* can't be all bad.

- That Davidito and Karen Zerby would be the two witnesses described in the Book of Revelation, and play a pivotal role in the whole end-of-the-world situation. Yeah. Okay, so aside from the fact that there hasn't been any evidence so far that there even is an end-of-the-world situation, Ricky ended up cursing both David's and Karen's names, left the cult, and committed suicide. Ricky will have no part in this prophecy, thank you very much, David Berg.

- That Berg would die in 1989, at age seventy, which was an extremely tenuous interpretation of a very boring part of the Book of Daniel in the Bible. He actually died in 1994, at age seventy-five, so those last five years would have been embarrassing. A spokesperson for the Children of God told reporters that 'he fell asleep in his sleep, peacefully' which is of course far more comfortable than falling asleep while you're awake, screaming.

- Finally, Berg predicted that Christ would return in 1993. Sure, Ariana Grande was born in 1993, but . . . nah. When Christ stubbornly refused to turn up in 1993, Berg explained it away by saying God had given the Children of God an extension in order to spread his word more and get ready for the REAL return of Christ. Which. Y'know. Any day now.

Incredibly, Berg's failed predictions only lost a few followers here and there. Still, forgetting to carry the one and making a predictive error is a damn sight better than losing a whole planet to a comet strike, so I guess everybody can take that as a win. Berg insisted he was God's prophet for our time, but it seems patently clear that God was just pulling his leg.

After Berg's death in 1994, his common-law wife, Karen Zerby – known within the cult as 'Maria' – took over, sending a lot of letters out to followers making quite sure they knew she was a queen and why. Included in her regal argument were incontestable gems like 'Jesus said that I am a queen, so that makes me a queen' – a statement backed up by just as many facts as those in other Children of God publications.

Today The Family International is, at least outwardly, a far more moderate organisation. The practice of Flirty Fishing was discontinued in 1987, partly because of the increasing threat of AIDS. Due to the practice of effectively fostering children with their 'aunties' and 'uncles' instead of their parents, and the movement of members internationally from commune to commune, investigations into child abduction occurred in more than one country, particularly once parents left the group and started looking into getting their children back. From the late eighties, raids targeting reported child abduction or abuse in Family homes occurred in numerous countries, the most significant in Argentina in 1989 and Australia in 1992.

Australia had its first Children of God home as early as 1972, shortly before the Earth wasn't hit by a comet. In May 1992, child services officers raided one home in Victoria and another in New South Wales on suspicion of child abuse. More than 120 children were removed from the homes and placed into temporary custody, but no evidence of abuse was found and the children were returned shortly after. Anyone reading Children of God literature would be gently excused for suspecting that children in the cult's homes were perhaps not being treated with the care they're entitled to, but authorities really do need actual evidence before taking children away from their parents.

Where cases were not so clear-cut, unfortunately due to a number of factors in the raids globally – botched raid management, the unwillingness of the children to impugn their parents and their inability to recognise their lifestyle as unusual – no arrests were made. Throughout its history, Children of God has given its members, including children, instructions regarding how to act when investigated or asked questions by 'Systemites', this coupled with a broad policy of individual name-changing and strenuous secrecy surrounding the identity and location of the cult's leaders, means it's a tough group to pin anything on.

Numerous leader-sanctioned document 'purges' were ordered in the cult's later decades, instructing Family homes to destroy or censor lists of potentially incriminating or contentious documents. One such instruction from 1991 urges: 'As our enemies are determined to stop at nothing in order to destroy us, so we should be willing to do whatever is necessary to prevent info from falling into their hands which could in any way endanger any of our precious Family', which is a cutesy way of saying 'hide the evidence'. Directives like this included requests to destroy any potentially damaging photographs and videos such as those containing 'nudie cuties'. Sure, just your stock-standard religious leaders ordering you to chuck out your naked photographs, another humdrum day in the Children of God, praise the Lord!

Unfortunately, to make tracking people between communes more difficult, orders were also given to destroy most photographs of friends and family, making it even harder for children to know or remember their relatives. Even in homes where nothing illegal was going on, it is unlikely that children were having a good time in the Children of God.

Destroying documents is a neat way of denying to authorities that the lifestyle choices of members are in any way ordered by leadership, and it's also a pretty efficient way of telling individual members who may be in trouble with the law that they're on their own. Nothing like washing your hands of responsibility in the flames of a pile of burning letters, right, cult leaders? In order to herald a new policy and avoid misguided persecution going forward, the group's charter, available on their website, now includes sweeping statements regarding the treatment of children and a code of conduct for members to abide by when dealing with children. It reminds adults in the cult that they are subject to the laws of whatever country they live in, which is a considerable relief after David Berg's opinions that System laws against incest and paedophilia are to be taken with a grain of salt.

Depending on your source and how biased it is, you can poke a stick at membership of Children of God peaking at around 20,000, and currently at a drastically more modest 3000-ish. It seems that once a cult starts operating within the law of the countries it settles in, and shaving away the bits that makes it unique, it becomes way less attractive to those looking for a truly alternative lifestyle.

In 2010, The Family International announced a 'Reboot', in which major changes to significant doctrinal teachings and organisational structure occurred, including an abandonment of communal living, and permission for members to pursue System jobs and education. Now with a notable web presence and – on the surface at least – the whimper version of its previous roar, it appears to be as benign a contemporary Christian offshoot as any.

'Missionary work' makes up most of the group's current mission statement, including building and providing for the underprivileged, although the witnessing side of the cult's projects are tinged with a little creepiness in its modes of infiltration. Providing 'character and faith building' kits for school teachers to order online, supplying 'educational material' to hospitals and institutions for the disadvantaged, bedside clown visits to sick children and public ministering via hugs, it's hard to remove thoughts of friendly but thorough indoctrination. It probably doesn't help that some of the 'positive-behaviour-enhancing' videos available for children are called 'Kiddie Viddies'. Still. In its current guise, the implication is that The Family International at least means well.

That said, despite the comparatively squeaky image of The Family International's contemporary manifestation, given its past stance on sexuality, the role of women and secrecy, it's probably a superb idea to give The Family International a miss. And, you know, don't join a cult.

AUM SHINRIKYO

IKUO HAYASHI, ONCE a doctor specialising in hearts and arteries at Tokyo's Keio Hospital, calmly dropped two newspaper-wrapped packages onto the floor of the train he was travelling in on the Chiyoda line, heading towards Kasumigaseki station. He was wearing a surgical mask like many of the passengers on the Tokyo subway system, but was also carrying an umbrella which had had its tip filed to a sharp point, like an unexpectedly sinister Mary Poppins. As the train approached Shin-Ochanomizu station, he stabbed his sharpened umbrella into one of the packages on the floor, releasing lethal sarin gas in fast-evaporating liquid form. Then, because Ikuo Hayashi was not an idiot, he quickly left the train.

Elsewhere, on other trains also headed towards Kasumigaseki and Nagatacho – where Japanese parliamentarians hang out on a normal working day like this was supposed to be – four other men with wrapped packages and pointy umbrellas also released sarin gas into carriages full of unsuspecting commuters. Just outside their destination stations, five more men waited patiently in parked cars, ready to drive the gas-bag poppers back to their communal home after a hard morning doing their Messiah's bidding. All ten men were members of Aum Shinrikyo, a cult you do not want to share public transport with. It was 20 March 1995, twelve people died, and thousands more suffered illness and injury. In addition to the human casualties, some of the trains in Japan were late, which hardly ever happens. A spoonful of sarin helps the Tokyo railway system go down.

Sarin gas is nasty, which is why people don't invite it to parties. It's a nerve agent, and when it's manufactured correctly it is odourless and very, very dangerous. It fiddles with the enzymes that tell your nerves to stop doing what they're doing, effectively making your nerves keep doing what they're doing excessively, over and over again. When those things are activities such as contracting your muscles or providing your eyes with gentle lubrication, a dose of sarin gas jams your nerves into high-achiever territory, squeezing out saliva, tears, vomit, and faeces, freaking your heart out and confusing the muscles you use to help you breathe. If it doesn't kill you, sarin gas will probably make you pretty sick for a long time, and will almost certainly make changing your underpants an urgent priority. The hot tip: don't breathe in or touch sarin gas.

The problem with doomsday cults, though – and Aum Shinrikyo is definitely the kind of cult that's obsessed with the end of both the world and humanity instead of more constructive things like fun and macramé – is that they think things like sarin gas are pretty cool. The story of how five smart blokes came to be releasing deadly gas during the morning commute starts, like not many stories do, with a vision-impaired narcissist and a spot of yoga.

Chizuo Matsumoto, who later changed his name to the far more punk rock Shoko Asahara, was born in 1955 into a poor tatami-mat-weaving family with no sight in his left eye and only partial sight in his right eye – a considerable impediment to the effective weaving of tatami mats. If Shoko's parents had sent him to a normal school it's possible that he might have felt less powerful than his classmates, constructing an entirely different future for him. In a school for the blind such as the one Shoko attended as a child though, the man with half an eye is king, and he used his dodgy peripheral vision to assert power and fleece other students of their money. They would pay him to be their eyes, and lead them out into the world for tea and meals, and in return he both stuck up for them and treated them quite, quite badly. When your schoolmates have to rely on you for things like the power of sight, you can some-times end up taking a couple of liberties. Not to foreshadow his future as a cult leader or anything, but here you've got a kid who assertively claims that he can perceive things others can't, using that skill to manipulate others into dependence and out of money. The writing, visible in retrospect to all of us with normal vision, was on the wall.

Shoko was well known but not well liked at school, and his standover-style of bullying resulted in multiple losses when he campaigned for student body president at different stages throughout his school career. Unluckily for the safety of Japanese citizens, this taught Shoko how to develop a grudge and really nurture it – a fantastic skill to master if you want to foster the singular drive required to start a cult a bit later. Sure, not all of Shoko's school-time ambitions and resentments were as practical as simply getting cranky over a political loss – he also professed a desire to one day be in charge of a robot army. At least his political aspirations had some potential application in real life, unlike his aspirations to grow a full, non-patchy beard, a dream unrealised for the rest of his life.

Two chance circumstances also helped steer Shoko towards cult leadership. In the late seventies and early eighties, when a recently graduated Shoko started dabbling in yoga, acupuncture, and traditional Chinese medicine, Eastern health and medical practices were exploding in Western mainstream culture. Awakening your *chi* was becoming more and more *chichi*, and a guru in the early eighties was like a scrunchie in the early nineties – all your cool friends had one.

Additionally, after World War II, freedom of religion was established in Japan after the disestablishment of Shinto as the official religion. Pre-war, Shinto and its emphasis on the holiness of the emperor had become intrinsically linked with the state, and it was more or less a requirement to be into Shinto. Afterwards, Allied organisations occupying defeated Japan figured that state-endorsed Shinto was a major contributor to the intense nationalism and highly structured lifestyle of the Japanese people, so the refreshed post-war Japanese constitution included a comparatively relaxed bit about no specific religions receiving state support, and people no longer being required to participate in religion. As a result, 'new' religions, or *shinshukyo*, proliferated, with many Japanese people even choosing more than one religion, picking what suited them from the spiritual buffet.

In the ensuing decades, as the initial orgiastic frenzy calmed down, the path was laid for potential sect leaders to serve up appealingly packaged bits and pieces of spirituality in an organised and focused way. Interestingly, more than a handful of these religions had a mildly apocalyptic flavour to them, appealing to those who felt that life and fate were out of their control. You know – party people.

So here comes Shoko Asahara, at just the right time. Selling shonky mystical medicines and running a yoga school. Getting busted by the police for selling unregulated pharmaceuticals, and chatting to more and more people about a grab-bag of concepts pinched from Christianity, Buddhism, Hinduism, science fiction, and anything else that made him look cool. He particularly liked the idea that Hindu god Shiva was the god of destruction, so effectively set himself up as the president of the Shiva fan club. John's end of days predictions in the Bible's Book of Revelation was another of Shoko's favourites, being the most predictable reference of any lazy doomsday cult.

While Shoko's complicated belief system morphed and developed over time, one constant was his misinterpretation of the original intent of the existing religions he borrowed from – in this sense he was one of Japan's most enthusiastic but careless cherry-pickers. For example, the Buddhist concept of *poa*, which is loosely a process of gently and seamlessly transferring your consciousness during death, became essentially a verb meaning 'murder' under the cute and cuddly Shoko. By the time Aum Shinrikyo became an actual religion, he'd even mixed in some concepts he'd heard about via Isaac Asimov's *Foundation* series of science fiction books and the predictions of Nostradamus, likely feeding his scientists-defending-against-the-end-of-the-world and there's-a-good-chance-I'm-the-Messiah fantasies in equal measure. If it sounded vague, mystical, loosely scientific and a teensy bit Armageddony, Shoko was into it.

Like many young men in their early twenties, Shoko found himself a wife and popped out a few puppies. Like drastically fewer young men in their early twenties, Shoko also popped over to the Himalayas, read a few books about spirituality (well, skimmed them), got a selfie with the Dalai Lama to look more legit, achieved 100 per cent total enlightenment – claiming he was the first guy since Buddha to do so, announced his discovery that he had unique, god-like DNA in his blood and whoops, proclaimed himself the Messiah. Certainly a lot of the things Shoko did in his twenties weren't absolutely legit, truthful, legal, or unlike manipulative scams, but at least he kept himself busy, y'know?

For additional, non–Dalai Lama legitimacy, Shoko distributed leaflets featuring a photo of himself levitating a couple of metres off the floor. Okay, one metre. And less possibly levitating than definitely bouncing off his knees. With an incredible amount of strain and effort showing in his face. In short, not levitating at all. The thing is, Shoko's target audience was so ready to believe in a non-materialistic, non-rigid borderline hippie that if a man clearly bouncing a short distance off the floor at very real risk of giving himself a hernia says he's levitating, sure, he's levitating. The photo was even featured in the definitely-believable-sounding *Twilight Zone* magazine in 1989. Shoko also claimed he could see through objects and meditate for hours underwater – all things that should have been pretty easy to prove, but when you're looking for a guru, I guess you just take their word for it.

Particularly surprising enthusiasts of Shoko's unscientific means of attracting followers were actual scientists. It could be equally confidently claimed that Shoko was a fan of scientists, because Shoko was a fan of smart people who could help him devise devices and substances instrumental to his obsession with world domination. He made it easy for scientists and tech-heads to join the cult by approaching and welcoming them, and ensured that they were the most comfortable and generously treated members of the group.

In 1987, Aum Shinrikyo considered itself an actual religion and, after a bit of nagging, convinced the Japanese government that it was as well, thanks to the government's new chill attitude towards new religions led by long-haired blind dudes who look like they just got out of bed for a glass of water. The name 'Aum Shinrikyo' is very loosely translated as 'Supreme Truth', and seemingly the truth is that if you hand your yoga students enough pamphlets, they'll believe what you say and do what they're told. Still, it's disappointing that they didn't keep calling themselves by their previous name, 'Aum Associations of Mountain Wizards', but maybe under that name they were just attracting too many hot chicks. Unfortunately for Japanese transport but fortunately for cults who want to be left alone, religious freedom under the law at the time meant tax breaks and a fair amount of immunity from prosecution – and even light investigation – from authorities. Put simply, these guys were free to look at porn on the internet without much chance of their mother walking in. Religious groups were even free to run businesses purely for profit, something almost unheard of today if you don't pay too much attention to the corners of most major religions. Once Aum was official, its membership increased exponentially, expanding to multiple compounds and boasting thousands and thousands of followers in a handful of countries by 1995.

Japan was good at a lot of things in the 1980s and 1990s, but it was spectacular at creating generations of computer and anime nerds – often referred to as *otaku*, although that's a term as ambiguous as 'nerd'. At the top of the brainy race at that time and in that place, things were overworked, impersonal, hyper-industrialised and completely unsuitable for the development of normal, casual social skills. The pressure on the academically gifted in Japan to achieve, achieve, achieve and furthermore conform, conform, conform, meant that some of them inevitably went looking for something with more meaning, a way they could make a difference in a sea of competitive sameness. Having not been a notable academic giant himself, Shoko wanted to surround himself with the kind of malleable but intelligent brains that could do his future dirty work for him – because his future dirty work required knowledge, skill, and inventiveness.

He needed science and tech nerds who wanted to break out of the norm.

And if there're two things science and tech nerds *love*, they are anime and playing out their resentment of society via violent apocalyptic fantasies. Aum Shinrikyo already had an interest in science and technology and bucketloads of violent apocalyptic fantasies – all they needed was a bit of anime and an incoming flock of followers was in the bag. The resulting anime films – kind of a cross between bad music videos and an overweight Astro Boy in his pyjamas – consist largely of an aesthetically generous cartoon version of Shoko Asahara flying around a cityscape in the lotus position. There are certainly better music videos, but there are few more effective advertisements for the tourism possibilities of transcendental meditation.

Potential recruits were targeted at busy train stations – these guys really had a thing for trains – and handed vouchers for free yoga classes. Once they were at Shoko's studio, they'd learn about breathing and meditation, sit through a bit of anime, and were given or encouraged to buy books written by Shoko. And guys? While we've got you, it would be super-great if you like, *only* read books by Shoko. And if you gave us any or all of your assets. And stopped having sex or eating any interesting food whatsoever. Just moving into a compound, meditating, reading, and handing over cash, m'kay? Great, see you tomorrow and we'll do the same thing all over again.

Shoko taught his followers about the struggle between materialism and spirituality, and claimed that proper religion is actually intensely scientific – a brave notion from a man who strongly hinted on a number of occasions that he could fly. Being reasonably interested in Buddhism as well – at least as far as it served his purposes – Shoko also spoke a lot about karma, and the fact that bad karma could be removed by putting yourself through physical suffering and intense ordeals. Surprisingly, nobody asked Shoko to babysit much.

The level of advancement and enlightenment each Aum Shinrikyo member reached within the cult was dependent on a cluster of factors – how much money you donated to the cult, how completely you cut your family and the outside world out of your life, and how robustly you could contribute to the diabolical chemical and technological needs of the master in his quest for obliteration. Certainly not, by the looks of things, how upbeat and chipper you were. In order to advance from mere follower to a member of the almost monk-like inner circle, whole estates were handed over to Aum, and if the families of members complained, they were simply threatened. Isolation from broader society was exceptionally important to Shoko, in theory because he didn't want his devoted members to be contaminated by materialistic and destructive outside influences, but in practice because outsiders can really get in the way of people signing their trust funds over to cult leaders.

No doubt still smarting from missing out on school-level political leadership, once he had an acceptable number of followers Shoko thought he'd try his hand at politics on a broader, national scale. With twenty-four of his followers and a party called 'Shinrito', he ran for Japanese parliament on an extremely sexy platform of objecting to sales tax. Good idea, not basing your political campaign on your other platform of total world domination and destruction, but still ultimately unsuccessful. All twenty-five Shinrito candidates lost, and they lost huge, even with rumours that cult members had falsified voting registrations in order to vote in the relevant electorates. It probably wasn't the sight of followers and party members campaigning in groups dressed in white and wearing oversized papier-mâché Shoko Asahara heads that lost them the election, but it's reasonable to propose that it didn't help. Still, Shoko blamed a rigged voting system and continued to fester with a seething hatred and lust for revenge, like a movie stereotype of a deranged psychopath stroking a white cat.

Aum Shinrikyo based itself in a number of compounds, with its main digs at a spot outside Tokyo near Mount Fuji called Kamikuishiki. A cluster of industrial buildings with tunnels and bunkers, like any self-respecting maniacal cult hangout, the camp boasted some extra-special rooms and buildings reserved for fun things like drug manufacture, making heaps and heaps of guns, fiddling with chemical and biological weapons, and a purpose-built body disposal unit, a bit like Disneyland without the queues or any fun. Days were spent not eating much, not sleeping much, not having sex much, doing a bit of yoga, meditating a bunch, and listening to both live and recorded sermons by Shoko that were increasingly about the world heading towards its explosive end.

The good thing about Aum Shinrikyo is that, as an odd kind of relief from the growing sense of dread and unease, they were into some truly kooky shit. For varying amounts of money, starting at lots and lots of yen through to absolute and utter craploads of yen, you could be the proud owner of the following choice products:

- 'Miracle Pond', a container filled with Shoko Asahara's used yet blessed and holy bathwater. Drink it straight or cook with it for only $300 an ounce! Floating pubes and soap scum not included, but some vials might have a little bit of guru wee in them.

- Alternatively, grab yourself a vial of Shoko's blood to drink for a mere $8000. Stop focusing on your Messiah's sermons about the evils of materialism and just buy some of his really expensive body fluids. What a deal.

- For a couple of hundred dollary-doos, you could also get your mitts on some clippings of Shoko Asahara's hair – hopefully from his head – to brew into a nice steaming cup of Messiah hair tea. No need to floss afterwards!

- If you're really serious, score yourself a 'Hat of Happiness' – an unwieldy helmet covered in electrodes available for rent at just $700 a month, or for sale at ten times that. See, Shoko himself would wear one of these hats and think really hard about Messiah stuff, so by wearing one yourself you can basically just absorb the Messiah's thoughts. I don't care what anyone says, that's a bargain.

The sale of such products – plus a couple of thriving businesses in the outside world like food shops, fitness centres, computer businesses and a babysitting service – kept Aum Shinrikyo well funded, particularly when supplemented by the sort-of-voluntarily-ish surrendered life savings of its members.

A lot of these incredible items – which scandalously never made Oprah's list of Christmas gift recommendations – were specifically intended for use in initiation ceremonies and everyday practices and rituals; activities designed to prove a follower's devotion to Shoko and Aum.

There was the 'Christ Initiation', in which an Aum member would take some LSD before sitting in an isolated individual meditation cell for twelve hours, tripping balls.

At 'Kundalini' level, aspirants were required to demonstrate that they could lower their heart rate, brain activity, and oxygen levels, a lot like a hibernating bear with occasional access to LSD.

The 'Perfect Salvation Initiation' involved wearing the afore-mentioned Hat of Happiness, erasing your previous thought patterns and replacing them with those of the guru. On LSD, preferably.

Generally speaking, any recruits who were seen as valuable to the cult – high-order scientists and technicians, for example – were subjected to gentler processes so as not to scare them off, but lower-level recruits were really put through the wringer to make sure they were made of the right stuff. To reach higher and higher levels of spiritual consciousness, members had to undergo these rituals and – perhaps most onerous of all – read Shoko's books.

From mid-1994, things progressed and most of the newly introduced initiations didn't involve as much absorbing of the guru's bodily fluids or thoughts. Later initiations could, for the most part, be summed up thusly: just drop some more acid.

It should be reasonably clear by now that LSD and other drugs were a super-important part of Aum Shinrikyo's spiritual methodology. Mind-altering substances helped people stay compliant, be ready to believe some truly wacky stuff, and made reading the Book of Revelation *amazing*, man. Plus, with all of those scientists on board, the cult could just whip up a fresh batch of acid whenever supplies were low. It's easy to convince your followers you have mystical powers when they're all off their collective tits.

On the darker flip side of initiations – if drinking a weird guy's bathwater isn't dark enough – were the punishments for disloyalty or not being devoted and pious enough, although the line is heavily blurred between initiations, punishments, forced improvement, and just bizarre practices. A lot of them involved drugs though, naturally. Aside from the impending doom of humanity, hallucinogens were one of Aum's most consistent themes. Former cult members have variously reported being dunked repeatedly in extremely cold water, drinking salt water until they vomited, being bound and hung upside-down for over an hour at a time, weekly bowel-cleansing (which actually sounds marvellous), and experiments exploring the effect multiple electric shocks of varying intensity have on memory. The latter were performed in the hope of developing the ability to effectively erase the recollections of followers the cult deemed untrustworthy. At least that's what cult members say, but it's pretty hard to trust the memories of people who have been subjected to memory-erasing experiments.

Followers were also suspended into scalding hot water for up to fifteen minutes, to train them to withstand high temperatures lest their enemies decide to attack them using high-intensity heat beams, an uncommon fear among rational, non-paranoid humans. Uncomfortable as the 'thermal training' must have been, the mental image of numerous Aum followers impersonating teabags is not without its appeal.

Deaths happened both inside and outside the cult, none of which are believed to be just coincidental or nobody's fault. Perhaps because of lingering resentment from his political failure at both school and in actual Japanese politics, or perhaps due to a gently developing megalomaniacal psychosis and blood-lust, it wasn't long before Shoko Asahara decided that his Aum Shinrikyo followers were a useful bunch of enemy-thwarting murderers.

The more followers you have, the more family members of followers you have on the outside sitting around getting suspicious and nosy, so every cult has to deal with the familial-interference problem. Shoko was a guy who didn't like to be criticised and, as a result, 1989 to 1995 was a bad time to be a journalist, lawyer, or politician who was critical of Aum as Shoko and his flunkies gave sceptic-silencing a red-hot go.

Tsutsumi Sakamoto was a lawyer who represented some Aum family members in their campaigns against the cult. He had also investigated Shoko's claims that tests conducted at Kyoto University had shown unique, messianic DNA in his blood and, not surprisingly, Sakamoto discovered that the boffins at the university had better things to do than test hippies with pretensions for god chromosomes, and no such test had been undertaken. In November 1989, Tsutsumi Sakamoto suddenly disappeared from his Yokohama apartment along with his wife and one-year-old son. Their bodies were not found until 1995, when arrested Aum members confessed to breaking into their apartment at 3 am, killing the family, and burying them. Police didn't investigate Aum too hard at the time of the murders because, under the good old Religious Corporations Law, they didn't want to hurt the cult's feelings.

Critical journalists, civilians who helped defectors, and anyone who stood in the way of Aum looking like a bunch of hard, cool guys were variously gassed, injected, or sprayed with chemicals with varying levels of damage.

In February 1995, 68-year-old notary Kiyoshi Kariya, who was trying to get his brother out of Aum Shinrikyo after already retrieving his sister, was kidnapped and taken to the Aum compound. Drugged with the intent of getting him to spill the beans on his sister's whereabouts, Kariya died of an overdose of a homemade truth serum and earned himself a trip to the cult's how-will-we-dispose-of-the-body department.

In May 1995 – after the Tokyo gas attack – a letter bomb was sent from Aum to Tokyo Governor Aoshima, possibly with the intent of distracting authorities from investigating and arresting the cult's leader. Fortunately for the governor, the bomb detonated before reaching him. Unfortunately for the governor's secretary's fingers, it detonated while the governor's secretary was opening it.

For a bonus murder round, Aum Shinrikyo had arrangements with the Yakuza – essentially the Japanese mafia – because people who manufacture drugs and people who distribute drugs like to hang out and talk about sweet sleeve tattoos. One of the top cult scientists, Dr Hideo Murai, was fond of personal television appearances claiming Aum's innocence, and was about to be arrested on suspicion of being definitely not innocent. Concerned that the doctor might spill the beans on gang involvement, a member of the Yakuza stabbed Murai during one of his live television appearances, the inventive little scallywag. Considering the fact that Hideo's extra-curricular hobby had been trying to figure out how to cause earthquakes, the Yakuza did us all a favour, really.

Perceived enemies of the cult were not the only victims – via punishment, over-zealous 'religious training', suicide, or quite possibly just parting their hair on the wrong side, at least twenty Aum Shinrikyo followers are believed to have been killed between 1988 and 1995. Early in 1989, a member of Aum Shinrikyo was accidentally drowned during a dunking ritual. Fellow member Shuji Taguchi, who observed the drowning and subsequent body disposal, decided it was an opportune time to leave the cult. Silly Shuji, people don't just leave cults. Potential deserters can't be trusted, so, allegedly while Shoko Asahara watched, Shuji's mates gave him a dramatic farewell – they strangled him.

Gruesomely, a lot of the bodies were disposed of via a purpose-built microwave crematorium, and once zapped, the bones were pulverised and scattered. No more waiting around for an old-fashioned convection corpse oven to cook your recently acquired cadavers down to a brittle consistency, no, sir. This is the nineties, and microwave technology can help you dispose of bodies in a mere fraction of the time.

Shoko, and by default the cult he oversaw, was utterly obsessed with death, in case the clues above leave any doubt. But see, it's fine. It's fine, because the bad people who died were only spending their lives gathering bad karma. Killing them was doing them a *favour*, see. They were *mercy* killings, with the added bonus of the killer receiving a heap of good karma credit, fast-tracking them to full enlightenment while they waited out the brief time between now and the end of the known universe.

So what exactly was Aum Shinrikyo's deal with Armageddon? Initially they were your stock-standard, run-of-the-mill doomsday cult trying to prevent the end of the world and be big heroes, then they gradually believed that they and they alone would survive the end of the world on a vaguely predictable date. It's quite difficult for cult leaders to retain their credibility if, once the date they've predicted a fatal cataclysm on passes without incident, their followers start to think that maybe they're full of shit. It's best to keep your predictions vague and readily mobile, claiming the ambiguity of divine symbols and God's fanciful and ever-changing whims. Shoko preached that, as conversion to his particular brand of pseudo-Buddhism converted bad vibes into positive energy, if enough people converted they would provide enough happy fun-time energy to save the world. After a while they just got sick of waiting, being ridiculed by the broader community, and incorrectly predicting the end of times, and decided to give the apocalypse a bit of a personal nudge.

Shoko was pretty sure that the end of everything would occur due to a nuclear-fuelled stoush between the US and Japan and guessed it would happen around 1997-ish or thereabouts.

Nine-tenths of the population of the world would die, with only the highly enlightened Aum Shinrikyo kids hopping on the salvation bus. All the other survivors would be free to live out their time in a nuclear wasteland, while Aum members, who wanted to do what they could to encourage animosity between the US and Japan, earned a shitload of karma thanks to indirectly killing squillions of people. Fun bonus!

In late 1994, Aum Shinrikyo's chief of military intelligence, Yoshihiro Inoue, even organised a clandestine raid on the secret files of Mitsubishi Heavy Industries, a company in Hiroshima that was party to countless Japanese military classified secrets thanks to their habit of manufacturing serious weaponry for the Japanese government. Impossible to imagine without getting the *Mission Impossible* theme in your head, Inoue and four mates – three of whom were actual flippin' paratroopers for no understandable reason except it was a great story to tell at parties – snuck into MHI in stolen uniforms and went on a downloading-weapons-technology-plans frenzy. It wasn't their only raid, either – due to the numerous high-calibre cult members who had worked within the tech and science industries, the wacky gang also managed to pilfer some secrets from NEC and a Yokosuka naval base. The raids were due in large part to Shoko Asahara's very strong desire to cut buildings in half with extremely large laser weapons. Go, he said. Go get me the plans for a hardcore Dr Evil situation.

Any self-respecting Dr Evil needs a large-scale imagined enemy. Shoko and Aum were not big fans of the United States and made their distaste broadly public, whether using America as a scapegoat to blame potential future apocalypses on, or attributing Japan's perceived problems to America's influence on issues like materialism, consumerism, and most probably mullets. To be fair, they also weren't massive fans of Japan either, and Shoko kept a hit-list of Japanese politicians he'd like to see assassinated. Jewish people were also on Aum's list of enemies, because Aum seemed pretty lazy when it came to looking for people to hate, and they figured taking Hitler's lead was a pretty groovy thing to do because Hitler was such a groovy guy. For reference: it's not, and he's not.

An unusual ally to Aum Shinrikyo, rumoured to be home to up to 30,000 Aum members at its peak, was Russia. The Aum message that had originally appealed so strongly to young Japanese workaholics who felt they were utterly at the disposal of their commercialised environment also worked a treat on 1990s Russians who felt they were utterly at the disposal of their government's whims and perceived bleak futures. With the Russians ripe for the picking, Aum campaigned heavily in Russia, buying radio time for daily sermons on stations broadcasting to various Russian and Japanese cities. High-ranking Aum members popped over to Russia frequently to relieve them of some of their relatively cheap assault rifles and transport helicopters, the latter with the intention of using them to squirt deadly gas over large areas. They didn't get around to much in the way of organising helicopter-flying lessons for themselves, but credit where credit's due – knowing where to buy a helicopter is really the biggest and most difficult step in the process. If there were two things that Russia was amazing at during the 1990s, it was constitutional crises and no-fuss international weapons transactions.

As the obsession with killing began to take hold, Shoko and Aum set to experimenting and practising chemical and biological warfare, at least until Shoko could convince his best scientists to build him a nuclear bomb and the aforementioned giant, building-slicing laser. Early experiments with botulism and anthrax didn't have the desired potential for fast-acting, widespread death orgies, so Aum's scientific heavies moved decisively from biological to chemical. That said, one anthrax test in Tokyo that failed to result in any serious human casualties did end up killing some birds and pets. *Pets*. Those *monsters*. The group's chemists started manufacturing sarin gas at least as early as 1993, and really took a shine to it. This is the one, they thought. This is the nefarious and sadistic gas for us.

Aum went to such lengths to practise their gassing skills that they bought a sheep and cattle station in remote Western Australia. The thing about Australian sheep and cattle stations is that they're really, really big – this one, Banjawarn Station, is just under half a million hectares – and they're a really, really long way away from everything else. You need a packed lunch and a spare tyre just to make it down the driveway to the letterbox. So, even though vast Australian outback farms are a bugger to get to, the phone reception is awful, and the freshness of the sushi cannot be guaranteed, they're ideal places to test chemical weapons. Australian Customs charged Aum around $20,000 worth of excess baggage fees in early 1993 to allow them to import a heap of gas masks, ditch diggers, hydrochloric acid, respirators and generators, but seemingly didn't ask them a whole bunch of questions about their intentions. It should come as no surprise at all to people who aren't customs officials that scientifically gifted nerds from Japan are not natural sheep shearers. That said, it wasn't until investigators found – regrettably only after the Tokyo gas attacks – twenty-nine sheep carcasses scattered about the station that all showed residual signs of sarin gas testing that authorities figured that maybe there was more to these international desert geeks than meets the eye. Also 'International Desert Geeks' would be a pretty good name for your electro-funk band, if you have one.

Now, nobody's saying that Aum Shinrikyo also conducted a nuclear bomb test at Banjawarn Station, but there *was* a loud noise in late May 1993, and there *was* a bright flash at the same time, and there *is* mineable uranium in exactly the same area, and the cult's psychotic leader *was* completely and utterly obsessed with building a nuclear bomb. Look, it could just be rumours.

Once they started to get the hang of the whole sarin gas caper, Aum members figured it was time to test some on humans. They decided the humans in question should be some court judges who they thought were about to rule against them in a real-estate-related case, so in 1994 some cult members drove a converted refrigerated truck to the apartment block the judges were staying in in Matsumoto, spraying sarin gas as they went. Their original plan was to gas the courthouse that the case was being heard in, but due to Aum's increasing habit of not getting things *quite* right, they ran a bit late and the courthouse had closed for the day. Seven people died, a hundred people were extremely sick, and not everybody's pets made it. The judges survived, although from all reports they did feel a bit iffy.

By early 1995, Shoko had pretty much decided that the end of the world, brought on by him and his mates but conveniently blameable on the US, would happen in November of that year, but funny things can happen on the way to Armageddon. Sick of people dying, Japanese authorities decided to hell with the religious protection laws – they'd better have a bit of a closer peek at Aum Shinrikyo. On 19 March 1995, police raided some Aum digs in Osaka and arrested three cult members on suspicion of abduction of another member who had decided he didn't want to be in a cult anymore. Shoko – although he *swears* he didn't, honest – decided that rather than a damaging, public criminal trial involving members that a paranoid cult leader couldn't be certain wouldn't dob him in, a bit of distraction was in order. It was time to speed up Armageddon and keep the police busy doing something that wasn't investigating Aum Shinrikyo. I mean, surely everyone would suspect the US government of a mass poisoning in Tokyo, and not a cult that had been manufacturing poison for a couple of years? Watertight plan, Shoko. Nice one.

The thing about sarin gas when it's well made is that it's odourless and very lethal. The thing about sarin gas when it's made by scientists who have only recently started specialising in making sarin gas and who are in a rush because their Messiah just brought the date of the apocalypse forward, is that it has a noticeable unpleasant odour and is a lot less lethal.

So on 20 March 1995, after a practice session on water-filled plastic bags at Aum headquarters, Dr Hayashi, four of his mates and five getaway drivers each headed towards the stations they were going to catch their death trains from, laden with sub-standard sarin and sharpened umbrellas, aimed at distracting Japanese authorities from prosecuting their Messiah and – fingers crossed – starting World War III. Each came prepared with a bottle of water to rinse their umbrella tip with, a syringe full of sarin antidote should they themselves be affected, and no doubt tightly clenched, nervous sphincters.

Five carriages, five men dropping packages of sarin on the floor, five pointy umbrellas stabbed hastily into each package. Thousands of people coughing, gasping, vomiting, drooling, struggling to breathe. Station attendants trying to help by carrying the pierced packages off the trains, unwittingly spreading the rapidly evaporating liquid further and wider. Trains – even those with sarin leaking onto their floors – continuing to operate in order to reach their scheduled stops on time. Evacuated passengers lying in the street, their faces streaming, some foaming at the mouth or bleeding from the nose. Hospitals overrun, ambulances late and wailing, media scrambling, stations emptying, doctors bewildered, panic widespread. Fifteen subway stations affected by gas. People dying.

A horrifying, terrible morning, and the worst terrorist attack in Japan's recent history. The attacks marked the end of the generously wide berth the authorities had previously given Aum Shinrikyo.

Between the gas attacks and the first of any arrests, more than one Aum compound was investigated, with police finding chemicals suspiciously similar to those used to both create and neutralise sarin gas. Shoko released some videos proclaiming, and in one case actually singing, his innocence. His excuses were about as convincing as his early levitation photographs. Aum had sarin antidote chemicals because the CIA kept trying to bomb the compound with gas, said Shoko. The other chemicals were there to help them make porcelain, medicine and fertiliser, said Shoko, conspicuously un-surrounded by porcelain, medicine or fertiliser. He also continued to broadcast radio speeches criticising the police, blaming them for the gas attacks in an attempt to make Aum look bad, and circumventing possible attempts to block his broadcast by again using equipment and signals provided by his buddies in Russia.

Finally on 16 May, Shoko was found by police hiding like a bastard in a secret underground bit of his Kamikuishiki compound, and promptly arrested. Impressively, police found millions and millions of yen hiding with him. Perhaps even more impressively, in the same quarters in which Shoko was found, police also discovered just under forty individually labelled glass vials, each with a single pubic hair inside. In contravention of his own sex rules, Shoko had been diddling select members of his cult and deftly plucking a curly souvenir afterwards. You have to hand it to him, really. And then wash those hands pretty quickly. There's no anti-bacterial soap too robust when we're talking about a guy with his own personal pube museum.

Since the attacks, at least 200 Aum Shinrikyo members have been arrested, with thirteen given the death penalty. During their investigation and trials, most were extremely forthcoming and even remorseful and apologetic, at least giving us some hope that the hold of a cult on a bright young thing's psyche can really sour once they're facing the death penalty for hurting or killing innocent, uninvolved strangers. Others, disappointingly, stand by their karmic reasons for killing people, and Shoko Asahara maintained that he had absolutely zero knowledge of any of the death plans at all. There are few things scarier than a stubborn, unrepentant mass murderer.

With so many attempted and actual attacks, and so many more that could have been planned had the cult's bigshots not been arrested, there's only one saving grace – one thing that stopped countless thousands more people being killed and injured. Aum Shinrikyo was incompetent. They were bad at releasing diseases to any significant effect. Bad at buying the right kind of anthrax. Bad at making giant lasers and nuclear weapons. Bad at buying helicopters that they knew how to fly. Bad at manufacturing full-potency sarin. Bad at averting suspicion. Bad at hiding and lying. If Aum didn't suck so much at doing so many things, the situation could have been far, far worse.

Still, how did they get away with it for so long? For starters, there was the freedom afforded to religious groups by authorities, a policy robustly re-thunk in the ensuing years. Additionally, evinced by the fact that members awaited execution for twenty-three years for a crime committed in 1995, the Japanese court system is criminally slow. Shoko's trial alone took eight years, which is longer than *Melrose Place* was on air. In 2004 he was sentenced to hang, with his execution taking fourteen years to actually take place in 2018. Not a fun way to spend a couple of decades if you're a victim of the cult aching for closure. Better news if you like the idea of evil, murderous psychopaths wasting away in a prison cell, gradually losing both their mind and their ability to not piss themselves. Despite convicted cult members testifying that they acted under his direct orders, Shoko maintained his innocence the entire time from condemnation to execution, claiming he knew nothing about any murders or gas attacks or drug manufacture. He also spent much of his time in court muttering and making nonsensical outbursts trying to distract the court proceedings, in much the same way that a big cowardly baby might.

The cult is still around to this day, albeit in a two-pronged, comparatively piss-weak form under constant scrutiny from authorities. The group split after some internal bitching and moaning about mission statements, so the two branches are Aleph on the one side and Hikari No Wa (or 'Circle of Rainbow Light') on the other. The rainbow guys are the milder version, but Aleph resembles Aum Shinrikyo more precisely and still talk a little more than is comfortable about vaguely end-of-the-worldy stuff. The cult still has an alarmingly fervent following in Russia, with local authorities there only thinking to outlaw the group in 2016 as a terrorist organisation.

In better news, the Religious Corporations Law that prevented Aum from being properly investigated was resoundingly tweaked after the gas attacks, with the aim of allowing authorities to meddle in plots to kill bulk citizens in the name of religion a lot earlier. Which is nice. The Clinton administration in the US, alerted to the fact that deranged gurus with enough techy followers can act like terrorists and pose a threat to governments and citizens – previously the domain of rogue nations with clear agendas – beefed up its defences against similar attacks and clamped down on access to hazardous germs via microbe banks. It's bizarre that the kind of reactive security measures that we're so used to today with our responses to terrorism were applied so broadly as a result of a group that started as a yoga class. There's the lesson, I guess. Don't trust yoga.

COLONIA DIGNIDAD

IF YOU'RE EVER in Chile and looking for a unique and unexpected tourist experience, head east from San Carlos and up a bit, pop into the Maule region just near the Perquilauquen River at the foot of the Andes, and walk up the road from Parral until you see some blokes wearing traditional German lederhosen, speaking German, and offering you a German sausage. While you're eating wurst and pondering dessert, you'd be excused for asking what a traditional Teutonic village is doing plonked here on the edge of South America. Simple! It's because it was once the site of one of the most heinous cults imaginable, started by an actual Nazi. Enjoy your strudel.

Just after World War II, when Nazis had finally cemented their enduring reputation as World's Worst Guys, many dyed-in-the-wool Third Reich dudes decided that Germany was an unattractive place to be. For starters, it was the first place people who wanted to kill and punish Nazis looked when they wanted to find Nazis to kill and punish. Secondly, they were pretty sure that the relatively victorious Russians were going to move in and turn everyone into Communists, and if there's one thing Nazis hate, it's Jews and gay people and the disabled and brown people and Communists.

One Nazi in particular, Paul Schafer, encouraged a large fistful of around 250 Germans, fuelled by his passionate sermons, charisma and unrepentant Nazism, to follow him to Chile, where he would become the leader of a Germanic utopia. The spot they picked felt kind of German-ish, surrounded by snow-capped mountains, rolling hills, and lush agricultural expanses ready for being planted with the fixings for spatzle and stollen and sauerkraut. Funded by hefty donations from his faithful, he bought up additional farmland surrounding a handful of existing German emigres, bullied a few Chilean nuns out of their church grounds, and set up shop. There, where if you squinted you could imagine yourself surrounded by the Alps rather than the Andes, the group hoped to preserve and celebrate their culture, dress, food, and language. An utterly blissful notion, save for the fact that Paul Schafer was a controlling, violent, power-hungry paedophile. He was just getting started, though. There was plenty of time yet to really let the darkest, squelchiest parts of his personality shine through.

The group called itself 'Colonia Dignidad', or 'Dignity Colony' with a distinct lack of irony for people who some-times wore leather shorts with long socks, an outfit with an arguable lack of dignity depending on who you are and how far you are geographically from a German beer hall. In fact, you could argue pretty robustly against both words in the title, unless your definition of 'colony' is the same as your definition of 'concentration camp'. It's probably not.

The fairly laid-back agricultural community had already been established when Schafer and his adherents arrived in 1961, but Paul really decided to make it his own, turning it into a thriving and industrious community with little time or energy to do anything but thrive and be industrious. Schafer had learned many things in *das Mutterland* that came in handy when transferred to settling a small chunk of another continent – discipline, how to organise a bunch of people into a well-oiled achievement machine, the importance of loyalty, and how to make truly excellent smallgoods. He was almost the ideal choice for the leader of a displaced, fledgling community, with just a handful of small personality-based drawbacks.

After a typical adolescence in the Hitler Youth, Schafer served as a medic in the Wehrmacht – that big army chock-full of Nazis – during World War II. Trying his hand at being an evangelical Baptist minister afterwards, Schafer was moved on from his position as church youth leader due to his superiors finding out about his grotesque habit of messing around with young boys.

Schafer established the 'Private Social Mission', a kind of 'cult lite' that was part baptistery, part heavily regulated community, and in an utterly unbelievable and legitimately horrifying move, part orphanage and children's home. Putting a paedophile in charge of a children's home is like stirring a bowl of jelly with a chainsaw – the jelly just has no chance at all. When Schafer was inevitably pulled up for molesting a couple of the children he was supposed to protect, he figured it was a good time to move on. Instead of suffering the inconvenience of arrest, Schafer got chatting to the Chilean ambassador to Germany, conveniently leaving out the bit where he was under investigation for kiddy-fiddling, and got himself an invitation to relocate to South America.

Schafer already had the loyalty of his community, thanks in part to his talent for enforcing rules and making people believe that his way was the right way. Likely unaware of his persecution for unsavoury behaviour with children, all Schafer had to do to get his flock to follow him to another part of the world was ask them to, with questions that very much sounded like he was telling them to. It was easy for Schafer to cover up his real reason for leaving Germany since a lot of people were leaving because things were unpleasant in Germany. Post-war, up to 9000 Nazis and sympathisers hopped it to South America, settling mostly in Argentina, Brazil, and Chile, often in rural German enclaves that had already been well established. In Argentina, President Juan Peron – a big fan of Hitler's fascist ideology – made entry to his country easy for anyone who sympathised with Adolf Hitler, Benito Mussolini, and miscellaneous other egregious fascists. Feeling that life in a balmy mountainous paradise might be preferable to a significantly crippled and grumpy Germany, South America found itself accepting great clumps of right-wing extremists. By the time Schafer and his loyal community had arrived, they were able to slip very easily into the environment they acquired thanks to the efforts and example set by many emigres before them.

Once settled in Chile, Schafer continued the habit of strict rule-enforcement over his moderately sized congregation, which meant that now, with the added bonus of geographical distance, he could gradually control more and more of the influences upon them. The colonists at the newly established Colonia Dignidad were forbidden from access to information or authentic news reports from back home in their insular compound, so as far as they knew things stayed unpleasant in Germany for a long time. They weren't aware of the great big strides that had been made towards reconciliation and rebuilding, so they continued to believe they were in a better place than their homeland.

As befits the paranoia of any psychopath with a desperate thirst for power, Schafer organised life at Colonia Dignidad in a way that ensured his continued position as its absolute and supreme leader. His followers were simply not permitted to regard anyone or anything in their life as more important than their loyalty to him – he must be regarded as the ultimate authority figure. He had a number of methods at his disposal for reminding followers that the admiration of any other entity was *verboten*, and he didn't mind shattering a few childhood illusions along the way. For example, children not born inside the cult who had been exposed to the idea of Santa Claus still got excited about his imminent arrival near Christmas-time, which Schafer considered an unwelcome threat to the purity of his leadership. Gathering the kiddies by the river, Schafer arranged for a man dressed as Santa Claus to arrive, then pretended to shoot him dead, and then made the children watch the 'body' floating away on the river's current. The children, not knowing the scenario was merely an act, believed that their proxy father figure had just murdered Santa. Paint it any way you like, that ain't right.

As reportedly charismatic and undoubtedly domineering as Paul Schafer was, the discomfort of others in his presence – even without the imminent threat of beatings, which we'll get to have fun with shortly – was partly due to the fact that he had a glass eye. The story of how he lost his eye would, when applied to any other one-eyed person, evoke moans of sympathy and horror. When applied to a sadistic bastard like Schafer though, it feels like it bloody served him right. As a child, little Paul had tied his shoelaces too tightly, and was struggling to undo a particularly troublesome double knot. Enlisting a fork for help, he tried prising the knot open with a prong, but being a young boy clumsy with utensils and slow to blink, he slipped and gouged a puncture in his right eye. To others: oh no! To Schafer: sucked in, you horrible perv.

As far as adults went, Paul Schafer dictated who married whom – not usually existing couples, and usually matches unlikely to want to sleep with each other – and frowned thoroughly and deeply upon the merest notion of sexual relations between an adult man and woman. Occasionally people within the compound did fall in love, but it seems that Schafer just wasn't interested in increasing the population of his congregation via traditional vaginal means, possibly as an extension of his general disinterest in vaginas as a whole. In the rare circumstances that a child managed to be born in the compound, remarkable considering how exhausted and void of libido everyone turned out to be, it was swiftly removed from its parents, lumped in with any other children of the same gender and similar age in common dormitories, and brought up by assigned group nannies that the children were required to call 'auntie'. Schafer himself insisted on being called 'Der Permanente Onkel' – or 'The Permanent Uncle' – one of the creepiest things Schafer insisted on, in competition with hundreds of creepy things perpetrated by a hot contender for World's Creepiest Guy. In fact, as not a lot of paedophilia was reported or known about publicly in Chile prior to the arrival and establishment of Colonia Dignidad's leader – Schafer really upped the average – after his crimes were known, a nickname given to paedophiles in Chile was 'Uncle Paul'.

Relationships weren't easy in the compound – men and women were strictly segregated except for some ceremonies and the production of the occasional promotional film, with even eye contact with the opposite sex being a strict no-no. If you developed a crush on someone, it could be literally months before you were within doeful-eye-contact distance of them again. Women were required to dress in dowdy, full-coverage, non-loin-inflammatory frocks, and the men in plain, no-nonsense clothing, embarrassingly decades behind fashion. Schafer himself was allowed to wear contemporary duds, though. Schafer was the boss, and Schafer liked to show he was the boss with natty threads. Genital contact was almost completely out of the question for Colonia residents, what with the erotic squelchy arts tending to distract people from farming, digging tunnels, and blind obedience.

Furthermore, all of the work – and there was usually about fourteen hours a day's worth – was done in complete silence, any communication punishable as always by heavy beatings. Private conversations and secrets were forbidden, adding a lack of gossip to the existing pile of joyless, drab situations at the Dignity Colony. Bad behaviour was often ascribed to possession of the wrongdoer by demons, and in Colonia Dignidad, exorcisms were conducted by beating the absolute shit out of the demons' host, like dust out of a carpet. There were many very good reasons that nobody referred to Colonia Dignidad as 'Funtown'.

Much like – oh, I don't know – Hitler and the Jews, Schafer knew that having a common enemy was one of the best and most efficient ways to unite people even if they're having a bad time, and the enemy he provided the residents of Colonia Dignidad was Satan. Satan *loves* lazy people, you see, so if you keep working from first light to last, you can avoid eternal damnation and, in theory, yet another beating. Satan made people resist authority, Satan made people ask questions, Satan made people want to leave the compound, and Satan made people disobey thousands and thousands of rules. Therefore, if one cult member defied Schafer or broke the rules or presumably sneezed too loudly, it was extremely easy – on the pretext that the sinner was riddled with Satan's diabolical whimsy – to get all of the other followers to report them or gang up on them. Effectively, with a common enemy and a small army of willing snitches, you had a colony that was more or less self-policing. Even if those with a rebellious streak persisted, there was still an arsenal of techniques – including shocks from a cattle prod, time spent in isolation in dark rooms, or massive doses of drugs usually used to treat epilepsy or schizophrenia – at the disciplinarians' disposal, although these were administered not by the tattle-telling masses but a trusted cluster of Schafer's lieutenants.

Drugs do a great job of making you more suggestible and willing to let other people make decisions for you. They can keep you in a relative stupor that transforms you into a plodding, pliable mass. Don't do drugs, kids, no matter how stridently your local cult leader insists. Particularly for those residents who voiced their objections to the people in charge about the way residents were treated, or questioned the rules or any of the very real immoral and illegal things they saw perpetrated at Colonia Dignidad, electric shock 'therapy' was useful for affecting the memory of the complainants. Nothing rattles the brain like a few hundred volts passing through it, and you can't keep making a fuss about something you've seen if you can't be absolutely sure you've seen it.

Although Schafer started life as a Baptist minister, it's genuinely difficult to say which religious pigeonhole the belief system at Colonia most comfortably fits into. Even when you consider how readily some breakaway Baptist groups occasionally go rogue and dance to the beat of their own extreme and questionable drums, there wasn't much of your classic Baptist guff left by the time Schafer really got into the swing of religious dictatorship. There's not a lot of information available about the religious doctrines Schafer enforced in camp, but it's fair to say that he chucked most of his Baptist preaching in the bin and instead opted for a singular, pure belief in one thing: Paul Schafer being the head honcho. All the characteristics of organised religion, like gathering for speeches, confession, and donating your time, toil, and money, could be channelled into the cult of personality without the messy need for actual doctrines.

Generally speaking, Baptist churches distinguish themselves from the vast smorgasbord of other Christian religions with two idiosyncrasies: they baptise believers when they're adults who know what they're doing rather than as babies who only know they hate baths, and each Baptist church can rule themselves autonomously without interference from any other church or main body. So, basically, once you've gone full immersion and washed away your sins and stuff, go nuts. Be a Baptist church of your own wacky governance and destiny. That's why rogue pockets such as the Westboro Baptist Church in Kansas in the US does things like picketing military funerals with gross statements regarding God's feelings towards the LGBTQI community, and why Paul Schafer could easily get a bunch of Germans to South America and then open a can of pious whoop-ass.

And open cans, Schafer certainly did. He considered discipline to be the absolute pinnacle of spirituality, yet was subject to little of it himself. Women and men were both beaten, and while women had some use to the commune as labour, and in infrequent cases as child-bearers, compared to the men and boys, women were seen as relatively dispensable and, even worse, descendants of Eve, the dirty original sinner. It's a horrible irony that in a place led by a despicable Nazi paedophile, women were the ones considered evil. Beatings were also an integral part of regular 'confessions'. At Colonia Dignidad, instead of the kind of confessions we're used to seeing in contemporary Catholicism – whispered admissions and penance to an anonymous absolver in a quiet, dignified wooden box – 'sinners' were brought before Schafer and his special cronies in a room, told what their sin was, and hit very hard, very often. If you resisted and denied any wrongdoing, you definitely got hit. If you agreed that you had sinned and begged for forgiveness, you also definitely got hit.

By 1973, Schafer had had a chance to really establish his own variety of dictatorship on a small scale, so when dictator-on-a-large-scale Augusto Pinochet came to power in Chile via a violent coup in that year, Schafer figured he'd found his new bestie. After a coup d'état – interestingly backed by the US government due to their general suspicion of anything resembling reds under beds – overthrew the democratically elected but disagreeably socialist Allende government, Pinochet made it very clear he was the new leader of Chile, and it would be very difficult to be any person who had a problem with that idea. During Pinochet's reign (1973–1990), more than 3000 people disappeared – most of whom turned up dead – and tens of thousands more were tortured. Having ideas at odds with those of Augusto Pinochet was an efficient way to get measured for a coffin so, put simply, Pinochet was really Paul Schafer's kind of guy.

Pinochet was super, super into torturing people who disagreed with him, or who he suspected had information about other people who disagreed with him. The problem was, Augusto and his gang of secret police operatives, the DINA (or Dirección de Inteligencia Nacional, which proves that the Latin languages can make anything sound nice), were a bit rubbish at torturing people. They hadn't had their jobs for very long, didn't have much experience, and through the mishandling of those without confidence or sufficient training in the excruciating arts, the people they were torturing kept inconveniently dying before they'd handed over any useful information. Happily, out at Colonia Dignidad, there was a one-eyed guy who was a proper expert at various forms of torture. Schafer had picked up a few tricks from those famously skilled torture-merchants, the Nazis, and he had followers who would do absolutely anything he told them, including torture. To top it off, Pinochet understood that Schafer found the idea of Communists and socialists altogether distasteful, so the two were destined to be bros from the get-go. Pinochet was all 'Can you do my torturing for me please, Paul', and Schafer was all 'You BET I can, Augusto, when can you drop them off?', and an enduring, sick symbiotic relationship was born. 'No, YOU hang up,' finished Pinochet, twirling the telephone cord around his finger. Schafer even facilitated a couple of guest lecturers, such as former members of the Gestapo, to teach Pinochet's men in his secret underground bunkers in a kind of sick torture academy. While Augusto had hundreds of torture camps dotted around the country, due to being a sadistic and paranoid bastard, Colonia Dignidad was the only one where you could get a really top-notch pretzel.

Basically, insurgents, rebels, and nay-sayers were rounded up and shipped off to bad torture places according to their individual interrogation needs. Torture techniques at Colonia Dignidad, a premium service, primarily involved holding prisoners in the various underground stone tunnels beneath the cult's compound and administering electric shocks to the fleshier, more embarrassing parts of their bodies while they were strapped to metal bed frames. It wasn't unusual to have an electrode or two under your fingernails, or up your bottom, or in the eye of your penis, or in your mouth, like an extremely upsetting game of Operation. Not one to rest on either his laurels or on currently existing torture technique, Paul Schafer even commissioned a spot of experimental research, testing prisoners who weren't even being interrogated at the time to see how much agony they could handle before becoming unconscious or dying. In almost any other field, this kind of devotion to refining one's art might be commendable, but when applied to torture, it's a little bit sickening. Dogs were trained to attack the genitals, and the different levels of prisoner tolerance to the trifecta of being hit, being electrocuted, and being hanged were tested. The underground torture chambers were efficiently soundproofed too, so despite the screams, most of the Colonia Dignidad's German residents were unaware that prisoners were being tortured in the camp, often literally beneath their feet.

In 1977, Amnesty International released a report about the violations it believed were occurring beneath Schafer's compound, so he sued them for defamation. How *dare* Amnesty International say that things were happening in his community that were definitely and absolutely 100 per cent happening. He lost the case, but the court proceedings took twenty years, delaying full publication of the report. Throughout the 1980s, Amnesty International continued their campaign and even convinced the German government to try a spot of investigating into the goings-on at the suspected torture cult, but before they could commence the investigation, the German government needed permission from General Pinochet. Weirdly Pinochet, the Grand Poobah of Torture Time, did not give his permission.

A number of people who disagreed with Pinochet at various volumes went missing during his dictatorship, with an alarming percentage of them last seen in or near Colonia Dignidad. While it was easy for the government at the time to ignore the relatives of locals marching and picketing, and generally kicking up a stink wanting to know where their disappearing family members were, it was less easy to cover up the disappearance of a US citizen. Boris Weisfeiler was a Russian-born American and mathematics professor at Pennsylvania State University, who shared the popular opinion that the Andes were quite pretty, and liked to hike through and around them. In 1985, probably confronted by a military border patrol in the middle of his bushwalk and unable to convince them that he had absolutely no interest in their country's politics, Boris was reportedly yoinked off to a mystery location, his backpack found later by the side of the Los Sauces river. Boris's sister Olga, who has not given up her campaign to discover what happened to him, maintains that the Chilean government's claim that Boris most likely drowned while he was hiking is garbage. No body has ever been found. One problem for Boris – aside from the whole disappearing-without-a-trace thing – was that he was Jewish. Some strong advice for Jewish Russian–Americans hiking alone in Chile under the Pinochet regime: try not to get taken to a Nazi torture camp.

Two years after Boris Weisfeiler disappeared, a Chilean informant claimed that he had been part of a patrol that arrested a foreign hiker that they suspected was a Russian spy and took him to Colonia Dignidad. According to one story, Boris was seen alive in the compound in 1987 but not since, and according to another he was executed within a couple of days of being kidnapped. Olga Weisfeiler has recruited lawyers, written to embassies, and garnered the support of the US government and the FBI, but despite the Chilean judiciary opening inquiries into Boris's disappearance, and even indicting eight officers with his abduction, nothing has come of it. In 2016 a Chilean judge closed the case, applying a statute of limitations with reasoning that the abduction was a common crime rather than a human rights violation, and lifted the charges against the indicted military officers. A cynical person might think that secrets were being kept and proper investigation and release of relevant documents were being intentionally stalled. A non-cynical person might think that too.

Paul Schafer was extremely talented at identifying the right people in power and befriending them, often with the help of wheel-greasing packages of homemade cheeses, smallgoods, and cakes. In return for all the tortures and disappearances, Paul Schafer and Colonia Dignidad enjoyed a long period of not being bothered by authorities and not being investigated for heinous crimes against children. Under fear for their own safety, even German diplomats in Chile looked the other way when their attention was alerted to the icky goings-on in the camp. Due to the relationship between Schafer and authorities, if cult members fled the compound and turned up at the German embassy for assistance and protection, they were simply reported to Schafer's cronies who turned up to transport them back to Colonia Dignidad. Through whatever means – possibly bribery with dangerous secrets, payment, or the exchange of favours – Schafer had built himself a robust network of protection that served him very well for several decades.

It also helped Schafer's cause if the wider community at large – from South America to Germany – thought the colony was a thriving mass of benevolent do-gooders, bent on the betterment of mankind and the charitable provision of baked goods and bandages to the surrounding poor Chilean families. To this end, a number of glowing promotional films were produced on-site. The promotional films were, in a word, bullshit. They showed women cheerfully churning butter, men cheerfully working the fields, children cheerfully playing and lending a light helping hand, and orchestras and choirs cheerfully oompah-oompah-ing their way through traditional musical classics from good ol' Deutschland. At a fundamental level, anything depicting the residents of Colonia Dignidad as cheerful was a complete lie and utter farce, but Schafer needed the outside world to consider the camp a wholesome, utopian wonderland doing non-stop good deeds truly worthy of your donations and warm fuzzy feelings. Gentle journalistic probes into the cult were semi-regular, so these films came in handy for averting too much scrutiny, along with glowing articles written in pro-Pinochet newspapers. In the rare circumstances where journalists, investigators, or ambassadorial staff were actually permitted to visit the compound, they would see a harmonious, charitable colony working for the collective good – all an act to keep Schafer operating his torture and slave camp a little longer.

The great thing about having a secure compound that's extremely difficult to escape from is that, by default, you also have a secure compound that's extremely difficult for people to get into. This made Colonia Dignidad an ideal place for people to hide, or lay low until people stopped looking for them. As a result, the compound hosted a number of guests of questionable ethics. The kind of people that good, upstanding people with normal reactions like us might shoot on sight. You know – people like high-ranking Nazis.

High-ranking Nazis like Walter Rauff, a horrible prick considered responsible for the death of over 100,000 Jews, Communists, and disabled people thanks to his participation in the invention and engineering of mobile gas chambers. Rauff dropped in on his buddy Paul for a cuppa, out of sight of war-crime investigators and autograph hunters.

High-ranking Nazis like Josef Mengele, who was given the definitely un-cute nickname 'The Angel of Death' during the war, which probably doesn't sound cute in German either. While working as a doctor in the concentration camp at Auschwitz, Mengele – for no good reason and with no empathy whatsoever – decided he would conduct genetic experiments, primarily on twins. The experiments included amputating limbs, intentionally infecting one twin with diseases, transfusing blood between siblings, and sewing twins together to form conjoined twins, just for giggles. He was also a bit obsessed with people with heterochromia iridum – those with one eye a different colour from the other – sometimes injecting chemicals into one of their eyes to see if he could change its colour artificially. Mengele avoided arrest until he died, because he was, quite evidently, a scumbag.

There was also a rumour that Hitler's deputy, Martin Bormann, had a brief stay at Colonia Dignidad after disappearing from Germany in 1945, but after DNA testing of a skeleton found in Berlin, scientists figured that he was the kind of coward who commits suicide rather than facing the war-atrocities music, not the kind of coward who flees to South America.

Mind you, for someone who professed to loathe Communism, to a degree and with several significant caveats, Schafer was running a Communist state. Everyone pitched in, everyone more or less owned the means of production, there was no class system or currency, and everyone was miserable – classic, text-book Communism. Sure, there was a despotic, unhinged tyrant in charge and technically nobody was allowed to leave or had any freedom whatsoever, but I'm sure if Marx had stayed alive long enough he would have ironed those kinks out. To the extent that sometimes Communism can sort of lean towards a totali-tarian dictatorship with free slave labour, Schafer totally had that side of it down. Guard dogs, hidden sensors that set off alarms should an escapee trip its tentacles, barbed wire, covert systems designed to eavesdrop on residents – all signs that you're in a cult, a prison, or an extremely difficult video game. Even if any followers had made it past the virtual buffet of deterrents, what then? Life is difficult for someone in a relatively remote part of Chile who only speaks German, fleeing from someone who is on extremely close terms with the country's sadistic dictator. Best you go back, accept your inevitable beating, and peel another 300 potatoes – it's safer.

As far as cult compounds go – and credit where credit is due, even if the people due the credit are too tired and drug-addled to accept credit – Colonia Dignidad was a bloody impressive one. Loads of farmland growing grain, potatoes and vegetables, a meat processing plant, a wheat mill churning out flour, a dairy churning out milk, a power plant churning out electricity, sleeping quarters, a hospital, a teeny little airport, a school, and a cemetery – as it was discovered later, both an official and unofficial one. On top of that, a machining workshop allowed them to maintain their numerous vehicles, they made their own bricks and tiles, and there was a radio communication centre that allowed a tiny minority of residents and several DINA agents to reach those on the outside. They grew and made enough to eat for themselves – particularly as they weren't allowed to eat much or enjoy anything resembling variety – with plenty of baked goods and sausage to bribe officials and sell to Chileans outside the compound walls, even in shops as far away as Santiago, the capital. Profit and self-sustainability are pretty easy when you have a few hundred silent slaves.

Obedience also stemmed from isolation – there were no televisions, radios, or even calendars permitted, so residents of the compound were free to stay focused on their narrow, singular world and keep their minds on the many, many jobs. Schafer and pals considered rest and fun to be the folly of the entitled, not the domain of the holy, and that eight hours of work a day was a bit on the lazy side. Colonia Dignidad residents were allowed one day off a year, on Schafer's birthday. Happy narcissism to you.

Disadvantaged locals outside the cult were offered treatment in the compound's hospital and education in their agricultural school, which furthered the group's image as a benevolent bunch of do-gooders. Locals admired the Germans for their work ethic, their industriousness, and the fact that they were so damn neat and tidy. A sign at the compound's gate declared that the high fence with barbed wire, armed guards, and watchtowers was 'Benefactora Dignidad', and so convincing was their proclaimed status as a charitable organisation that they were given subsidies and grants by the Chilean government. Admittedly it's a lot easier to get money from the government when it's headed by one of your best mates who likes to send you his favourite torture victims.

If you're a really good cult leader capable of ensuring slavish devotion from your followers, you know to keep them teetering somewhere at the midpoint between just enough energy for unpaid labour and too exhausted to rebel or have sex with each other. An even balance between a broken will and a strong work ethic means things get done without many messy insurrections, and at Colonia Dignidad there was a crapload of space in which to get things done. From a not even modest starting point of 15,000 hectares, through acquisition – sometimes negotiated, sometimes forced – the colony burped itself out to over 35,000 hectares. As it grew, any residents working out in the distant fields away from the more built-up areas of the compound were given a free armed guard, just to make sure that distance from the central administrative buildings didn't manifest itself into thoughts of rebellion or escape.

The horrors of Colonia Dignidad were given the cinematic treatment in the 2016 movie *Colonia*. In it, Emma Watson plays a character who infiltrates the cult's compound when she suspects that her anti-Pinochet boyfriend, Daniel, played by Daniel Bruhl, has been kidnapped and is being held there. Of considerable relief to viewers, the film washes lightly over the sexual abuse that was a feature in any other telling of the cult's story and focuses instead on the torture and beatings, and Schafer's dodgy dealings with his buddies in the Chilean military elite. *Colonia* makes it seem like it was fairly easy to enter the cult – knock at the gate, change your clothes, survive an interview with Paul Schafer – yet fairly difficult to peel a large pile of potatoes. That said, it does stress the twin points that it was exceptionally hard for a would-be escapee to leave the compound or the country at the time, and that Emma Watson looks adorable in plaits.

Like so many cult leaders before and after him, in Schafer's state-within-a-state the strict rules were only intended for the underlings, with luxury and spoils to their glorious leader. Tragically for hundreds of children, for the disgusting leader of Colonia Dignidad, 'spoils' equated to the worst kind of abuse.

So. The paedophilia. It was not good, and if discussion of such things puts you in a very bad place, then maybe skip this bit.

Schafer was only semi-secretive about his taste for young boys within the cult, convincing his congregation that he believed the children to be possessed by demons, but enlisting some of his closer elite to assist with associated awful tasks like bringing new children into the camp, or keeping them sedate and agreeable with drugs. There were definitely two tiers of society in Colonia

Dignidad – the regular residents who toiled and obeyed and were subjected to harsh discipline, and Schafer's more intimate group, those granted some privileges, who helped him mete out the discipline and kept the compound running and secure. A bit like prison guards, you might say, if you were going to call Colonia Dignidad a prison, which you definitely should. Many children were subjected to 'therapy', which included being given sedatives and electro-shock therapy, in theory to help exorcise the demons, but in reality to make them compliant. Every night, at least one boy would be required to stay in Schafer's bedroom. Schafer would quote Jesus by saying 'Let the little children come to me', and whether or not you believe in Jesus, you'd have to agree that's a pretty shitty way to have the meaning of his words twisted.

Schafer was crafty but relatively indiscriminate in his selection of rape victims – the children of cult members and boys from the local area were all fair game. As the cult was seen as a charitable organisation, Chilean parents willingly sent their children to its school and hospital, wanting better service for their kids than could be provided elsewhere locally. One of the overblown promotional videos from Colonia Dignidad claims that over 25,000 Chileans had received free medical treatment in its hospital. Many children were even adopted into the cult from poor families in the surrounding area, sometimes legally, often not. Children were unable to tell their parents about the abuse, as those born into the cult didn't always know who their parents were, and those adopted into the cult only had adoptive parents on paper – realistically they were completely at the mercy of Schafer.

Children spent their early lives watching all the adults being obedient to Schafer, and all the older kids doing the same, and everything being under his power and according to his directions, so to them it was just normal that he was the only authority figure. To a child in the commune, Schafer was basically God. And when a strict God asks a child to his bedroom and makes him do things that confuse and frighten him, that child knows he has to obey, lest they be sent to Hell. It's reasonable to imagine that actual Hell would be preferable.

In 1990 when Pinochet was finally overthrown and replaced with the much milder-mannered and less-likely-to-overlook-torture-and-child-sex-abuse president Patricio Aylwin, Paul Schafer likely knew his days were numbered and that Colonia Dignidad could not continue in the same way it had for thirty-odd years. The freedom to be the horrible place it was had only been possible because of outside officials – including German diplomats, making them distinctly unpopular with German citizens back home – turning a blind eye and facilitating its own atrocities. With the previous regime's torture camps around the country being shut down and raided, many of the more sinister practices within Colonia Dignidad's walls ceased. The commune was renamed Villa Baviera, they were investigated for tax evasion, and their official status as a charity was withdrawn, ironically just when they finally eased up on being horrible assholes.

Mothers of children who had been raped within the cult, smart enough to not take their concerns to local police but head straight for the capital, had their complaints turned into arrest warrants in 1996, and their claims were backed up by doctors reporting evidence of forced sexual contact. People were finally having their tired, broken voices heard, and in contrast to their courage, with the kind of shrivelled and puny testicular fortitude characteristic of a cult leader, Schafer ran and hid, first in his underground bunkers, then elsewhere outside the camp. He hid from an arrest warrant issued in 1996 for multiple counts of child sex abuse. He hid from his own trial in 2004, conducted in absentia, that convicted him of paedophilia. During repeated raids of the compound, Colonia Dignidad residents insisted that Schafer was dead, trying to put the authorities off his fetid scent. Unluckily for Schafer, the parents of sexually abused children tend to want to see a paedophile's body before they stop baying for justice, as they should, and maintained their pressure on investigators.

Schafer hid for nine years, and was finally found in Buenos Aires, Argentina, in March 2005, a pathetic figure in old-man slacks and a cardigan. He had been found not by Chilean authorities, who were generally frustrated by the limitations applied to investigations conducted by officials outside Argentina, but by a journalist and lawyer free to work in other countries, urged on by relatives of the abused and ex-members of the cult. When captured, it was reported that Schafer just looked up at his captors and asked, 'Why?' UM, BECAUSE OF THE RAPES AND TORTURE, MATE.

Other cult members were arrested and charged as well, mostly Schafer's bosom-buddy upper elite, on various counts of unbelievably evil stuff. One of the worst of the Schafer cronies was Hartmut Hopp, Colonia's main doctor guy and one of Schafer's closest affiliates, who was convicted in Chile in 2011 of human rights violations and aiding and abetting the sexual abuse of minors. Mostly responsible for handing out the drugs that pacified the residents and stopped them wanting to willingly do rude things to each other, he also spent his time helping Paul Schafer do rude things to very unwilling victims. Hopp is, in the succinctest of terms, an appalling bastard. Hopp hopped it back to Germany, sneakily eluding Chilean border control soon after being convicted of his crimes – nice one, Chilean police – and almost unbelievably lived in Germany in freedom, far from the shit hitting the fan. Under German law, the government does not extradite its own citizens, so more than a decade after Hopp fled his crimes he relaxed, did the gardening, and walked down to the shops for milk and newspapers. Finally, in 2017, the Chilean judiciary convinced the German judiciary to agree to jail Hopp in his own country. There is a general feeling held by victims of Schafer and Colonia Dignidad that neither country is really doing all they can to bring the bad guys to justice and compensate the little guys, and it's reasonable to suggest that that feeling is warranted.

When the compound was finally raided around the time of Schafer's arrest, due to Schafer's strong connection with his buddy Pinochet, investigators found the largest non-military weapons cache ever discovered in Chile. The cache did not muck around, and included rocket launchers, grenades, military rifles, sarin gas, mines, explosives, missiles, and some more adventurous and loopy items like dart-shooting cameras, .22 calibre pencils, and a walking-stick-shaped gun. Lethal walking sticks are certainly a novelty, but, man, cults sure do love sarin gas. If cults wrote a BuzzFeed article entitled 'The Top Ten Gases for Making Your Paranoia Manifest', sarin would be in the top three, easy. In addition to the weapons, the bodies of scores of political prisoners were found, and in some cases their cars – buried on the grounds – were unearthed. If you weren't so cross at Schafer for being the entire bottom rung of the humanity ladder, you'd have to hand it to him for really getting stuff done.

In 2006, Paul Schafer was found guilty of twenty-five counts of child sex abuse and sentenced to twenty years in prison. Twenty-five counts, when the real count was likely to be in the hundreds, if not thousands. Twenty years for a very long history of enslavement, abuse, restriction of liberty, the worst imaginable kind of criminal sexual misconduct, and being a nauseating, power-driven cock-knuckle.

Despite the fact that by now hundreds and hundreds of people would have liked to have seen Schafer wasting away in a lot of discomfort in jail for as long as possible, he died at eighty-eight, five years into his twenty-year sentence. We can only hope that for those five years he at least had a painful, thrombosed haemorrhoid. We can only hope.

In 2016, 120 ex-members of the cult understandably filed a class action against the Chilean government and the German embassy for allowing the horrific conditions and practices at Colonia Dignidad to continue for as long as they did. In 2017 the Chilean and German governments agreed to form a joint commission to document the crimes committed within Colonia Dignidad, and to co-operate on a memorial for the victims that were abused, tortured, and killed there. Probably too late but still a reasonably decent gesture. Joachim Gauck, the German President at the time of the class action, expressed regret that the German embassy in Chile had turned away Colonia Dignidad escapees seeking help, but offered a resounding *nein, danke* when it came to offering compensation, using the excuse that they didn't establish the dictatorship in Chile. Widespread criticism continues to be levelled at both the Chilean and German governments for dragging their feet with investigations, convictions, and reparations. It's like nobody wants to admit any responsibility for allowing a Nazi paedophile torture cult to thrive for more than thirty years.

These days, Colonia Dignidad as Villa Baviera is unrecognisably watered down, a German-themed tourist destination with German music, a restaurant, a petting zoo, a souvenir shop, and an annual Oktoberfest knees-up. They even do weddings, because what's more romantic than saying 'I do' in the same place an old sadist used to force children into sexual acts? If you can stomach the history, you can also order some pretty authentic German food, including reportedly excellent sausages. By all reports the tourism is only moderately successful and Villa Baviera is suffering financially. That's a weird mix of emotions, when all is said and done. You want the victims of a power-hungry sadist to have a chance to finally thrive once they're out from under his thumb, but at the same time going for a holiday at a rapist's hell prison seems ultimately distasteful. If you do stay there though, try not to be distracted by the deep excavation pits you might see on some of the hillside, where Chilean officials went digging to look for the bodies of political prisoners. It might put you off your pork knuckle.

HEAVEN'S GATE

ALMOST EVERY DISCUSSION of the Heaven's Gate cult starts with the same imagery.

Thirty-nine people, all dressed in the same black, homemade, baggy tops, loose black trousers, black and white Nike Decade sneakers, all with the same amount of change in their pockets, all with a purple square of cloth placed over them like a shroud, all in the one house. All dead.

The mass suicide in a mansion in Rancho Santa Fe, California, was, when it was discovered on 26 March 1997, one of those news stories that makes you stop what you're doing, stare at the radio or television, and swear very quietly and very slowly under your breath. To anyone not on a steady diet of fringe cult behaviour, it was very, very weird.

The originators of Heaven's Gate had the kind of names that would be more at home on a Country and Western Greatest Hits album than at the helm of a suicidal science fiction cult:

Bonnie Lu Nettles and Marshall Herff Applewhite. Having :
superb names wasn't enough for them, though, and disappc
ingly throughout their questionable careers as cult leaders, 1
changed their names frequently as their theories about the w
and its fate evolved and developed.

Like many cult leaders, Marshall Applewhite was raisec
extremely religious parents, and his father was a roving preac
That said, most people raised by extremely religious par(
don't eventually become cult leaders, so the correlation betw
having a goddy family and leading a bunch of devoted follov
down a bizarre and dangerous path remains tentative.

Applewhite Senior was a conservative Presbyterian mini:
in Texas, and by all reports conservative Presbyterian minister:
Texas in the mid-twentieth century – in fact quite a lot of peo
in Texas in the mid-twentieth century – had reasonably strc
views regarding homosexual and bisexual people, so Marsh
grew up, got married, had children, and kept his bisexuality
secret as possible. Repression of sexuality became one of his k
recommended skills as a cult leader later in life, so it's likely tl
the habit started out of perceived self-preservation in his yout
Most of the people who have tried to figure out the origins
Marshall Applewhite's unusual path in life factor his sexuality
as a very significant influence. Of course, rumoured depressio
paranoia, and mild psychosis could probably be factored in ;
well, but it's enough to say that, as far as potential for extrem
personality-trait cocktails go, Marshall was working with som
pretty top-shelf ingredients.

After briefly toying with the idea of becoming a religious minister himself, Applewhite got himself a master's degree in music and enjoyed some time as a performer, choirmaster, and music professor. He taught at the University of Alabama, but by all reports universities in Alabama in the mid-twentieth century, like their Texan counterparts, took a dim view of either lecturers having relationships with students or homosexual relationships in general, and Marshall was invited to leave when it was discovered he'd had both in a single, convenient package. The affair was the beginning of the end for his marriage, and he separated from his wife, dabbled in a few jobs and opened a deli for a short time, but as far as a singular life direction was concerned, he was at a bit of a loss. Until he met Bonnie.

Bonnie Lu Nettles was a nurse, mother, frequent *Sound of Music* watcher, and recent divorcee who knew a bit about Christianity but was mostly fascinated by the occult, astrology, and UFOs. She liked having people over to the house to chat about astrology and to summon the nineteenth-century monk she swore spoke to her directly from the afterlife – just normal housewife stuff. She didn't look like an occultist, or medium, or astrology nut, or cult leader. Bonnie looked like a middle-aged, intensely normal mother of four. She seemed unremarkable, which is remarkable considering she was later regarded by quite a few people to be actual God.

Bonnie and Marshall met in 1972 at a Houston hospital where Bonnie Lu worked and where, depending on whose story you pay attention to, Marshall was either visiting a sick friend or seeking physical or psychiatric treatment himself, reportedly for either

a minor heart problem or to cure himself of his homosexuality. Marshall was deeply troubled by and significantly ashamed of the fact that he was bisexual, primarily because people can be dicks and can't help sticking their puritanical noses into things that they're frightened of. You could do a spot of projecting and consider that if Marshall hadn't been made to feel bad about his sexuality, his life might have taken a very different, much less scandalous path, but nothing is certain. The world and hormones and brain-wiring and God and aliens work in mysterious ways.

Whatever Applewhite was at the hospital for, when he met Bonnie Lu Nettles he was sure he'd met his spiritual soulmate, and that the meeting had been divinely ordained. Bonnie had always been obsessed with astrology and the mystical, and both she and Marshall had long suspected they had a purpose beyond the pedestrian on Earth. The pair bonded quickly and thoroughly, and for all intents and purposes, bar the romantic or sexual, became an inseparable kind of platonic power couple.

It wasn't until Applewhite and Nettles spent a bit of downtime brushing up on the Book of Revelation that the penny dropped and they realised who they were and what their mission was: preparing the world for its end. Good old Revelation, friend of potential apocalyptic doomsday obsessives everywhere.

Two of the pivotal figures in the Book of Revelation, and the two that really pumped Marshall's and Bonnie's nads, were the two witnesses, symbolised as two olive trees and two lampstands in Bible John's freaky reverie. The witnesses are pretty terrifying, with the ability to breathe fire, smite enemies worthy of smiting, and control oceans and the sky. Controlling the sky is very good for planning a picnic, but the other skills are a real bugger if you don't want to scare the children. The main job of the two witnesses is to try to turn as many people as possible towards God, then to be killed and soon after resurrected, at which point God will summon them up to Heaven and start the ball rolling properly on the end of the world as we know it. Cute, right? Well Marshall the music teacher and Bonnie the nurse really felt a close affinity with those kids – the ones that breathe fire and smite – especially the hanging out in Heaven as God's special guest stars bit. Marshall and Bonnie started their whole thing by calling themselves 'The Two'.

That was it. It was their job to prepare people for salvation, encouraging them towards the highest form of evolution possible – they called it The Evolutionary Level Above Human – and then facilitate their removal from Earth to the heavens, before everything on Earth went to shit.

But Bonnie and Marshall weren't married to their original names any more than they were married to each other. Sometimes they expanded their title to 'The UFO Two', due to their noteworthy addition of aliens into their interpretation of the Christian Bible. Sometimes they were 'Bo' and 'Peep', possibly due to Christianity's relentless insistence on using sheep as a metaphor. Sometimes they were 'Guinea' and 'Pig', perhaps to signify that even they were subject to their alien gods' whimsical experiments. But mostly they were 'Do' (a deer, a female deer) and 'Ti' (a drink with jam and bread), a neat junction between Marshall the music teacher's musicality and Bonnie's intense love of *The Sound of Music*.

Like Bonnie and Marshall, the cult also changed its name throughout its history, depending on its philosophy, focus, and the whims of its creators. In 1975 the group was called Human Individual Metamorphosis – with the acronym 'HIM', and later Total Overcomers Anonymous, Anonymous Sexaholics Celibate Church – a whirlwind of potential contradictions – and finally Heaven's Gate. Whatever they were called, their particular brand of earnest space kook hit the market at just the right time.

In seventies and eighties America, two things struck a chord in people who had enough time on their hands to go looking for something better, for a way to improve themselves and the world, and for a way for humanity to evolve: new age spirituality, and UFOs. Anywhere the two overlapped seemed to many people to be the ultimate in forward-facing progress. Practices like yoga and meditation became exponentially popular, as did the idea that not only were we not alone in the universe, extraterrestrials were super-smart and had important messages to give us about enlightenment and rising above being just mere people.

In addition to people being swept up in a frenzy of alternative spirituality and UFOs, Marshall and Bonnie's theories espousing becoming better than other humans and gathering your reward of being whisked off the planet to a better place had a strong attraction for a very particular kind of people: broken ones. A huge percentage of the people who responded strongly to the Heaven's Gate message had either recently undergone an experience that they were having trouble adjusting to, or they had a long history of feeling maladjusted to mainstream society. For those people, the idea of an escape, where there was no pressure to engage with society, or to date, or to face up to normal worldly problems, or even to figure out what to wear in the morning, was one that was exciting to buy into.

Alan Bowers lost his wife to divorce and his brother to a boating accident at the same time. Margaret Richter joined after the end of a brief, dud marriage. David Van Sinderen was an environmentalist desperate to save the Earth and seek something better. Cheryl Butcher was a shy computer expert described by those who knew her as a loner. Alphonzo Foster never really fit in to life on Earth, and floated around until he found Heaven's Gate. Brandy Nelson was a wheelchair-ridden artist with a failed marriage. Some people do therapy, some do drugs and alcohol, some wait for time to heal things. These people, and others, sought eternal betterment in the arms of a gently fatalistic cult with a UFO twist.

Because of this gleeful and enthusiastic abandonment of their existing lives, and the fact that Heaven's Gate had a rare lack of hidden agenda or secret leader behaviour – hidden from and secret to the cult members, that is – there were no specific rules around leaving the cult, and members were free to go at any time, no harm done. This was a cult with an open gate and an unusually low level of paranoia. If there's such an oxymoronic thing, it could be argued that Heaven's Gate members were willingly coerced. One surviving cult member semi-joked to the media that they all wanted to be brainwashed, and thought there was joy in it. Surviving cult members are notoriously bad at jokes.

Mind you, despite the fact that it was easy to leave, that's not to say that leaving the cult wasn't seen as generally a bad idea among its members. In a nutshell, the group believed that they'd be plucked from Earth by the same aliens who had populated the planet thousands of years ago, and then they'd be taken to Heaven while the world died. Once their general beliefs are considered, it becomes clear that staying with the cult meant that you'd be rescued from a doomed existence by a vastly superior race, and that leaving the cult put individuals at a much higher risk of being left behind on a planet with no future with a bunch of losers. In fact, Marshall Applewhite claimed that to *not* 'exit' in the Heaven's Gate way seemed a lot more like suicide than what they were planning. While nobody really seemed forced to do anything, within the Heaven's Gate mindset, making a decision to leave the only group that assured salvation would be seen as a senseless and extremely peculiar thing to do.

In recruiting, Bonnie and Marshall didn't appear to try to change people's minds, or convert them from their former way of thinking to theirs. Rather, what worked for them was making their message available to groups that likely contained people for whom their message struck a chord, and resonated with them as something they felt they'd been waiting to hear their entire lives. They advertised relatively low-key meetings via posters and flyers, and instead of preaching and proselytising, they collected the phone numbers of anyone whose spiritual lightbulbs had clearly been lit and called them later to gently introduce their theories. Once there was mutual agreement that the recruit and the cult had the same basic philosophical objectives, the recruit was encouraged to drop everything, sell everything, and join Bonnie, Marshall and friends on the road.

And they were on the road a LOT. After a particularly well populated meeting in Waldport, Oregon, in September 1975, about thirty of them just packed up and left. For the first chunk of the cult's existence, they led a robustly nomadic lifestyle, with a bit of camping here, a bit of gentle ministering there, a spot of philosophy re-juggling in the spaces between. Their recruitment efforts ebbed and flowed, with one last big push around 1994, when they suspected a UFO visit was imminent. They even paid for a full-page ad in *USA Today* at the time entitled 'UFO Cult Resurfaces With Final Offer' – seemingly not at all bothered with the 'cult' label. While members were encouraged to cut ties with the outside world, including friends and family, occasional phonecalls and home visits were permitted, which meant that media investigations and the interference of authorities egged on by concerned parents and siblings were present, but kept to a manageable minimum. At this stage the cult wasn't bent on doing anything nefarious, they simply believed that the world was a terrible place and too much contact with it would besmirch the evolutionary purity they were striving for. You know, the usual.

Membership numbers fluctuated depending on how strict the rules were and where the constantly developing theories of Marshall and Bonnie were at during that specific time, including Bonnie's predictions about the end of the world and the imminent arrival of UFOs, which were only consistent in that they didn't materialise. She liked to guess that she and Marshall would be killed and martyred by a certain date, or that the world might end at a particular time in a particular way, but, inconveniently, it never did. But faith is faith, and for a core of those who had given up everything to follow Bonnie and Marshall, their errors were just hiccups. They were in it to win it. Even some members who quit and left then returned, dissatisfied with the lowly drones in the outside world, plodding through their lives without meaning. At least within Heaven's Gate they had ideals, routine, and more-or-less believable theories about life.

So. Their theories.

The big one, and the one that fed most of their other little ones, was that thousands of years ago the Earth had been populated by aliens as an experiment – planted on the planet as if it was a garden – and the successful experimental subjects that had evolved to a level above human would be collected by the aliens in a spaceship while they left the rest of the world to die. Sure, it seems crazy when you put it all in a sentence like that, but when you really look into it over several long paragraphs and with an open mind, it also seems crazy.

Heaven's Gate beliefs seem a little less out there when you consider that they were based very much on the same principles as modern Christianity – a deity, a terrestrial effort towards sinless perfection in order to earn eternal life somewhere beyond the sky, an end-times salvation – but with Heaven just replaced by outer space for the most part.

Human bodies were called 'vehicles' and were merely the means by which souls or spirits got around. Anything that was considered human was seen as base and primitive, with the main goal being to evolve to a higher level. It was proposed that their souls were just temporary extra-terrestrial 'walk-ins', adding a modified version of reincarnation to their philosophy. The same alien being could exist in one human vehicle for a while, then when it was finished with it, pop itself into a fresh one. This in turn allowed Marshall Applewhite to claim that he was Jesus incarnate – a common claim among cult leaders, although not usually as creative. See, the first time Jesus – the alien spirit version – inhabited a human vehicle, the world simply just wasn't ready for his wacky bearded coolness. The Jesus vehicle had its alien soul popped into it in its thirtieth or so year by John the Baptist – obviously – and then went around telling everybody the manner in which their world would end, in between being super-nice to everybody. Folks at the time couldn't handle his intense realness, so he got back into his holy space-ship and decided to come back later. The second time around, he chose Marshall Applewhite as his vehicle, and you have to admit that the idea of the return of the Messiah as a wild-eyed, bisexual former music teacher is a bit delicious. Further to that, Marshall fitted Bonnie neatly into the equation by dropping large hints that she was actually God. Look, with no sex and one partner declaring the other to be the ruler of the known universe, it wasn't what you'd call a conventional relationship, so what's one more layer, right? Technically it meant that Bonnie was Marshall's father, which if nothing else would have been extremely confusing to family members at Christmas-time.

Never one to shy away from a gardening metaphor, Marshall told students that their alien creators would harvest the spiritually evolved, leaving normal humans, the equivalent of weeds, behind and effectively turning the soil – digging the remains of their evolutionary experiment back into the earth with the worms, the dog bones, and the eternally damned souls. Less calming as a horticultural analogy was the idea that this digging in or spading under of the Earth's soil would probably manifest itself as a cataclysmic disaster, ending humanity for all time. Enjoy tending your little windowsill herb garden with that image in your head.

Initially, Applewhite and Nettles believed that each person would be taken – body and spirit – physically onto a visiting spacecraft. But in 1985 Marshall was forced to face a reality that shook an important belief adjustment out of him: after a two-year fight against liver cancer, and the surgical removal of one of her eyes, Bonnie Nettles died at age fifty-seven, leaving her body behind. When someone who you think might be God claims that their body and soul will be whisked away on a space-ship and then they die, leaving behind a body, it's really one of life's most inconvenient spanners-in-the-works.

The classic What Happens When We Die? question had to be re-addressed, and quickly. Marshall took a little bit of time to recover from the rattling departure of his soulmate, then reorganised his thinking, and made an announcement to his followers, who might have been at risk of leaving if it wasn't something they could believe.

It was settled. When the aliens were ready to swing by and pick everyone up, they would just suck their souls into the space-ship, not their bodies. Their physical vehicles would remain on Earth to rot among the base, unsaved masses, while their evolved essences had the UFO ride of a lifetime. The problem was, in order to all catch the same spaceship, all of those who were qualified for entry to the Next Level would likely have to die at the same time. The two main ways that Marshall thought their souls might be made separate from their bodies en masse were in an incident where they died as a result of persecution from authorities, and he used the case of the Branch Davidians at Waco as a specific example while he was waiting, or by their own hands, in a dignified manner. All they had to do to make sure their souls were available was to free them of the bodies, the souls' vehicles. As they waited and waited and no violent authoritarian persecution seemed imminent, it was likely they'd have to go with Marshall's second option. They had to crash the cars to release the passengers. They had to kill themselves.

It's very important to note that, from all the evidence, not one of the departing members of Heaven's Gate considered themselves to be committing suicide. They were not dying, they were abandoning their bodies, and fully expected to be given new ones aboard the spaceship. They were not leaving existence, just Earth and all its human complications and simplicities. They even went to great lengths to put a statement on their website claiming that they were against suicide, and to make reassuring videotapes to be viewed after the event, explaining that they did not consider themselves to be ending their lives.

All the cult needed was a clear sign that the UFO – the craft that would transport them from this world to the next – was ready to pick them up, like the mother of a teenager swinging by in a station wagon outside a party. So they waited. And while they waited, they lived their lives in a very specific way.

Moving from camping grounds to rented houses, life in the various Heaven's Gate compounds represented a symbolic break between the external world and the previous lives of members, where mammalian urges, impulses, and habits muddied the clear path to the Next Level, and the world created by Marshall and Bonnie, where free will and independent thought were things of the past. Members gleefully subjected themselves to lives where every tiny detail of daily existence was overseen, regimented, and precise. And Heaven's Gate members freaking *loved* it. Say what you will about having free will, but the idea that somebody else makes all your decisions for you must be pretty freeing and relaxing, especially if none of those decisions involves wearing skin-tight clothing.

Absolutely none of the decisions involved wearing skin-tight clothing. In fact, Heaven's Gate members were required to wear baggy, shapeless clothing to minimise any hint of their gender or sexuality. They even shared all their clothing, so it was as generic in style and size as possible. Long loose pants, voluminous shirts buttoned to the neck, and gender-defying bowl haircuts meant that no time was spent considering one's physical appearance, and as little time as humanly possible was spent finding any of your fellow cult members attractive.

Being sexual was just not on the menu at Heaven's Gate. Sexual urges were things that humans had, not those seeking to achieve the evolutionary level above human. To achieve that level, most of the practices in the compound sought to overcome base human habits – taking pleasure in food, sexual urges, individuality, emotions, and free will.

Most of the time that members were awake and not over-coming fundamental person-ness, they were listening to Marshall's lessons. Heaven's Gate members were often referred to as 'students' and called their own entry into the cult the day they entered the 'classroom'. The subject of the lessons was always a mix of theory – what the history of 'humanity' is and what happens next – and instructions regarding how to reach the Next Level. Some of Marshall's videotaped lessons are available to watch online, where his ability to combine hardly any interesting sentences with extremely long, rambling diatribes without blinking much is on full display. Even with the subject matter and Marshall's wide-eyed delivery, the videos become pretty boring pretty quickly.

Still, the lessons were exactly what Applewhite's followers wanted to hear, and they strived constantly and meticulously to be the kind of people that judgemental alien overlords in space-ships would feel compelled to pick up and take away. Along with the lessons were lists of behavioural guidelines and 'offences', also made available on the Heaven's Gate website and categorised under 'major' and 'lesser' offences.

The behavioural guidelines were really a roadmap to conforming, being compliant, and not questioning the authority of Do and Ti – the former holding court in this world, and the latter communicating, conveniently through Do, from a world beyond. One guideline asked students if they could follow instructions without adding their own interpretation, to which presumably nobody answered, 'Depends on your definition of interpretation.' One was an instruction to avoid being clumsy, which raises questions regarding whether anyone is ever intentionally clumsy. Extremely sensible behavioural guidelines suggested followers avoid being aggressive, insensitive to others, or procrastinating, while others extolled the virtues of doing a job thoroughly, showing restraint, and being consistent. Some of the guidelines, such as the one that asks students if they use a higher gas flame than necessary when cooking, or more toothpaste than is required, were troublesome in that to find out how much flame or toothpaste is appropriate, one must automatically break the guideline about asking obvious questions.

The list of major or lesser offences provided a little more detailed instruction to followers regarding how to conduct themselves. There were only three major offences: deceit – whether doing things secretly, keeping secrets, or lying; sensuality – allowing yourself to become aroused either in thought or action; and breaking rules. So one of the biggest rules was to not break any rules, meaning that if you broke any of the other rules, you also broke that one. Two for the price of one – that's pretty good value as far as offences are concerned.

The lesser offences listed on the cult's website are where you really start to get a sense of exactly how much self-control followers were expected to exercise, and how little they were allowed to make decisions for themselves.

Students should not trust their own judgement, or use their own mind, or want to be seen as good.

Students should not compare themselves to others, have likes or dislikes, or offer suggestions to their teachers.

Students should not have private thoughts, or put themselves first, or want their own way.

Students should not be vain, or 'vibrate' their own femininity or masculinity, or have inappropriate curiosity.

And students should not exaggerate 'vehicular symptoms', which presumably means that they should absolutely minimise any behaviours or ailments that come off as a bit too human. No man-flu, for starters.

Even tighter day-to-day rules emerged as the group learned to live with each other – shower for exactly six minutes, use exactly this much syrup on your pancakes, go to bed at 9:54. Different dietary restrictions were experimented with, like fasting and the lemon detox diet, but all members would undergo them at the same time. The rules helped members shed their sense of self – if everyone's doing the same thing in the same way at the same time every single day, they are no longer their human selves. In evolving to the level above human, they became more or less empty shells, receptacles for Marshall's and Bonnie's lessons. Watching Marshall's videotaped lessons, it's sometimes hard to understand why his followers found him so compelling. Hard until you remember that they literally had nothing else going on.

As there were so many rules to remember, the group had a neat way of self-policing. Each member had a 'check partner', or 'personal dibber-dobber', if you will. Pairings were made according to whoever was least likely to have any affection whatsoever for the other, and each was required to monitor the behaviour of the other. In fact, taking any action without running it past your check partner first was the first on the list of lesser offences, and it was advisable that most of your thoughts – and you were encouraged to have as few as possible – were shared with your check partner to make sure they were all hunky dory with the good old above-human ideology. While she was alive, Bonnie Nettles was Marshall Applewhite's check partner, which meant her death left him in a bit of an emotional and procedural pickle. He had to make his own decisions and check himself before he ultimately wrecked himself, but still often consulted Bonnie telepathically wherever she was in the 'Next Level'.

A side-effect of all this checking with each other and not putting yourself first and not being vain or aggressive was that the Heaven's Gate camp – and eventually house – was a really, really nice place to be. Selfishness just wasn't acceptable, jealousy was hugely frowned upon, and all the pancakes were exactly the same size – it's no wonder that many members who spent any time away from the cult couldn't wait to get back. This place was the capital city of Polite Town. If hugging had been allowed (it wasn't) nobody would have ever got anything done.

Every cult needs a way to sustain itself financially, and usually can't survive purely on tithes and trust funds, and Heaven's Gate's preferred method of earning some extra cash was via fairly advanced computing and an extremely 1990s version of web design. Not to paint all sci-fi UFO nerds with the same brush, but demographically speaking there's considerable correlation between being into aliens and being into computers, so the members of Heaven's Gate were ready to surf the surfing-the-internet wave into money town. The cult even had its own web design business called 'Higher Source', and while you can still visit some of their work on the internet, be warned that viewing nineties web design from a twenty-first-century aesthetic perspective often leads to disappointment. They certainly knew what they were doing for the time, but it was likely a relief when two cult members inherited a couple of hundred thousand dollars and everyone could relax for a bit. Paying bills can be a tedious pain in the arse when you're busy planning your genetically superior escape to another galaxy.

Every visit outside – for groceries, errands, or paid work – was noted in a daily logbook, with all money spent listed meticulously in a ledger.

Each member was given a new name, and the method of renaming was borderline whimsical. It was simply three letters – usually consonants – crammed together without vowels and followed by 'ody'. Rkkody. Mrcody. Srfody. Wknody. Yrsody. It's like they were the world's least fun Teletubbies.

In a seemingly reckless leap away from the shunning of the outside world and the cheap foibles of mere humans, a handful of popular culture artefacts were allowed to be consumed within the cult, being primarily *Star Trek*, *Star Wars*, *E.T.*, and *The X-Files* videos. Considering more than one episode of *The X-Files* had a storyline about a cult, it's cute to imagine a room full of people with bad haircuts in baggy clothes watching telly, pointing at the screen and saying, 'Hey, look, it's us.' In fact, one of the Heaven's Gate members could have pointed at the screen during *Star Trek* and said, 'Hey, look, it's my sister.' Nichelle Nichols, who played Uhura in the original series of *Star Trek*, lost her brother Thomas in the Heaven's Gate suicides. Spooky.

If you look at it one way, many of the modifications Heaven's Gate followers made to their lives were minor if taken individually – a bit of fasting, a haircut, a spot of exactitude when it came to making pancakes. It's only when all of the many modifications are seen as a whole that they seem overwhelmingly strict. With one exception. One of the modifications that eight of the male followers made to their lives to achieve purity was definitely, no matter which way you poke it, extreme. See, even with the bowl cuts and the bad clothes, some members found their own members a little troublesome, and struggled daily against that wretched, domineering mistress: horniness.

The solution that occurred to those (mercifully) few who were not confident of controlling their groinal urges was to undergo castration, or its fancier title: gonadectomy. Eight cult members volunteered their testicles to appease their judgemental overlords and stop their niggling fixation on sex. Granted, the first home-surgery procedure was wholly botched and ended up with one guy in hospital to have his distended ball-bag drained, and the rest of them were left at the comparatively deft mercy of a Mexican gonad specialist, but it did the trick. Heaven's Gate members commented afterwards how free they felt without their bothersome testicles. Marshall Applewhite was one of those who got the snip, rounding out and finalising his lifelong worry over what he considered his carnal mis-wiring. He wasn't altogether convinced that castration was the answer, and it was one of the few policies that wasn't either his or Bonnie's idea, but suggested by their students. Marshall even consulted the departed Bonnie telepathically to see what she thought about the separation of followers from their nuts, but Bonnie wisely decided not to answer the spectral phone that day. The castrations proceeded with some trepidation, as castrations should.

The actual suicides of the thirty-nine members of Heaven's Gate can be broken down – somewhat grotesquely – into how they planned it, what they had on them, how they died, and what happened immediately afterwards.

In 1995, news reports started alerting people to the appearance of the Hale–Bopp comet, roughly two years before it was expected to come close to Earth, and also two years before the unrelated release of Hanson's hit single 'MMMBop', a complete coincidence. When reports of an approaching comet happen, every telescope geek in the world points their lenses at the sky, and squillions of photographs were available. And the thing about space is, there's a lot of stuff in it. So when lots of space nerds are taking lots of photographs of a comet, at least one of those photos is also going to contain bits and pieces of other stuff, often indistinguishable from scratches on lenses, flares, reflections, blips, dust, and random splodges. But when you're a cult that's spent the last twenty-odd years waiting for a big, clear sign that your ride is here, a photograph of a comet that might possibly be accompanied in a photograph by a scratch, flare, reflection, blip, dust, or random splodge can look very much like a comet accompanied by a UFO with your name on it. The Heaven's Gate cult was excited, and updated their website with the leading announcement 'RED ALERT – HALE BOPP BRINGS CLOSURE TO HEAVEN'S GATE'.

In October 1996, the group bought themselves some alien abduction insurance – a thing that is still actually possible to do – which would pay out one million dollars to any abductees' beneficiaries who could prove that an abduction by a being not from Earth had occurred. Most alien abduction insurance policies pay out extra if the abductee is impregnated and, as we don't really know the ins and outs of alien nookie, the impregnation cover is offered equally to men and women. No payouts have occurred so far.

In March 1997, the days leading up to the suicide – or exit, as that's what cult members called it – almost all the students of Marshall Applewhite recorded a five-minute exit video, ostensibly to explain the actions they were about to take and to reassure their loved ones that they were making what they considered a joyous choice. And the thing is, the videos are incredibly convincing. The people speaking to camera, sitting on plastic outdoor furniture in the lush green grounds of the Rancho Santa Fe mansion, are serene and happy, and when you try to equate happy people with suicide it does extremely weird things to your brain. We're used to equating it with depression, or people having an otherwise very bad time, not people who are giggling with excitement in front of a video camera.

The night before the comet came closest to Earth, the entire group went out to dinner in Carlsbad, near San Diego. Everybody had a chicken pie. Everybody had a salad. Everybody had a piece of cheesecake. And presumably every waiter working in the restaurant that night had a story to tell their friends.

The Away Team – so named after teams sent off-ship on investigative missions in *Star Trek* – were all wearing the same homemade sweatpants and tops, and they'd purchased their thirty-nine identical pairs of Nike Decade sneakers. Initial reports of the suicide when it was discovered claimed that thirty-nine men had died, so effective was the androgynous uniform – a minor victory for a dead cult leader who strove to eliminate sexuality. In early 1997 members had fifty sew-on arm patches made that read 'Earth Exit Monasteries', changing them to patches they had made closer to the exit date that read 'Heaven's Gate Away Team' – for no better reason than it sounded more directly like the *Star Trek* reference. The sneakers had been bought a short time earlier, for the bargain price of $548.45 for the lot. That's $7.03 per shoe, which is meaningless but once you think about doing the maths, you pretty much have to do the maths. It's bizarre suicide sneaker maths, we may never get another chance.

Heaven's Gate was the best and worst thing to happen to Nike Decade sneakers. Prior to the horrific crime-scene photographs that made them famous, Decades were considered one of the daggiest Nike varieties, popular with dads and people in the market for unimpressive budget-level trainers. There's just no way the shoes would have been discussed over watercoolers globally or sold on eBay twenty years later for thousands of dollars without the grotesque cachet that being the uniform-of-choice for an array of UFO-obsessed corpses provides. Still,

Nike probably did the smart thing and discontinued the line within weeks.

Every member had $5.75 in their pockets – the standard five-dollar note and three quarters they carried whenever they had left the house in the past, noting it in the ledger. The five dollars was to avoid accusations of vagrancy, and the three quarters were for phonecalls, just in case. There was conjecture at the time that the identical change was symbolic, to show that they were leaving the house for the last time; others say it was just to confuse the hell out of whoever found them. The odds are really pretty good that whoever found them was already confused enough without the ultimate identical pocket change jape, but you do you, Heaven's Gate.

Over three days, according to the instructions in a document they'd written called 'The Routine', handfuls of members swallowed overdoses of phenobarbital washed down with pudding, apple sauce and some vodka, and allowed themselves to slip out of consciousness with plastic bags on their heads. After each group's death, with the exception of the last two remaining, members neatened their bodies, removed the plastic bags, positioned their shrouds, and tidied the scene. The last two bodies still had the plastic bags over their heads. By the time they were found – first by a recent ex-cult member under instructions sent to him by the cult when they were still alive, then by the authorities he anonymously called – the house reeked of early decay. Some of the cult members had been dead for three days.

The deaths of the Heaven's Gate members brought the idea of brainwashing to the fore in the media and in academic circles at the time, fuelling the anxiety of concerned parents and enthusiastic panic-merchants in equal measure. Debate raged over whether brainwashing was even a thing. If it wasn't, then a lot of folks who had made their money as 'deprogrammers' and 'exit counsellors' – those who helped reverse presumed brainwashing in escapees or those recently kidnapped from cults – would be out of business. Deprogrammers and exit counsellors essentially stage interventions upon the recently exited, usually with family members and friends of the cult member actively present, until the harangued member reneges and agrees to become a normal, non-culty member of society once again. Deprogramming has a terrible success rate. This is partly due to the fact that, as with someone with a gambling problem or a leisure cyclist who insists on wearing lycra past noon, there's often no good way to get a person to give up their crutch – or crotch in the case of the cyclist – unless it's their idea to.

Whatever your definition of brainwashing is, and whether or not you believe it's possible, it's easy to imagine that the friends and family members of cult members in general, and Heaven's Gate members in particular, would be desperate for any explanation for the behaviour of their loved ones that isn't just that they willingly chose to end their own lives to hitch a ride on a UFO. It's hard enough to believe that an adult would willingly allow themselves to get a bowl cut, so brainwashing is a neat, compact explanation that puts the responsibility squarely on the shoulders of the cult leader. By believing in brainwashing, loved ones have the tragic luxury of also believing that the friend or family member they lost didn't make an extremely terrible decision willingly. It's much easier to think of your sister or daughter as a victim of a powerful deviant than as someone who would wholeheartedly believe in one.

Of course, if your definition of brainwashing is the kind of thinking that results from choosing to live life according to unbelievably strict rules, isolating yourself from the rest of society, shunning a life that absolutely wasn't working in your favour, abandoning your sense of identity, and only talking to people who have exactly the same beliefs as you, then sure, go nuts, brainwashing's a thing. By this definition, the members of Heaven's Gate who took their own lives were brainwashed. The question is moot, though. Regardless of whether or not they were brainwashed, they're gone, and they're not coming back.

Okay, so they're not *all* gone. A couple of members opted out of the exit mission – they chickened out, or they felt their calling was here on Earth, continuing to explain and spread the Heaven's Gate message. One or two even continue to maintain the Heaven's Gate website under the legal entity 'The TELAH Foundation' (The Evolutionary Level Above Human), although thankfully without updating its intensely nineties GeoCities vibe. But Heaven's Gate as a functioning entity is essentially gone.

Even though he was directly responsible for the death of thirty-eight people – thirty-nine including himself – it's difficult to feel the same animosity for Marshall Applewhite that you might feel for other cult leaders who were also responsible for the deaths of their followers or outsiders. The thing is, even though it's likely that most crew members of the Heaven's Gate Away Team would still be alive if they'd never met him,

Applewhite really seemed to believe his own theories. He wasn't cheating anyone. He wasn't knowingly deceiving anyone. He wasn't imposing rules about fasting upon his followers and then sneaking round the corner for a surreptitious cheeseburger, or enforcing celibacy and then inviting his nubile devoted out to the back room for a special cuddle. As far as we can tell, Marshall Applewhite was a sincere cult leader. It's interesting to think that after his own guru – Bonnie Lu – died, he may not have wanted to go on, and it's not outside the realm of possibility to suggest that he interpreted his own suicidal thoughts as the universe's new plan for him. Just as he never wanted to be a cult leader by himself, perhaps he also didn't want to die by himself, and worked that idea into his broader, spiritual narrative.

Still, though. To be on the safe side, maybe don't become a cult leader in the first place, eh.

BRANCH DAVIDIANS

IMAGINE A FIRE.

No, bigger than that. A really big, really hot fire. Nobody's really sure who started it, but all around the outside of the fire there's a bunch of tanks, jeeps, cars, and all manner of military and official-looking men. They're tired, because they've been there, waiting, for fifty-one days. They have lots of guns and lots of frustration because they've been trying to get David Koresh and his Branch Davidians out of the building that is now burning. And they've failed. They've failed pretty significantly.

Inside the fire are around seventy-six people who have spent the last seven weeks definitely not leaving. Now, tragically, they're sealing the deal and will never leave alive, or even as recognisable human shapes.

In 1993, the Branch Davidians' compound at Mount Carmel near Waco in Texas burned to the ground, and a stack of bodies burned with it. At multiple points over the fifty-one days that the compound was under siege by federal agents, there would have been excellent opportunities for each side to make some sensible, peaceful decisions. But they didn't, and now there's a dark, charry smudge on the ground near Waco.

The problem likely started in 1959 when the owner of an extremely cool name, Bonnie Sue Howell, welcomed her son into the world, fathered by a since-disappeared but also coolly named Bobby Wayne Howell. Bonnie Sue thought for a bit, and then named the baby Vernon Wayne Howell. It seems that, by this point, all the cool names had run out.

Vernon's childhood could be politely described as inauspicious and impolitely described as a bit of a shitfight. He didn't know his father, he was partly raised in the boozy house of his grandparents, and when he was seven his mother married his stepfather when he was fresh out of jail, and the new couple liked to party with a seedy crowd. Using religion as both an escape and a small means to gain attention, Vernon showed promise with his ability to memorise huge tracts of the Bible and could regurgitate the whole thing by heart at age twelve, but showed very little promise anywhere else. Despite being able to read and absorb the word of God just fine, he suffered from a learning disability and was considered at school to be – put nicely – a bit dim.

History shows us that, through no fault of their own, people called Vernon who can recite Bible passages verbatim are not customarily the most popular kids in high school, such is our warped society. History more favours people who get outside into the sunshine regularly, and you could say that, at least in adulthood, Vernon Howell pretty much made a career out of staying inside. He didn't do overly well in school, and left in the mid-seventies at sixteen, perhaps partly because the other kids used to call him 'Mr Retardo'. Here's a tip, kids: if you're going to tease someone at school, remember that, at some point, some of them are going to want either vengeance or a chance to finally feel powerful. A lot of the time, especially in places where it's pretty easy to buy guns, those things don't end well.

Once he'd left school, Vernon played to his strengths and spent a lot of time at the Seventh Day Adventist church in Tyler, Texas. He discovered some confidence and let it blossom robustly into arrogance, catching the attention of church elders. But despite his clear devotion to scripture and his gift for keeping younger churchgoers in thrall when he waxed biblical, they eventually threw him out in 1981 for his constant challenges to authority. See, they don't say this on the news much, but churches haaaate it when you tell them they're wrong. So Vernon went off in search of a new church.

The Branch Davidian sect existed before Vernon Howell found it and settled in. It was an offshoot of the Davidian Seventh Day Adventist church, itself an offshoot of the Seventh Day Adventist church proper, so here's where we look into a bit of Seventh Day Adventist history in the area. It might start off boring, but it ends up with people essentially trying to make a zombie, so sit tight.

We can't talk about the Branch Davidians without mentioning Victor Houteff, who was around in 1929 grumbling about the state of the Seventh Day Adventists and hollering for reform. He thought the Adventists had become too caught up in worldly pursuits and had forgotten that their true mission was to prepare for the imminent return of Jesus Christ and live simply, which just sounds like a super-fun time. In traditional entrenched religion style, the Adventists didn't think very much of people who disagreed with the way they did things (as I mentioned earlier), so they kicked Victor out. It makes you wonder how many religions and denominations there'd actually be today if churches found a way to make peace with dissenters in ways that didn't involve kicking them to the kerb. Four, probably. Eight, tops.

In 1935 in a huff, Houteff decided to screw 'em, and started up his own rig on an uninspiring mound a few kilometres out of Waco and called it Mount Carmel. He invited some like-minders to come hang out with him and wait for Jesus and the spooky end times associated with his return. The group grew their own food, kept their lifestyle to a bare minimum, and wrote books and pamphlets that kept membership dribbling in at a relaxed rate.

When Victor died, his wife, Florence, took over the role of Chief Waiter for Jesus, and got impatient about the big guy's return, starting to look for clues and signs so she could put something definite in the calendar. Definitely not just picking a number at random, Flo picked 22 April 1959 as the big day that heavy stuff would go down. Spreading word of her prediction and the specific date, she called for all Davidians to gather at Mount Carmel to await the day of reckoning. Some sold everything they owned to make the one-way pilgrimage. There wasn't enough room at Mount Carmel for almost a thousand pilgrims, so many set up tents and camped. Excitement mounted as 22 April approached.

Nope.

As you may be aware, Jesus did not come back and destroy the world in 1959, so Flo had a bit of egg on her face. Her error wasn't great for the strength of the Davidians' resolve, and as is the wont of offshoots of the Seventh Day Adventists in particular, many people left to start their own offshoots, and Flo slunk off from the Mount Carmel compound with her embarrassed tail between her legs.

One of the offshoots was headed up by a guy called Ben Roden, who had not had the opportunity or numbers to challenge Florence Houteff before this point. He took over the Mount Carmel compound in 1959 and called his particular group the General Association of Davidian Seventh Day Adventists, because he was running low on imagination. Again, due to a lack of creativity, Ben predicted that Jesus would be coming back to make sweeping changes to the world, but he was smart enough to not put a date on it, having learned from Florence's mistake. Instead, he provided the vague directive that Jesus would come back when everyone was spiritually mature and pure, so basically any time between right now and sometime in the future, but probably pretty soon so comb your hair. Smart move, Ben.

Inconveniently dying himself in 1978, leadership of the Long Name That Includes the Word Davidians was hotly contested between Ben's wife, Lois, and Ben's nasty, violent shithead of a son, George. George Roden was the kind of guy you really didn't want to get upset, but unluckily for everybody, George Roden got upset at nearly everything. George Roden got upset if you didn't believe his claims that he was the Messiah, the chosen one, the big cheese. George Roden got upset if you questioned his authority. And George Roden got upset if you made best friends with his mother, tried to undermine him, and wanted to snatch the Mount Carmel compound from right out under him. Here's hoping nobody tries to do that, eh.

After leaving school and not making that much of himself, Vernon turned up at the Mount Carmel compound at age twenty-two. Not long after in 1984, he married Rachel Jones, a girl of fourteen, which is, you know, not great. But it was under God's instruction, you see, and he works in mysterious, sometimes only-just-legal, sometimes pretty gross ways.

When Vernon joined the Rodens' group, 68-year-old Lois Roden warmed to him immediately, drawn to his gentle, convincing interpretations of Bible chapters and possibly the comely neck-curls of his almost-mullet. There are oft-repeated murmurings that Vernon partly ingratiated himself to Lois via the use of his penis, a fact which must have really stuck in George Roden's craw – he might have been a violent psychopath willing to do some fairly extreme things to establish his power over the religious group, but he considered having sex with the cult's leader, his mother, unavailable to him as a point-scoring option. He had *principles*.

George kicked up a stink, claimed Howell had raped his mother, and in 1984 chucked him out of the compound. Surprisingly for George, Vernon took a large chunk of Roden's followers with him, as they preferred Vernon's comparatively calm and non-psychotic approach to worship and Bible study. The exiles took up camp in Palestine, Texas, a hundred miles away, living like the homeless in campsites and rough huts. No point living nice in permanent buildings if the world's about to end, right?

Like any sane, calm, non-terrifying Messiah, in 1987 George Roden decided that the only way to prove who was really and truly God's representative on Earth was to see who could bring a corpse back to life. Off he popped to the compound grave-yard, shovel in hand, and exhumed the remains of Anna Hughes, a Davidian woman who had died twenty years before at the age of eighty-five. That had to be one desiccated, shrivelled-up corpse, but George liked to play his sick power games on the 'difficult' setting. He placed Anna's body on a makeshift altar and draped her in a cloth bearing the star of David, because by this point nothing is really all that weird.

George lay down a challenge to Vernon: whoever could resurrect Anna Hughes first would be proclaimed the proper Messiah. Presumably George didn't think he could win an arm wrestle, which might have been an astronomically less horrifying and gross solution to – let's face it – an imaginary problem. It's important, if not obvious, to note that nobody breathed new life into a twenty-year-old pile of gristle and bones. Vernon saw his chance to get rid of George though, and alerted authorities to the fact that a mad bastard was interfering with dead bodies over in yonder compound. The police needed proof though, the sticklers.

Ready to claim that they were just breaking into the compound to photograph evidence that Roden had unlawfully exhumed a body, yet dressed in fatigues and armed to the back teeth, Vernon and seven mates snuck into Mount Carmel. They were sprung, and what ensued was, stereotypically for Texas, an old-fashioned shoot-out. Despite hiding behind a tree that later had eighteen bullets gouged out of its trunk, George Roden was only mildly injured in his chest and hand, shot by Vernon who was sheltering behind a broken-down car.

Unsurprisingly, George took offence to being shot in his own compound, and he called the police. Vernon and his crew were arrested for attempted murder, and extremely significantly, when the police showed up to arrest them and confiscate their weapons, they acquiesced calmly, and willingly surrendered their weapons. Authorities came to arrest them. They didn't resist. They gave up their weapons. Let's see if that information seems particularly poignant at some stage later in this story.

The 1988 trial ended in a hung jury, so Vernon and his fellow raiders were sent home with their weapons for a vegetarian pizza and ice cream party. The officers who signed the weapons back out are probably kicking themselves right now, but live and learn.

George's immediate fate was less satisfactory. Due to being prone to flying off the handle in a broadly illegal way, George got in trouble for a number of different petty crimes including tax evasion, having not paid tax owed by the Mount Carmel compound for some considerable time. George was shitty that he wasn't granted an exemption for being a religious organisation, and sent letters to the courts detailing how much he hoped they'd contract AIDS, an act not recommended for anyone who wants a lenient ear come trial time. Totally coincidentally, the courts found an old restraining order that his mother had filed a decade before that had never been enforced, so they thought it was a pretty good time to enforce it. George was no longer welcome in the compound.

Vernon could see his time had come. He swooped into Mount Carmel while George Roden wasn't allowed anywhere near the place. Vernon arranged for his own followers to help pay all the outstanding taxes owed, and started work building new digs, clearing the compound of legal trouble and ingratiating himself to practically everyone. By 1989 Vernon was the leader of the Branch Davidians.

Eventually George Roden moved to Odessa in Texas, hacked his roommate to death with an axe, spent most of his remaining years in a hospital for the criminally insane, and died of a heart attack during an escape attempt in 1998. Stay in school, kids.

Back at Mount Carmel, Vernon Howell settled well into his role as leader, concentrating mostly on leading the Branch Davidians in Bible study, particularly the Book of Revelation.

Holy *crap* cult leaders love a bit of the Book of Revelation. The last book of the Christian Bible's New Testament inspired Aum Shinrikyo's Shoko Asahara to release a bunch of gas on the Tokyo subway, and Do and Ti of Heaven's Gate were sure that they were the two lampstands mentioned in its pages. Normal, non-murderous Christians have a lot of trouble with the Book of Revelation, due to its non-linear storyline, its bizarre imagery, its incomprehensible plot and its unconfirmed strong influence from some major hallucinogens. Historically a lot of Christians have even argued against its inclusion in the Bible. But Vernon Howell loved its convoluted trippery like a cat loves showing you its anus, and he devoted most of his life to interpreting it.

For Vernon and the Branch Davidians, the most significant parts of the Book of Revelation were the lamb, the twenty-four elders and the fire, oh, so much fire. Relatively speaking, they spent hardly any time unlocking the mysteries of, for example, the four beasts covered with multiple eyes, which was a shame. Those guys are awesome.

In the Book of Revelation, the lamb is an animal that's sometimes assumed to be Jesus, but that Vernon interpreted as the cool thing that loosens the seven seals on the piece of paper that the instructions for the end of the world are written on. Basically, the lamb is the thing that kickstarts the end of the world and leads the faithful safely through it, and not just a cute woolly creature gambolling blithely in a meadow, or something that tastes delicious with potatoes, peas and a light herby jus. The lamb in the Book of Revelation is badass. Vernon Howell wanted very much to be badass. He was the chosen one. He was the lamb. He was going to kickstart the end of days and save the faithful, leaving the sinners to eat his dust.

Then there's the twenty-four elders, who are found in the Book of Revelation all dressed in white with crowns on their heads, sitting on a throne each. They're broadly interpreted as the ruling committee of the church, although there's a lot of argument and guesswork on that point. Suffice to say, they're important and would probably have some role in ruling the world after the end of days, or at least get cushy jobs in administration and take care of most of the paperwork.

Vernon decided it was up to him to create the twenty-four elders in the form of his own children. Sure, fathering twenty-four children might mean he'd have to have a load of sex with lots of women, but he was saving the world, man. A little bit of sacrifice was warranted.

Finally, the Book of Revelation has a lot of fire in it, mostly once the end of the world gets pretty serious. It's raining down from the sky in bits – sometimes mixed with blood, which is cute – and a third of all mankind is killed with fire before you've even reached the tenth chapter. Fire has a starring role in the end of the world in the Bible, so it's not a completely crazy notion to suggest that Vernon wouldn't mind going down in flames if push came to shove. In theory. Of course.

Around the time he established himself at Mount Carmel, Vernon Howell made one of his few good marketing decisions and changed his name to David Koresh. The 'David' part was a nod to the biblical King David, who – no biggie – basically founded Jerusalem as the capital of Israel and in the right light is kinda an ancestor of Jesus Christ. No less pompously presumptuous, the 'Koresh' part of Vernon's new name is from the Hebrew 'Cyrus', who was – no biggie – just the king of the first Persian Empire and the dude who conquered Babylon according to the New Testament. Overachievers, the lot of 'em, but whatever – everybody can agree that David Koresh is way more punk rock a name than Vernon Howell.

Speaking of things that aren't punk rock, David Koresh nee Vernon Howell considered himself quite the musician. In the late eighties Koresh recruited for the Branch Davidians enthusiastically in California, Israel, the UK, New Zealand and Australia, and was pretty successful – the followers that died in 1993 in the Mount Carmel compound were from six different countries. New followers were partly drawn in by Koresh's gently charismatic style and good manners, but the main attraction to him and his church was that he could just explain the Bible like nobody else. People were fascinated with his opinions about the scripture, and his incredible way of linking one part to another part. He also used music as a recruiting tool – inviting potential followers to jam sessions and peppering his sermons with sporadic bursts of strumming and song.

It could be argued, however, that the reason Koresh spent time in California wasn't purely for recruiting purposes. California was where record deals were made, and where up-and-coming musicians – if they were any good – were discovered. The thing is that the 'if they were any good' bit is so, so important. Listening to Koresh's music would not strictly be considered doing yourself a favour. At its very best, it was badly recorded, stylistically immature folk music. At its second best, it was exactly the same as the worst guy who ever brought his guitar to a party, but instead of 'Wonderwall', he's playing Christian rock. The Bible tells us that many things are an abomination, yet weirdly never mentions Christian rock. Irony has never really been Christianity's strong point.

Koresh even handed out business cards with the word 'MESSIAH' emblazoned across the top and the subtitle 'Cyrus Productions'. Under his own name on the card was printed 'Guitar, Vocals', and that was next to the words 'Steve Schneider: Music Manager'. There were a number of references to Bible passages on the back of the card, which is in all honesty probably not the exact vibe record companies were looking for, but they also weren't looking for people who first wrote terrible songs and then sang them badly. The business cards still come up for auction every now and again, fetching a couple of hundred dollars on average. Do yourself a favour.

Steve Schneider: Music Manager would develop very much into Steve Schneider: David Koresh's Second in Charge. A former university lecturer in comparative religion, and a wannabe evangelist, Schneider joined the Branch Davidians in the mid-eighties, dissatisfied with his previous experience with the Seventh Day Adventists. He became the main point of contact between the Branch Davidians and reporters and authorities in the outside world, both before any of the fateful 1993 trouble and during negotiations with authorities during the siege that ended in Waco's most famous fire. It seems for most of the time he was associated with David Koresh, from endeavouring to help kick-start his music career to trying to help a bunch of cult members not die in a shower of bullets, he did the best he could, under the circumstances. In return for Schneider's devotion, bullish stubbornness when dealing with outsiders, and tireless work, Koresh slept with his wife and got her pregnant. When you believe there's a chance someone might be a prophet sent directly to Earth by God, it seems you'll let them treat you like you're an unpopular girl trying to get into their clique in high school.

The Branch Davidians were, at the heart of their beliefs, a religious group that was keenly focused on a complex series of interpretations of the Christian Bible. Under Koresh's guidance, they didn't read passages from the Bible in isolation or even necessarily in chronological order, but played off one passage here against another passage there, gleaning meaning not from one or the other, but by their contrast and juxtaposition. It wasn't just making shit up for their own ends *per se*, but it was definitely a distant cousin of making shit up for their own ends.

And David Koresh really, really loved Bible study. In a rudimentary chapel in the Mount Carmel compound furnished with plain wooden bleacher-style seats, Koresh would talk for hours – six hours was normal, fifteen hours was not unheard of – about the concepts and characters of the Bible. He would invite discussion and debate, or initiate call-and-response *Ferris Bueller*–style interpretive tutorials. And wherever there were references in the scripture to one individual who might have the key to it all, or who would lead the faithful to Heaven, or would initiate the next cataclysmic phase in world history, Koresh made one thing clear: that dude was him. He would be the next guy to feature in God's earthly plan.

The two other themes that a great deal of the Branch Davidians' Bible-interpretation focused on were constant and significant too. The first was that Jesus was going to come back like, *really* soon. And the second was that when Jesus came back, it was going to be messy as hell. There was going to be a fight, there was going to be death, there was going to be fire, it was going to directly involve the Branch Davidians, and it was going to absolutely feature David Koresh in a pivotal role.

In 1991, Koresh began to prepare his followers for war. He taught them how to shoot guns and performed telltale paranoid adjustments to areas of the compound. A series of tunnels was dug underneath the buildings, a watchtower was erected, and an old bus was buried to serve as a potential bunker. If only he'd focused instead on landscaping or polishing cement floors to a high shine like you see on normal non-cult renovation shows, he might still be alive today.

In habits inherited from the Seventh Day Adventists, Koresh enforced a vegetarian diet free from alcohol and caffeine. In a move less strictly Adventisty, in around 1989 he also decided that he was entitled to take any nearby ladies he wanted as his spiritual wives. According to Koresh, God wanted him to have lots of sex. God wanted him to have sex with virgins. God wanted him to make twenty-four children. God apparently spent an awful lot of his time thinking about exactly the kind of nookie that David Koresh should be having, and that kind of nookie was: all of it. Koresh worked harder trying to justify his sexual proclivities by using the word of God and the Bible than he ever did ironing a shirt or getting a haircut. For all the women David Koresh was bedding in God's name, here's hoping God also wanted him to spoon them afterwards and call them the next day.

The problem was, not all of the women Koresh took as wives were legally old enough to behave like wives do. There's little doubt that Koresh slept with girls as young as twelve and thirteen, and there are stories that he bragged about bedding girls a fair bit younger. He was much more determined to follow the laws he found in the Bible than the laws he found in the actual law, which is a really, really shitty way of excusing the fact that you're a sex predator. He'd tell girls that if they were good, then one day they'd be worthy of being one of his wives, giving them cheap Star of David necklaces to symbolise their readiness. A little bit like marking them for a prize, except the prize is a weedy Bible nerd with delusions of grandeur. And the parents of these girls were fine with the whole scenario, because someone that God had chosen as his prophet had in turn chosen their daughter as his beddable follower. Of all the things you might excuse Koresh for, or at least argue your way into reasonable acceptance, his blatant and pathetic need to get laid is his most heinous characteristic. That guy at the bar who tells you lies just to get in your pants has nothing on David Koresh.

Not content with taking just unmarried ladies as his spiritual wives, by 1989 Koresh had decided that he wanted every female human in the Branch Davidians to be his wife, particularly the hot ones. He told all the married men in the cult that they were no longer married, sorry, and that he was the only person allowed to have sex. Well, their wives were also still allowed to have sex, provided it was with him. Koresh explained to the religiously cuckolded husbands that he was merely shouldering the burden of sexuality in the group, believing that – for others – sex was a gateway to pain and deceit. The men would meet their perfect mate in Heaven. The women had their perfect mate right here on Earth, and it was studly David Koresh. Just so, so convenient. Koresh called this new hand-me-your-missus policy 'The New Light', because calling it 'I'm Putting My Wang in Your Wife' was too crass.

Hilariously, and a source of great pride to Antipodeans, it was at this point that a couple of Australians immediately left the group. The end of the world and all that is fine, but Aussies'll be buggered if you tell 'em they can't root their wives. Fair suck of the sauce bottle, Koresh mate. Jeez.

One of the functions of David's wives was to incubate heirs for him. He was still aiming for twenty-four children to match the twenty-four elders in the Book of Revelation, but when push came to shove, depending on whose evidence you rely on Koresh only managed seventeen, still a pretty decent effort all considering. Due to the group's relative isolation and their attitude towards the laws of the outside world, the birth certificates of many of the children born within the cult do not specify who the father is. But the father of those children was, in so, so many cases, David Koresh.

In addition to really-quite-probably sex with minors, Koresh, and under his instruction many of his followers, reportedly also nudged the edges of just plain old child abuse via a number of violent punishments. Regardless of anyone's contentious feelings around the subject of spanking as a form of discipline, stories from ex-cult members claim that Koresh really pushed the envelope. Reportedly for crimes as mild as not wanting to hug him, or crying when they shouldn't, children as young as eight months old were paddled on the buttocks until they were

ZEALOT: A BOOK ABOUT CULTS

bruised. Claims of abuse were later oft-quoted by authorities as one of the tipping points for taking action on the Branch Davidians, but there has been an inconvenient lack of substantive evidence that it actually occurred.

The steady stream of guns and gun parts making their way from the surrounding areas of Texas into the Mount Carmel compound was astounding. Traditionally it's been pretty easy to buy guns in Texas since Texas began, especially when compared to some other parts of the United States, and it was even easier at Texas gun shows, where you just needed a driver's licence, a pen to sign a form, and enough money to buy guns. Branch Davidians attended and dealt at gun shows, were frequent customers at gun shops, and ordered additional items by post. Mail-order guns for a cult, for just the price of a stamp, plus loads of fun with the bubble-wrap afterwards.

Despite comparatively generous gun laws, it was still a lot easier in Texas to buy semi-automatic weapons like AR15s than it was to buy fully automatic weapons like M16s. Even if you bought AR15s and the parts to convert them into fully automatic firearms, you had to have a special licence to do so, and pay a fee to the government. Branch Davidians were not paying those fees or acquiring those licences, but they were purchasing instructional pamphlets and videos that taught people how to convert guns like AR15s. Coincidences, and bullet casings, all over the place.

Unsurprisingly, the government had the compound under surveillance. The 120-or-so Branch Davidians weren't easily fooled though, and were pretty sure that the two college students living in a house across the road from the compound were undercover agents. They weren't stoned all the time for one thing, which was a dead giveaway. Additionally, the 'college students' were in their thirties and drove cars that would have easily passed a roadworthiness test, and when a couple of suspicious Branch Davidians knocked on their door with a six-pack of beer, they didn't let them in. Sorry, if you're a college student and a neighbour drops by carrying beer, they're coming in. Days with free home-delivery beer are the best days of a college student's life. Those beer-refusing, almost middle-aged people with disposable incomes were definitely Bureau of Alcohol, Tobacco, and Firearms (ATF) agents.

The ATF knew something was up inside the Branch Davidian compound. The Branch Davidians knew they were being watched by the ATF. It was only a matter of time before the whole situation came to a head. There was a strong scent of raid in the air.

So. The raid on the Mount Carmel compound and the subsequent siege. Before we get into the details of the world-renowned clusterfuck, it's important to note that almost everyone involved tells a different story, and almost nobody involved did a great job. There were terrible decisions made on all sides, lies told by all sides, and bravado-fuelled incompetence on all sides. The Waco tragedy is basically a textbook example of what it looks like when white men in positions of power compete to see who has the biggest penis.

The ATF was absolutely sure there were too many of the wrong types of guns in the Branch Davidian compound, and were understandably nervous about the extent to which the religious group was looking more and more like an organised military outfit. The jurisdiction of the ATF was reasonably narrow and focused primarily on the use of illegal firearms. They had strong suspicions that there were illegal, unlicensed guns inside the compound's walls, but they didn't have as much evidence as they would have liked. As a result, they were happy for rumours to circulate about other allegedly illegal activity within the cult, such as child abuse, to make their raid more palatable to onlookers.

The two big dates are 28 February, the day of the initial raid, and 19 April 1993, the day the siege ended in death and flames, with forty-nine days of messed-up histrionics in between. The day of the raid, the ATF wanted to surprise Koresh and the gang with arrest and search warrants, and timed their arrival for the part of the day that most of the members of the group would be scattered out and about, working. But a cameraman on his way to help cover the raid had lost his way and asked a postman for directions. The postman was David Koresh's brother-in-law. Uh-oh spaghetti-oh. Thanks to this tip-off, the Branch Davidians were concentrated inside, ready to receive guests with their guns raised.

Because no story set in Texas is complete without a minimum of two good old-fashioned Texan shoot-outs, a gunfight ensued. Nobody agrees on who shot first, but four ATF agents and six Branch Davidians were killed, meaning loads of tiresome paper-work for the bureau. It also meant that the FBI could now be called in. While firearm infringements don't tickle their fancy much, the slaughter of government agents tickles their fancy very much indeed, with both hands. They were in.

The FBI was quite comfortable and experienced with the finer points of negotiating with a much broader variety of trigger-happy activists than the ATF, and the ATF had a reputation for flashy displays of aggression, so there's no telling how extremely terrible things would have been if just left in the hands of the latter. Still. It wasn't good.

Negotiators on the outside made contact quite quickly with David Koresh and his second, Steve Schneider, on the inside. Koresh revealed to the feds that he'd been shot in the wrist and hip. This would have been better news for the agents, who were hoping he would come out for treatment, except for two things: firstly, his wounds were treated competently by other cult members, and secondly, David Koresh would absolutely love any situation that would make him look like a martyr.

On the second day of the raid, ten children were released, and the FBI brought some tanks in to menace the compound's perimeter, proving the government to have very robust testicles indeed. With the exception of special lines directly to the federal negotiators, phone lines out of the compound were cut.

Later in the raid, a nine-year-old girl was released with a note pinned to her jacket which announced that once the children were out, the adults would die, which is a pretty depressing thing to find pinned to a child's clothing that isn't a descant recorder proficiency badge.

Negotiations dragged and cult members dribbled out gradually, but there was still up to a hundred people left inside, tired, cold and angry. At least they weren't hungry, though – along with all the guns they'd been buying and caching, they'd also been stockpiling military food rations, so there was no telling how long those still inside could survive.

Over the ensuing days, Koresh and the Branch Davidians tried all sorts of tactics to avoid emerging from their fortress. Koresh conducted multiple phone interviews and was featured on CNN and Dallas radio, the attention-seeking boffin. He filmed himself in videos that he leaked to the press, showing himself as a faultless besieged martyr with battle wounds, surrounded by his children. Most of his participation in negotiations consisted of what the agents called 'Bible babble', streams of religious doctrine and unrequested sermons, which aside from being no help at all in resolving the stand-off, would also have been unbelievably boring.

On the third day of the siege, Koresh sent out a one-hour tape of a specially recorded sermon, promising to come out of the compound as soon as it was broadcast on radio. It was broadcast, but he didn't come out. God told him to wait.

Koresh promised to come out of the compound just after Passover. Passover passed, but he didn't come out. God told him to wait.

Koresh promised to come out of the compound just as soon as he'd finished writing a manuscript detailing his interpretation of the seven seals in the Book of Revelation. He didn't finish it, and he didn't come out. As the kids at school who used to call him 'Mr Retardo' knew, he was a really slow writer.

Questionable tactics weren't purely the domain of the Branch Davidians, though. Techniques used by the FBI and ATF to try to irritate the cult members into coming out with their hands up were manifold, and all at least as annoying as a teenager trying to get their own way. Electricity was cut off and reconnected at whim, depending on how willing Koresh was to communicate and negotiate. Bright lights were shone into the compound all night, and agents played extremely loud music over large speakers, including Tibetan chants, Christmas music, and Nancy Sinatra's 'These Boots Are Made For Walkin''. Sorry, but if you want people to stay in a cult compound forever and ever, play them *any* of the bangers and guaranteed dancefloor fillers from Nancy Sinatra's back catalogue. Idiots.

The FBI refused to send milk for the children into the compound unless more of them were released. When cult members sent videos out to the waiting authorities that included vision of any of the children inside, they were kept secret from the media in case they generated too much sympathy for Koresh from the public. Against the advice of the negotiators, tactical rather than diplomatic measures were instigated against the compound residents, escalating the situation and really bugging the shit out of everyone. Agents claimed that they wanted to raise stress levels within the compound to make more people want to come out, but the people who they were trying to put pressure on were people whose fingers were literally on triggers. It was just a terrible, terrible idea.

By the twenty-third day, the frustrated FBI started considering tear gas as a non-lethal technique for getting everyone out, but they needed special clearance for that from Janet Reno, the attorney-general. She ummed and aahed, suggesting alternatives like cutting off the water supply instead, so the FBI were like look, we'll just use a LITTLE bit of tear gas, just to make them cry a TINY bit, and it's probably fine to use on children, and then everybody will all come out and shake hands and they'll wipe their tears away and we'll be heroes. Easy.

'No,' said Attorney-General Janet Reno.

'Please?' said the FBI.

'Oh, okay,' said Attorney-General Janet Reno. She just couldn't stay mad at the FBI.

There's a story from one FBI agent who claims he saw a sign in the window of a compound building held up by a cult member that said 'Flames Await' which, if nothing else that had gone down in the last month and a half did, sure put some very bad writing on the wall. Mind you, people on both sides have claimed at various times to have seen all sorts of writing on all sorts of walls, but the truth has been so clouded with ideological agendas by now that the sign in the window might as well have read 'Eat flame, bozos!' for all the reliability of the 'reliable' eye witnesses.

On 19 April, with a last bit of warning over the loudspeakers, the feds moved in. Combat vehicles with booms attached inserted tear gas into compound buildings through windows and holes poked in the walls. Seemingly the FBI didn't consider that an outfit that had stockpiled military-grade weapons and military-issue food rations might possibly have also stockpiled gas masks, but live and learn, right? Maybe next time.

Walls were knocked over, agitation skyrocketed, the situation became panicked, but only nine cult members came out of the compound at the thought of imminent danger, and they were immediately arrested. On this, the last day of a long, terrible siege, most of the Branch Davidians spent breakfast and morning tea shooting back, but by lunchtime, fire had started in at least three areas of the compound. It spread quickly and burned fiercely, and firefighters weren't allowed anywhere near the burning buildings for a long time for risk of being shot. The compound was literally and metaphorically toast.

After the fire had died down, seventy-six Branch Davidians were found dead inside the compound, and according to FBI reports, many of them died of knife or bullet wounds, not from the fire. It looked very much like some of them had killed each other and themselves, with Koresh sporting a bullet wound right in the middle of his forehead.

Investigators also found hundreds of firearms, millions of rounds of ammunition, and forty-eight guns that had been illegally modified to convert them into fully automatic weapons, if a little melted. So many of the other claims about activity within the compound's walls – that there was child abuse, paedo-philia, and spooky levels of mind control – have never had any substantial physical evidence to back them up, but here was proof of illegal firearms activity. Except for the smouldering rubble, the extreme damage to their reputation, and the burnt corpses scattered all over the place, the ATF must have found some comfort in the fact that their original hunch was right.

Seven of the Branch Davidians were tried and jailed for a mixture of manslaughter and firearms offences. The announce-ment of their sentencing would likely have been given a lot more attention in the media had it not occurred on the same day that OJ Simpson went on the run from the police on suspicion of murdering his wife and hogged all the limelight. All said, it wasn't a good time for investigations that hoped to quickly and efficiently uncover the truth.

There is a load of questions about the Branch Davidians and the siege in particular that still haven't been adequately answered, despite more than one federal investigation and inquiry. It's hard to tell, though, whether they're not answered because there are no answers, or if they're not answered because of the competing agendas of all the people who might otherwise be able to answer them.

Those who strongly and sometimes violently defend the right to religion and gun ownership – a great combination to have at garden parties – are often ready to defend every action David Koresh has ever taken, including in some cases the very, very likely instances of sex with underage girls.

On the other hand, those in government who made decisions about the raid, siege, and final tear-gas attack are not traditionally the kind of people willing to admit mistakes.

And those who were there, on both sides, holding guns, are not the kind of people who like to admit they were wrong, or mistaken, or idiots.

Both sides seemingly escalated the situation unnecessarily. Both sides had decisions made by macho aggressors who could have made better, more peaceful ones.

Why such a heavy-handed raid? The ATF could have served a search warrant to Koresh at the compound, but made the decision instead to launch a surprise raid. If it *had* been a surprise, there's a small chance it might have worked, but factoring in a tip-off means that a group of people hell-bent on a fiery end-of-days battle were expecting them. Awkward.

And how much did the ATF know about the Branch Davidians' obsession with Armageddon? If you know that a group of armed people fantasise about going into battle as a trigger for the apocalypse, do you really head over there to surprise them with guns and armoured vehicles? From quite early in the piece, Koresh had nicknamed the Mount Carmel compound 'Ranch Apocalypse'. There's a clue in there somewhere.

Who shot first? On the first day, when people on both sides were killed, each blames the other for initiating the shoot-out. In the obvious *Star Wars* cantina stand-off comparison, neither the ATF nor the Branch Davidians could agree on who would be Han Solo, and who would be Greedo.

Why didn't ATF agents just detain David Koresh when he was out for a jog or getting supplies? A lot of people have asked this one. It's a pretty good question. Koresh didn't go out a lot, but people in Waco reported seeing him every now and again. The ATF claims that they wanted to both arrest Koresh *and* search the compound for weapons, but there's more than one way to skin a cat and raid a cult.

And finally, who started the fires? There's considerable debate on this point, and it's true that some of the gas cartridges the FBI used had the potential to be flammable in certain specific situations. Based on subtle hints, such as the fact that Davidians in general, and Branch Davidians in particular, have gone on and on for years about how their ends will probably be met in a great fire, and several little bits of evidence – all of them contested, of course – that the fire was started from within the compound, suspicion obviously falls on the cult members. Additionally, dying under siege from the government in a big fire would have made Koresh's predictions come true – he'd prophesied an event like this, so his credibility had never been greater, or more public, than when those fires started. Unfortunately it's hard to say 'I told you so' when your hair is on fire.

If – and it's still an if – David Koresh and the Branch Davidians had goaded the ATF and FBI into a violent siege in order to nudge their enclave towards a fiery Armageddon-esque end at the hands of the government, they wouldn't have been the first cult to find that kind of scenario appealing. Aum Shinrikyo, The Peoples Temple, The Family, and Heaven's Gate all fantasised about being participants in a battle between themselves and authorities. If you get a chance to martyr yourself while you're under attack from the really big, important people in power, that means you've successfully rattled some significant cages with your alternative theories about life, so your theories about life must have merit. Considering David Koresh's obvious narcissism, it's not unbelievable to imagine that once he managed to get the attention of the big dudes – the FBI – he figured he'd made it.

Americans have stayed angry about Waco for a long time, with some taking it to extremes. On the second anniversary of the fire at the Branch Davidian compound, Timothy McVeigh used his anger at what he perceived as the injustices suffered by its inhabitants as part of his reason for bombing a building in Oklahoma City and killing 168 people. When you decide to kill people to express your anger at people being needlessly killed, suffice to say you're not helping.

And when you decide to dig your heels in and not back down instead of finding a way to negotiate a compromise because you need everyone to think you're a tough guy, that's also not ideal. Clearly the Bible can be interpreted in many messed-up ways to justify a thousand terrible things, but the bit where it says we should turn the other cheek? That's a good bit.

RAELIANS

On 5 July 1996, Dolly the sheep was born. Dolly was a clone, and the first mammal to be born successfully as the result of cloning. When journalists and the scientific community asked the smart people at the University of Edinburgh and their mates at biotechnology company PPL Therapeutics for evidence that Dolly was, in fact, a sheep that had been cloned in a laboratory, they said 'Sure!' and showed them the evidence. Dolly lived at the university, popped out a few lambs, and died at the ripe old age of seven.

On Boxing Day 2002, Baby Eve was born. Maybe. Baby Eve was a clone, and the first human to be born successfully as the result of cloning. Allegedly. When journalists and the scientific community asked the smart people at Clonaid and their mates at UFO-based religion the Raelians for evidence that Baby Eve was, in fact, a human that had been cloned in a laboratory, they said 'Look, we'll get back to you' and then absolutely didn't.

There's little evidence that Baby Eve was born or lived, nobody has spoken to her parents, and not one piece of evidence has been offered or uncovered to suggest that human cloning took place.

Not all cults are bad. In some cults nobody is killed, nobody keeps anybody prisoner, nobody poisons anybody's mind against the outside world, and nobody tries to get away with putting their genitals where they shouldn't. Some cults are just peculiar and tell a couple of porkies about human cloning.

The Raelians are peculiar and probably don't clone humans, but otherwise they are pretty much okay. Depending on how much of a stickler you are, they might not even technically be considered a cult, provided you ignore the charismatic leader who tells you he's in direct contact with God, the (admittedly very reasonable) membership fees and tithing requirements, the bishops, the for-the-leader's-use-only concubines, and the executive-level secrecy. But wherever you put your pin in the is-it-a-cult graph, the Raelians are definitely too interesting to ignore, even without killing anyone or trying to predict the exact date the world will end. When all is said and done, the Raelians are actually pretty upbeat. They're sex-positive, inclusive, hate racism and homophobia, and campaign loudly against numerous global injustices. Their story doesn't centre around anything evil or even a bit iffy – their story centres around the stories that they themselves tell, and around a suave-as-all-heck little guy called Claude. Plus their stories have aliens, sex robots, and boobs in them. You can't beat that.

Born in 1946, Claude Vorilhon was a relatively normal little French kid, although he was passed from mother to aunt and back again when his father – who, by all accounts but Claude's own, was definitely not an extra-terrestrial – abandoned him and his mother, Colette. Much later, Claude would claim that his own birth was the result of a holy alien-being coming to Earth and impregnating his mother, which, while hard to swallow, is a lot more entertaining and aspirational than the classic 'Dad went down to the shops for a packet of smokes and never came back' scenario. Other than that mild narrative hiccup, there wasn't much remarkable about Claude's childhood save for the fact that he might not have got enough love and attention at home.

In a textbook move for a boy who didn't feel like he got enough love and attention at home, young Claude dreamed of being either a pop singer or a racing car driver, and he almost achieved both. Modelling his man-about-town, thoughtful singing style on that of equally French but more talented Jacques Brel, he performed in insignificant venues around Paris and came to the attention of a reasonably unimportant record label. He released a handful of songs in the mid-sixties under the name Claude Celler, packed with intensely French-sounding whimsy and sentiment of only moderate appeal to people with money in record shops. Props must be bestowed for the title of one though, 'Monsieur, Votre Femme Me Trompe', which loosely translates to 'Sir, Your Wife is Cheating on Me'. If you're going to be the leader of a worldwide religious movement in later life, it's important to have a lyrical sense of humour right from the get-go. Even later, as the leader of a successful global religious movement, Claude has continued to write and perform songs, defiant in the face of virtually zero demand.

At twenty-five, Claude started an automotive magazine called *Autopop*, which peculiarly went its entire three-year lifespan without winning a World's Most European-Sounding Car Magazine award. Being the founder and editor of a car rag allowed Claude to also become a test-driver of the cars featured within it, and he even raced a little, albeit with no reliable record of any success save for his own reports. Basically out of pop star, racing car driver and cult leader, he only had one dream left to fulfil and he wasn't even thirty yet.

Claude married the charming but entirely secondary Marie-Paul, who incubated two children for him while he incubated a thriving and robust ego. Aware that Claude was cheating on her and neglecting his parenting duties in favour of cars and people who weren't her, Marie-Paul in turn incubated a deep resentment and the marriage didn't last.

Then one day shortly before Christmas in 1973, as is so often the turning point for anyone's life story, Claude was visited by aliens. He was just taking a circuitous route along the side of a volcanic crater in central southern France on his way to the office, and boom, spaceship, right in front of him. Other people's claims that this extraordinary event took place just as he was getting sick of running an automotive magazine are mere coincidence and not good sport, although for corroboration purposes it is a true shame that Claude was completely alone at the time.

The ship that confronted Claude was shaped like a bell, no doubt to ring in the biggest change in his life, or at least to signal the beginning of a few decades of UFO-based religious yarns. A tiny little guy came out of the ship proudly and calmly, impressing Claude with his uncharacteristic lack of short man syndrome for a person under five feet tall. The little guy introduced himself as Yahweh and said he had come to visit Claude specifically, dropping a couple of utterly palatable but philosophically huge nuggets of information. The first nugget was that he, the little spaceship guy, was a member of the Elohim, fathered Jesus, and had created the Earth and everything on it, no big deal. The second nugget, just while you're recovering from the first one there, mate, was that he, the little spaceship guy, was Claude's true father. The alien gave Claude a new job – that of messenger and prophet, and a new name – Rael. Y'know, like in 'Israel'. That information may come in handy later.

For the rest of this story, you really, really need to know who the Elohim are. Originally 'Elohim' was one of the names for God in the Hebrew Bible. There it's singular, but for some – and definitely for Claude – it's a plural. Claude believes that not only does 'Elohim' refer to a bunch of dudes, but those dudes are aliens. And they're not just any aliens, but extremely accomplished alien scientists. The Elohim started us, and at some point they will want to come back and meet us, to see how we turned out. Or at least that's what they told Rael. All by himself. On the side of a volcano.

You'd think a single visit from an alien who told you you're Christ's half-brother and that your motor-racing journalism days were over would be enough, but nope. A couple of years after first being visited by the Elohim, Rael found himself again having his day interrupted by a UFO, and this time they took him up into their ship with them and onward to their home planet, where Rael hung out for a while. He met his half-brothers Jesus, Mohammed and Buddha, and they sat around talking about the weather, ancient and modern history, recipes, standard God stuff. Rael noted that robots, barely distinguishable visually from humans, did all the work on the Elohim planet, so everyone could just relax and let the robots work, from growing food to preparing meals to cleaning – even running a cloning machine like the one that Rael saw being demonstrated when the robots made a clone of his mother and himself – everything. Just efficient, versatile, do-everything robots on God's own planet. Marvellous.

Interplanetary convenience robots even do sex, as Rael found out. During his tour of the Elohim planet, Rael was offered the products of a sex robot–making machine and decided on six perfect women of different races and – seemingly importantly according to Rael's detailed description – different hair colours. Claude and the six nubile automatons all took a bath and then retired to the bedroom, Rael delighted with how submissive and filthy multi-racial sex robots can be. Yep, Rael went to another planet and had sex with robots while Jesus and Buddha were sitting in the next room. If that's not enough to make him a credible Messiah, nothing is.

It's important to note that the Elohim have about 25,000 years' worth of scientific and technological advancement over us – embarrassing – so even the simplest, most rudimentary examples of their world would seem like the most incredible miracles to us. Your great-great-grandmother would have considered the oldest non-internet-enabled Nokia phone to be the satanic work of a terrifying and diabolical wizard, so the technological advances of a civilisation tens of thousands of years ahead of us would seem to our eyes to be the work of gods. Which leads us nicely into Rael's neat trick of incorporating the stories of the Bible into his theories of the universe, thank you so much for asking.

These alien scientists from outer space created all of us, the human race, in a laboratory, which you might think would fly in the face of the idea of both evolution *and* the story of Creation, but not so fast, buddy – Rael has an answer for almost all of your questions about science and the Bible. He even calls Raelism an 'atheistic scientific' religion, yet is still more than happy to accept the Bible as a more-or-less accurate interpretive document. The Elohim told him that the Bible just *seems* different from the funkier true story because of the incredulity of humans at the time it was written and their inability to accurately translate from Hebrew. But the vibe of the Bible is more or less on the right track. That's the thing about Raelism – however far-fetched it seems, the religion's theories about the origins of humanity, the nature of life on Earth and the future of mankind are its most fascinating and impressive features, a bold claim when you consider its leader's range of competitively fascinating hairstyles over his lifetime. Mind you, Raelians believe that having long hair is like having antennae to increase your telepathic transmission power so, yeah, all of the stories are pretty good. But even topknots aside, absolutely part of Rael's considerable appeal and influence is his ability to explain almost everything and answer almost every question using his theory of adapted creation and evolution. He's very clever for a man who spends almost all of his time in outdated, early *Star Trek*-looking leisure wear.

Go on. See if there's a question about the Bible that Rael can't answer.

How do you account for dinosaurs, Rael? Easy – dinosaurs were just the result of the alien scientists mucking around and experimenting. Even birds of paradise were merely the result of a competition between the scientists to see who could create the most absurdly colourful flying things, so dinosaurs aren't such a stretch, are they? The alien scientists were just like children making monsters out of plasticine, but with 25,000 years' worth of technological advancement, and they spelt it 'pleistocene'.

What about Noah's Ark, Rael? Okay, so the Bible *almost* got it right here, in that God – the Elohim – saw that mankind was going off on the wrong track and that most of the Earth's inhabitants should be destroyed. Sure, two of each animal should be saved, and a handful of worthy humans, but the rest of the facts in the Old Testament are a bit off. The government on the Elohim's distant planet decided to wipe out humans with some nuclear missiles, and asked Noah to build a spaceship stocked with the DNA of all the animals he wanted to survive the massive tidal waves that the blast would inevitably create. Once the Earth's radioactivity had returned to liveable levels, Noah simply made clones of all the animals. Except unicorns, obviously. Noah could not *stand* unicorns. Fuck those guys.

And what of Jesus Christ's ability to perform healing miracles on Earth while he was the prophet, Rael? Lasers. Jesus Christ healed people by using lasers. The Elohim taught Jesus how to use lasers using science. Done. Next question.

Adam and Eve? See, they were the result of the first human genetic experiments in the first laboratory on Earth. Duh. Earth was barren, so after mucking around with plants and animals for a while, the Elohim decided it was time to make something out of their own DNA – only taller and stupider, obviously – and there you have it, loads of little Adams and Eves all over the place.

This guy. THIS GUY. Not only does Rael have an answer for everything, he would be absolutely kickass at an alien-evolutionary-creation-science-themed trivia night. Get him on your team.

Not that the half-brother of Jesus Christ would even *have* you on his trivia team. See, Jesus Christ, Buddha, Mohammed and Rael all have the same dad, which is the same guy that came out of the spaceship to hang with Rael in the first place. Rael understood that whenever the Elohim figured that Earth needed a prophet to remind its inhabitants of their true origins and destiny, they'd select a particularly pure and pert Earth lady, get her pregnant with divine DNA, and nine months later she'd squeeze out a holy messenger. This had happened at various junctures over the last few thousand years with Buddha, Mohammed, Jesus *et al*, and now they were all kicking back, having lunch in space. Nice.

While showing him their planet, the Elohim told Rael what his missions were. The end goal for Raelians is to greet the Elohim upon their return to Earth in a purpose-built embassy that would afford the big sky guys somewhere to land, somewhere for the faithful to gather to greet them, and somewhere where they rely on having diplomatic immunity. Simply put, no alien race that created a few million humans as an experiment wants to return to the laboratory only to be arrested and subjected to hours of tiresome paperwork, so they needed a safe haven with a short runway – they simply must be honoured with an administratively watertight embassy. The Elohim would likely arrive once humans had stopped using science and technology for war and dirty climate change, and instead started using it for togetherness, harmony, immortality, and endless sexy times. It was Rael's job, the Elohim told him, to spread the message to us all, including misguided scientists, that we need to head in that direction. The peaceful, non–nuclear apocalypse direction, in matching white pyjamas.

Originally Rael was hoping to build the Elohim embassy in Jerusalem, partly because, according to the Bible, Jerusalem clearly has a lot of meaning and important references for the Elohim, and partly because somewhere in or near Israel would really make the wordplay in Rael's name make total sense. Additionally, and in news that would have given Hitler haemorrhoids, while most humans have been conceived in a laboratory, Raelians posit that Jewish people are a legitimate race co-parented by humans and the Elohim – a holier race than the rest of the schmucks, so Jerusalem makes sense.

Unfortunately, the authorities who decide who does and doesn't get to build alien embassies in Jerusalem have never been too keen on the idea for a multitude of reasons, and successive governments keep rejecting Rael's request for embassy land. One large reason is that Raelians insist that the embassy be granted exterritoriality and not be subject to local laws, and governments aren't often easily convinced of granting that favour to aliens. Another small reason may be that the Raelian logo is a swastika wrapped inside a star of David. Certainly, one of the Raelians' stated aims is to remove the swastika's negative connotations, which they say are only a result of the symbol's enthusiastic adoption by Nazis. Raelians rightly claim that, originally, the Sanskrit swastika symbol symbolised luck and peace and love and eternity, used by many groups that aren't, in fact, genocidal bastards. That's all well and good, but regardless of what your intentions are, when people see a swastika they definitely still think about Nazis, and trying to change that is like trying to make people ignore Gary Glitter's conviction for paedophilia and just enjoy his music. Lukewarm attempts have been made to change the Raelian logo so that the centre is now a cute little swirl rather than the unavoidable reminder of the Holocaust, but Raelian websites and medallions worldwide are still saturated with the swastika version. Like neo-Nazism and herpes, that thing just won't go away. Still, despite the fact that authorities in Jerusalem have had several legitimate reasons for not permitting an extra-terrestrial embassy to be built in their city, after at least seven flat rejections, it's fair to say that Rael went off Jewish people a bit. It took them a while, but the Raelians even publicly withdrew their support of Zionism in 2015, declaring themselves the 'true Jews'. Jewish people just *love* it when people do that. And if you ever run a cult, remember: don't go too publicly hard in favour of a bunch of people and claim they're the children of gods unless you're absolutely sure they want to be seen in the playground with you at recess.

The Raelian movement moved its main base to Canada in the early nineties and started needling the Canadian government for the green light to build the alien embassy there instead. Considering the Canadian government had already refused to grant the group even the slightest tax exemption for being a religious organisation, the Elohim would be foolish to hold their holy breaths waiting for Canadian embassy-building approval and Earth visas. As far as finding a place to greet the aliens upon their return is concerned though, the Raelians do need to get a wriggle on – the Elohim need a place to land with full acceptance from the human race by around 2035 or they'll consider letting humans torch themselves in a nuclear apocalypse, just for chuckles. Any country willing to host an embassy for extraterrestrials and enjoy the obvious resulting intergalactic tourism benefits should put their hand up, quick sticks.

Aside from the as-yet unbuilt embassy or, if you want to include it, wherever Rael bases himself at any time, there is no recognised permanent Raelian base. There is no Raelian compound that followers live in, or even visit. No walls, gates, watchtowers, or barbed wire. Rather, personal contact with other Raelians is facilitated via seminars and gatherings in the countries where membership is high enough to warrant them, much like self-improvement conferences but with a far higher likelihood of seeing some nipples. Attendees listen to lectures by Rael, who is still very much enamoured with the sound of his own voice, or in his absence, a senior member of the movement. They fast, hug, meditate, get nude, and attend a range of workshops pitched at different levels of perviness – a spot of blindfolded caressing perhaps, a bit of a nude afternoon chit-chat, or an educational interlude during which you inspect your own anus in a mirror. Almost all of each seminar's attendees – and there are fewer attendees than Raelian publicity would have you believe – wear medallions featuring the Raelian logo. Lord knows that if cults ever stop existing, the entire medallion industry will go down with them.

In addition to the myriad of seminars, there's also a bewildering array of Raelian causes promoted on each country's organisational website, each with an additional website of their own and a snappy name. 'Clitoraid' lobbies for the protection of women against female genital mutilation, and campaigns for donations towards a 'pleasure hospital' in Burkina Faso where they hope to perform clitoral restorative surgery on victims of mutilation. The hospital has had trouble opening, as government and medical authorities in the African nation aren't too sure about authorising a hospital run by UFO enthusiasts, but Clitoraid has managed to work through smaller clinics. One of their YouTube videos shows women working for Clitoraid conducting a 'vibrator wrapping party', packaging gentle, no-contact sex toys to send to their recovering patients to welcome them back to the world of orgasm. Some say this is a nice gesture, some say it's cheapening the seriousness of female genital mutilation and making it more about sex than human rights. In particular, Clitoraid's 'Adopt A Clitoris' campaign, in which Westerners are encouraged to donate money towards restoration surgery, is seen as being pitched at somewhat the wrong angle. Although Clitoraid's heart may be in the right place, the provincial ownership connotations of adopting an African woman's clitoris doesn't sit well with the broader idea of empowerment.

In other movements, 'Rael's Girls' aims to remove the stigma associated with working in the sex industry, and 'Go Topless' supports what Raelians believe is a woman's constitutional right to overcome sexism within the law and get her tits out in public. Rael's Girls doesn't seem so intent on the plight of men working in the sex industry; however, Go Topless does make a point of campaigning for either the right for women to bare their chests or, alternatively, for the law to be changed so that men are also required to cover their nipples. Despite their claims, sexual equality is a shaky bowl of jelly within the Raelians.

There's 'NoPedo', a movement that invites people to dob in Catholic priests they suspect of paedophilia, and offers the services of Rael's Girls to step in and cure them of their deviant sexual practices. And 'One Minute for Peace' urges people to meditate for one minute, spontaneously or at organised events, so that their combined brainwaves can improve the world and lower crime rates. They say studies have been conducted regarding the link between meditation and crime rates. They say a lot of things.

'Proswastika' aims to selflessly rehabilitate the image of the swastika, restoring it to its original, pre-Nazi meaning of positivity, and 'Paradism' campaigns for a system of government that nationalises the undertaking of all human work and law enforcement by robots. No humans work, all humans share, everybody who's made of meat relaxes, and presumably the robots all go topless and are incredibly proficient at drawing swastikas. Look, it sounds all right.

The thing is, while all of these causes and movements have their own website and domain name and logo and mission statement, they don't actually *do* all that much. Even Clitoraid, which has achieved the most, has fallen way short of its stated aims. Raelians are accomplished at giving things catchy names, and sending girls in bikinis out to campaign for things with website addresses paint-smeared across their well-maintained torsos, but they're not absolutely fantastic at action. Raelians have two main missions – spreading the word of the Elohim and building an alien embassy. In more than forty years, they have spread the message of the Elohim to thousands, but have only made a couple of tiny models of their proposed alien embassy, without so much as a foundation laid. They're talkin' loud. They're sayin' nothin'.

Perhaps the most significant example of plenty of talk accompanied by no identifiable action is the Raelian obsession with cloning. Raelians believe that cloning is the key to immortality, and immortality is the key to wandering around not working, eating food that has grown itself, and having consensual sex with whoever you like for fun. In the Raelian version of immortality, we do still each grow old and wrinkly and start leaking from places we didn't used to, just like we do now. But in their world, our personalities have been uploaded to and stored in a giant supercomputer by very technologically advanced aliens, much like Facebook but infinitely more important and with a much more lax attitude towards nudity. Then when we die, our bodies are reproduced genetically by a bit of cloning, and our previous personalities are neatly popped back in to our new bodies via download. Followers of Rael agree that, upon their death, a mortician is allowed to chip a teeny bit of bone from their skull – located roughly where other people think the third eye is – to put into storage as a record and to facilitate the physical cloning. These little chips are rumoured to be stored on ice in a bank vault in Geneva, Switzerland, but damn it, it's so hard to get those Swiss bank accounts to cough up their secrets, so we may never know if there's a real genetic cloning skull fragment bank in Switzerland. The only secret those guys can't keep is Toblerone, bless 'em.

So if cloning is how we will all reproduce and achieve immortality in the future, what of sex? According to Raelians, go. Go get your sex. We don't need sex to reproduce if cloning is humanity's future, so it's purely for pleasure now. Rael strongly emphasises to his followers that sensual pleasure builds neural pathways and generates extra brain cells, so sex for pleasure actually makes you smarter. Heterosexual, homosexual, bisexual, kinky, queer, fine, fine, fine. Get it however you like (with consent), with whomever you want (with consent), with as much contraception as you deem fit (with consent), and if your tastes are a bit unusual and/or not generally considered legal or moral, you can go have sex with robots as soon as they're invented so you're not hurting or inconveniencing anyone (consent optional but implied in the robot's programming). Raelians have even suggested sex robots for Catholic priests, so that those among the order who have paedophilic urges – and let's face it, there are more than a handful – might be less inclined to act out on a human victim if they have a convenient robot available. It's an intensely uncomfortable idea. And provided the Catholic church maintains its stance on celibacy, a pretty good one.

Happily, paedophilia, rape, and other acts where consent isn't part of the whole shebang are robustly frowned upon, and anyone practising acts from the heinous end of town is swiftly excommunicated from the religion. Admittedly excommunication usually only lasts for seven years, as that's the time it takes for all the cells of the body to regenerate, the Raelians say. Maybe if you don't have any of the cells you had when you were a rapist, you aren't a rapist anymore? Worth a shot. Science, everyone.

But for those with sexual urges within legal, if still moderately pervy parameters, it stands that not all horny people want to wait until high-quality sex robots are invented – they want to lambada with real live human people NOW, please. While women have never made up more than a third of Raelian membership, it likely doesn't do recruiting efforts any harm to note that very sexy women indeed are a large part of the cult's visibility. Almost all the promotional and casual imagery of the Raelian movement you can find includes one of two things: pictures of Rael, or pictures of hot chicks. Indeed, perhaps a tenth of the pictures are of Rael surrounded by hot chicks, everything an aspirational space geek needs to know to pick a cult to join. The pictures make it look very much like Raelian membership is upwards of eighty per cent nubile, up-for-it ladies. Sure, there's also a lot of pictures of people holding inflatable aliens, but when you buy a ticket to a naked breast double feature, sometimes you have to sit through a few alien-origin-story previews. It's worked spectacularly well, too – there are tens of thousands of Raelians in upwards of eighty countries including the US, Canada, Australia, South Korea, Saudi Arabia, and Japan.

What kind of people join the Raelian movement you may ask, if you want the most obvious answer of all time? Hmmm, let's see, who would join a movement where aliens are gods and you have a fifty to eighty per cent chance of having sex with a robot? Proper, card-carrying nerds is who. The Raelians is almost wall-to-wall awesome super nerds, with a smattering of new age hippies who like the idea of free love and spiritual beings from outer space. Overwhelmingly, recruits statistically come from a Catholic background, which probably has a lot to do with the fact that a lot of concepts and rituals within Raelism smell faintly of Catholicism, but with a far, far broader attitude towards sexual freedom and much more comfortable clothing. In fact, great chunks of Raelian literature hint that it is superior to Catholicism in particular, in parts to an almost bitchy degree. Rael will take every opportunity possible to stick it to the Catholics, the quirky rabble-rouser.

Once a no doubt horny person decides to become a Raelian, they can pick a date to become baptised. The four significant dates in the Raelian calendar are 13 December, the anniversary of Rael first meeting the Elohim; 7 October, the anniversary of Rael's second meeting with the Elohim; the first Sunday in April, when human beings were apparently first manufactured; and 6 August, the anniversary of the Hiroshima atomic bomb.

Hiroshima is significant to Raelians because it marked the beginning of 'The Age of Apocalypse', which is when humans started using technology advanced enough to obliterate humanity, and also the time at which people reading this might get a much darker version of the 'Aquarius' song from *Hair* in their heads. Sorry.

Raelian baptism looks a lot like Catholic baptism, with two significant differences: firstly, it's performed on consenting adults, two words not always used together at all times in Catholicism. Secondly, rather than the water symbolising the cleansing of sin and new life as it does in other ceremonies, in Raelism the watery part of baptism is called 'transmission of the cellular plan', and it is both extremely cool and unbelievably lame. Participants sign a piece of paper renouncing any previous religious affiliations, and they're good to go.

Provided the baptism is performed at 3 pm, when it is assumed that an Elohim spaceship will be at just the right spot above you in the sky, the water on your forehead will act as an effective conductor for your genetic imprint. You see, the Elohim have a supercomputer on their ship that records all thought and human action, and when the Raelian bishop touches your forehead, he's just uploading your code to his big spy bosses, and water acts as a really strong WiFi signal. Once your code has been uploaded, the Elohim have a record of you being part of the club, and they also have something to download into your cloned body after you die, as long as everything goes to plan.

For the majority of Raelians, it sort of stops there. They're baptised, they might go to the occasional sensual meditation conference in their part of the world, make a donation or buy a book or two, and keep track of Raelian news on their demographically appropriate website, but not much more is required. It could be strongly and easily argued that those people aren't in a cult.

It's more difficult to argue that Raelians at higher levels in the cult – admittedly the minority compared to the more casual members – aren't in a cult. They're part of what's called the 'Structure', and in ascending order are the Assistant Organisers, Organisers, Assistant Priests, Priests, Bishops, and Guide of Guides or Planetary Guide, the last being Rael himself. More is required of the Structure than of normal members, as they're enlisted to help with Rael's mission to spread the word, assist with seminars, perform baptisms, build an embassy, and see if they can get a ticket to the Elohim planet for being a good sort.

There's also the extremely exclusive Order of Angels, women of the highest level of genetic excellence who have been specifically chosen to act as ambassadors for the Elohim when they eventually arrive. They're required to be celibate except for with each other and the Elohim (when they get here), and make themselves available as surrogate mothers for cloning experiments, should the need present itself. While they're waiting for all those things to happen though, they basically have sex with Rael, because technically he's at least half Elohim. You have to take your hat off to Rael for essentially recreating the Playboy mansion but dressing it up as a holy alien mission statement. Angels are required to wear the symbol of a feather on a necklace for identification as a member of this special elite, something that feels – when juxtaposed against the broader Raelian sex-positive stance – a teensy bit like they are being marked as incubator concubines.

Interestingly the Order of Angels is all female, which indicates that the Elohim are all male and all heterosexual, another clue that the Raelian sex-positive and gender-equal stance may just be for press releases only. On the outside, Rael presents himself as a pillar of equality, but on the inside he's just Pepé Le Pew in a tracksuit.

The free-for-all attitude that Raelians have towards sex, contraception, and generally agreeing that humans should be able to do whatever the (literal) fuck they like with their bodies has historically miffed conservatives in general and the Catholic church in particular. And the objection isn't just to the Raelians' love of rampant, protected nookie – the cult wholeheartedly supports abortion, the development of nuclear power, mucking around thoroughly with genetically modified food, and enthusiastically engineering the genetics of humans. That's enough to put three-quarters of the world's lobby groups in hospital with severely clenched sphincters, a fact not lost on Rael. Controversy means publicity, and publicity means Rael's mug on screens and magazines. Rael likey.

But doing whatever you like with your body (with almost whoever you like) as a Raelian does not extend to things that are likely to besmirch your gorgeous alien-designed meat carriage. Cigarettes, drugs, excessive alcohol, coffee and tea are frowned upon as they cloud people's ability to be the best experiments they can be in their genetically engineered bodies. Raelians will happily, and nudely, hand out condoms and advice for coming to terms with your own asshole during their seminars, but do not expect a steaming cup of International Roast anywhere near the conference room.

Building alien embassies and keeping Rael's leisure suits clean is an expensive undertaking, so Raelians are expected to give the movement ten per cent of their income for embassy purposes and an extra one per cent to facilitate Rael's leadership and speaking tours and presumably elastic bands for his topknot. By all reports though, tithing isn't all that robustly enforced, and donations for various Raelian projects of debatable efficacy are sought instead. Playing the long game, members are strongly encouraged to leave generous considerations for the Raelian movement in their wills, something sure to delight bereaved family members.

A large proportion of the Raelians' cash flow comes from the sale of books, available in multiple languages, that explain Rael's message and extensively complex theories, and there are absolutely loads of them. You can get the main gist of the whole Raelian belief system just from the titles, which are almost without exception explanatory to the point of obvious, and absolutely crammed with spoilers. Still, the books are undeniably the kind of thing you'd take off the shelf in the shop and flip over to see what they're on about, provided you're not easily offended by low-budget, unsophisticated graphic design.

Want to know about Rael's attitude towards evolution? You could start with the book *Intelligent Design: Message from the Designers*, to hear all about how we came about and what bits of the Bible really mean from an alien perspective. A good one to follow up with might be *The Message Given to Me by Extra-Terrestrials: They Took Me to Their Planet*, especially if you want to hear about the time Rael saw himself recreated in a big clone-making microwave oven on the Elohim planet and how he relaxed afterwards with a cluster of nubile sex-robots before zooming around with his anti-gravity belt. I mean, if you're into that kind of thing.

The self-explanatory literary journey continues with gusto, from *Sensual Meditation: Awakening the Mind by Awakening the Body*, in which you can learn how to nudge each of your senses awake while sitting naked in your living room, and how to free yourself from those fuddy-duddy medieval scientists that told us masturbation causes blindness. It broadens with *The Book that Tells the Truth*, which feels like it's as likely to tell the truth as one of those clothing stores that has the word 'Fashion' on the sign outside, yet very few fashionable items inside.

We can learn about whether Raelians say yes or no to human cloning in *Yes to Human Cloning: Eternal Life Thanks to Science*, and we can find out if humans were created scientifically by reading *Humans Were Created Scientifically*, a volume that comes printed in a handy, easy-to-read Manga version. In all of the books – whether teaching about the theory of Geniocracy, in which societies are run by a ruling class of geniuses, or the vaguely sexist *Let's Welcome Our Fathers from Space* – Rael carefully reminds us that our bodies are our own, and what our histories and destinies are as a race, and that he is a super-sexy genius from outer space. Mind you, he can remind us of that with just a wink and a smile. Oh, Rael.

For the more technologically advanced or time-poor, the Raelian message is succinctly – but by no means stylishly – packaged into digestible three-to-five-minute chunks on RaelTV, the cult's YouTube channel. The number of cults using YouTube as a way of promoting themselves, recruiting, and keeping their message consistent is increasing, reducing the need for resource-heavy on-the-street recruiting and the inconvenience of costly physical isolation. You don't need a remote compound with expensive electric fences if your followers are already self-isolating in their bedrooms with their computers. If your content is what those people are looking for, you can join an entire tribe of people together while they're sitting by themselves, for just the cost of an internet connection.

So we've read the books and we've had our coding uploaded to a spaceship and we've accepted that we're genetic experiments engineered by aliens and we've gone to a seminar where we got a massage from an old guy with a grey ponytail. It all seems quite harmless, and while some of the things we've heard and read don't necessarily seem like they're provable and true, we don't feel like we've been lied to either. The leader makes us feel good and hopeful and sexy, and all he asks for in return is a very affordable amount of money and our undivided attention and admiration. That should probably be enough. Let's stop it there.

Let's not stop it there, says Rael.

In 1997, less than a year after legitimate, university-supported scientists cloned the first sheep and called it 'Dolly', the Rael-supported company called Clonaid was born. Clonaid was an offshoot of the Raelian company Valiant Venture, which sounds like the kind of company someone's dad in an eighties teen movie would work at, and was originally based in the Bahamas like all reputable and definitely true scientific human cloning companies are. The purpose of Clonaid, headed up by Raelian senior bishop Brigitte Boisselier, was to clone humans. The company's public message focused on a mission assisting infertile or gay couples to have a child containing the DNA of the parents, provided they helped fund Clonaid's research and equipment via substantial financial contributions. Donations were also sought from parents whose children had died at a young age, with a potential promise to recreate their child via cloning. Certainly, those parents could be seen to benefit most from cloning, but put another way, you could be at least part-way forgiven for suggesting that Clonaid targeted emotionally vulnerable, low-hanging fruit for their funding.

In hypothetical parentheses next to Clonaid's mission statement was the whole immortality thing. Sure, couples that couldn't normally have children containing parental DNA can now have children containing parental DNA, but more importantly we take a giant leap towards the next phase of humankind. You remember the next phase: everyone lives forever, sex is just for pleasure, pizza party fun time every day until the end of never.

Additionally, to indulge their love of cloning, asking people for money, and making up names for stuff, the Raelians also started programs called Clonapet – for storing the DNA of treasured pets for future cloning – and Insuraclone – for storing the DNA of treasured people for future cloning. Both programs were very much built on the donate a lot of money now, reap the benefits once we've figured out how to do it later model, a Raelian special skill.

Brigitte Boisselier, a legitimately trained scientist with high levels of expertise in things that aren't necessarily cloning, went about gathering both donations and very high tech cloning equipment. Whether or not Clonaid was going to be able to produce a cloned human was – and is still – in question, but whether or not Clonaid was going to be able to produce a heaving mountain of publicity was clearer.

Unbelievably, not everybody in the world was excited when Clonaid announced its intentions to clone humans. In some parts of the world it was illegal to even try it, in other parts governments refused to fund it and strongly discouraged private companies from attempting it, and in any of the parts that contained religious people who got miffed whenever anyone except God played god it was frowned upon very hard indeed, using all the forehead muscles. The Vatican and other religious organisations unsurprisingly condemned Clonaid's intention to mess with God's normal procreation plan, and the Food and Drug Administration in the US hindered their plans further insisting that their permission, which they were not prepared to give, was required before any cloning was allowed to occur. But Rael was undaunted. He'd met God, and God said it was fine. Nobody would tell where the cloning was happening, or nobody knew, but high executives in the Raelians and in Clonaid assured everybody that it definitely was happening.

In December 2002, Brigitte Boisselier announced that a child called – at least in press conferences – 'Baby Eve' had been born as the result of Clonaid's cloning process. Boisselier claimed Eve had American parents, but was born outside America, and that . . . that was about it. No verified pictures of the baby, certainly no DNA evidence of the child being a genetic clone of its mother, and no actual proof that the baby was even real. The publicity was exceptionally real though, with Clonaid – and by default the Raelians – being frenziedly discussed on a global scale and parodied on *Saturday Night Live* a little bit.

But in for a penny, in for a pound, and in the ensuing months Boisselier announced four more cloned baby births and even produced a photograph of a newborn in an incubator in hospital to support her claim. It may not have been made clear to Brigitte the kind of material fussy journalists, governments, and high court judges deem 'acceptable evidence', however it's reasonably certain that snapshots from a possibly random delivery ward of a baby that could be anybody's are not it. Boisselier claimed that all five babies were in perfect health, which was a relief. It's always so sad to see fictional little babies suffer.

The Raelians continued to claim they were cloning humans as an ongoing project, hinting that many important people and celebrities had secretly backed them with funds and DNA, hoping to get their important selves replicated someday. The claims were accompanied with the usual Raelian level of deep, convincing evidence. None, mostly.

It's not all roses, puppies, UFOs, and book royalties, though. The Raelism movement has been the victim of persecution by many, many enemies, mostly people in governments that prefer organisations to do unreasonable things like pay tax, tell the truth, and not claim they've made world-changing scientific advances without providing any proof.

When the French government did that stereotypically French-sounding scoffing laugh at the Raelians' plea to be seen as a proper religion for tax purposes, the religious movement found themselves in dangerous arrears for tax they were supposed to pay on book sales, the cads. Rather than pay the tax, the Raelians went underground, feigning disbandment, the cads.

When the Raelians handed out brochures to the parents of Catholic school children in Geneva claiming that their kids were at a much higher risk of being interfered with by priests than most people, the local vicar sued them for libel. He was unsuccessful, because the judge rightfully pointed out that the Raelians weren't denouncing *all* Catholics. Just. You know. The ones that try to have sex with children. In fact, the Catholic church had a number of objections towards the Raelians' obsession with nitpicking their religion, kicking up a stink when, for example, Raelian followers handed out crucifixes to high-school students in Montreal and invited them to throw them into a fire. Rael and the Pope have a long-standing bitch-fight, and if they don't make up soon people will assume they're in love.

Rael's stance on cloning had him about-faced by South Korean customs when he tried to enter the country for a sensual meditation seminar, and Rael does *not* like being said no to. He claimed that Catholics in the Korean government were behind the decision to deny him entry, because he can*not* just let that

Catholic thing lie. He instructed his followers across the world to protest the ban outside their South Korean embassies, loudly and proudly. In some areas, upwards of six or seven protesters showed up.

It's virtually impossible to tell if Rael believes his own theories and stories, or if he's a straight-out charlatan, in it for the money and glory. One thing is absolutely certain though, visible from pop star to racing car driver to leader of a global cult proclaiming to be Jesus's half-brother and trying to convince people he can clone babies: Rael is an absolute slut for attention, and he's very good at getting it. You can't fault him for realising that, if you're going to be merely mediocre at your first two career choices, invent a third career where you're a prophet of the gods. And the more Rael's followers see him on websites, television, and in the news, the more convinced they are that he's an important person to be listened to.

Now preferring to be referred to as 'Maitreya Rael', 'Maitreya' being more or less the Buddhist version of a returning prophet, Rael and his movement haven't really seemed to have done much harm. It's not a fantastic human trait to ask people to pay for an embassy that has no tangible prospects of being built, based on a story that has the storyteller as its most important character. But all things considered, particularly after tales of mass suicides, gas attacks, sexual abuse, and blatant, legitimate fraud, if you absolutely had to join a cult, you could do worse than the Raelians.

Still. Best not to, eh.

RAJNEESHEES

IAN LESLIE, A reporter for the Australian *60 Minutes* program, sat across from Ma Anand Sheela, the deputy of the leader of a religious group that originated in India called the Rajneeshees, on camera. The interview had reached a tense point, where Ian had started to question Sheela about the group's habit of infiltrating and overtaking towns around the world with hundreds of orange-clad group members. The movement had a commune in Fremantle in Western Australia and was planning on opening another near Pemberton in the same state, which was really starting to get on everybody's wick. The Rajneeshees had an undeniable talent for pissing people off. Sheela was, without doubt, the powerhouse that generated that talent.

'Sheela, whatever your plans are, we don't want the Rajneeshees. We don't want the Orange People in our town,' said Ian, referring to the nickname many people gave to the cult members' preference for dressing in citrus hues. It's likely that he had a fair idea of who he was talking to and would have known how deliciously inflammatory that statement would have been to her.

'What can I say?' responded Sheela, ice water in her veins, predictably rising to the barb. 'Tough titties.'

It was a defining and memorable moment for the Rajneeshee cult, and one of the very rare times that the phrase 'tough titties' has ever been heard on a serious prime-time current affairs program. How fitting that it was in bloody Australia, by a bloody sheila called Sheela. You can still buy t-shirts that bear Sheela's image accompanied by the emblazoned phrase 'Tough Titties'. People are weird.

Sheela was only the second in charge of the Rajneeshees, but a clear frontrunner in the Most Influential Cult Leader's Assistant of All Time pageant. But we can't talk about Sheela without talking about the Bhagwan. Bhagwan Shree Rajneesh – who will just be called 'the Bhagwan' from this point forward to save time – was a calm, reassuring guru with a twinkle in his eye, an array of natty headwear, a long beard, and an almost obsessive devotion to his favourite chair. The Bhagwan delivered almost all of his lectures from a stage to rapturous hundreds while he sat, almost engulfed, in an outrageously comfortable-looking winged armchair that nannas in nursing homes would certainly kill for. If the Bhagwan had knitted a blanket in that chair with a tabby cat on his lap, it would not have looked out of place.

Originally an incredibly widely read professor of philosophy, the Bhagwan realised pretty early that the philosophical statements of others – lightly bastardised and delivered with big eyes, a long beard, a guru vibe, and an armchair – were like crack to middle-class white people who were spending their gap year looking for easy-access enlightenment. The winning formula was expanded to include a healthy enthusiasm for wealth, hedonism, and sex, so it was a dream combo for thousands who wanted to feel spiritual without having to give up their luxuries and nookie.

The Bhagwan attracted attention – and subsequently followers – by emphasising the points of difference between his movement and more traditional religions, and by making outrageous statements for attention. He referred to Gandhi as the cleanest ignorant man in the world and badmouthed him based on his policy of shunning technology and affluence. The Bhagwan wrote literally hundreds of books about tantric sex, love, meditation, and self-improvement, endearing himself to even more potential followers, particularly those in the patchouli-scented and self-help sections of the bookshop.

You could barely invent a religious movement or guru more perfect for attracting middle- and upper-class Western followers looking for enlightenment into its billowy folds. It ticked pretty much all of the criteria. For one, it appeared and flourished during the explosion of new religious movements of the late seventies and early eighties, when people with spare time found traditional religion more and more irrelevant, and went in search of something cooler, sexier, and more contemporary. It combined at least a surface veneer of Eastern mysticism – the coolest and sexiest of mysticisms at the time – with a healthy respect for capitalism and funny jokes. It advocated meditation, laughter, organic vegetables, love, peace, and sex, and invited those with suitable amounts of money and time to come and lay their heads on its lap. Plus it was based in India, the jewel in the hippie-attracting tourism crown, so you knew it had to be good.

The Bhagwan set up an ashram in Pune, a busy and relatively affluent city southeast of Mumbai. The ashram was gorgeous, green, peaceful, and would definitely have been given at least a four-star review on TripAdvisor. Tens of thousands of Americans, Australians and Western Europeans flocked to its nicely mani-cured six acres of spiritual-seeming resort-esque grounds.

A bonus of the Pune ashram being gated and separated from normal day-to-day Indian life outside was that it allowed Western visitors to feel like they were on a pilgrimage, but also let them visit the India they imagined without having to deal with the real India down the street – the dirtier, less-hygienic, more poverty-stricken one that would have made them feel guilty. It cost a lot to visit the ashram, which made sense – it would be silly for a guru to espouse the virtues of being wealthy without the same guru ensuring that you had to give him some of your own money to hear him say it.

The Bhagwan knew what he was doing when he named things around the place, too. It's unlikely that any scholar of Indian religion would entertain the idea that the Bhagwan was a proper guru teaching proper, traditional Indian religious tenets, but the title 'Bhagwan' – or more correctly 'Bhagavan' – loosely means 'guru' or 'god' in Hinduism. He called his followers 'sannyasins', which in Sanskrit refers to someone who has renounced their material possessions and emotional ties to live as spiritual a life as possible. For a guy who really liked material possessions, calling his followers sannyasins was a good way to remind them that, look, possessions were super-important to him, and in theory they're also good for you, but it's even better if you give yours to him. To be fair, the Bhagwan stressed that, in his movement, sannyasins renounced their egos rather than their possessions, again a principle that didn't seem to altogether apply to the Bhagwan himself. Traditionally Indian sannyasins wear yellow, orange, or ochre-coloured clothing, so the Bhagwan threw that requirement of his followers into the package for good measure. Nothing like feeling you belong to a free-spirited group like the vague appearance of a uniform, eh?

So. The Bhagwan managed to get everyone to flock to his ashram, but what would they do while they were there?

They would wear orange and red clothes like good little sannyasins and accessorise their outfits with necklaces featuring a picture of the Bhagwan on a medallion like good little feeders of guru-based narcissism.

They would listen to the Bhagwan who, in his gentle, assured, carefully enunciated way would hold daily lectures called 'discourses' in which he'd discuss his philosophies, sometimes in English and sometimes in Hindi, for a couple of hours to a rapt crowd. The discourses would take place in the morning, and on most afternoons the Bhagwan would entertain smaller audiences and initiate new sannyasins, giving them a new name and their Bhagwan necklace. Just something to remember him by, in case the trip to India specifically to listen to him speak wasn't enough of a reminder. By all reports and a fair whack of video evidence, the Bhagwan was an incredible speaker, mixing philosophy and psychology with liberal doses of humour and risqué jokes, like the Benny Hill of the subcontinent.

Followers would have loads and loads and loads of sex, because the Bhagwan preached that the release of sexual energy and being in touch with yourself as a sexual person was the well-lubricated road to enlightenment. You had to face your sexual inhibitions to rise above them, so organised sexual encounters were sometimes quite confronting and, to those not aware of the theory behind them and the consent of the participants, might have looked more than a little bit rapey. Even in the gentler encounters, sannyasins were encouraged to have the loudest, wildest, freest, most spontaneous sex they could, with as many people as they liked. As a result, they also spent a fair chunk of their time treating loads and loads and loads of gonorrhoea, extremely regularly.

And perhaps more frequently than any other activity, they meditated. Devotees of Rajneeshism weren't just doing your stereotypical bog-standard sit-cross-legged-and-say-ohm meditation either. A number of different types of meditation were practised in the ashram, but by far the most noteworthy was a type of meditation that the Bhagwan would probably claim he invented called 'dynamic meditation'. He claimed that Westerners found it difficult to sit quietly and shut up for any length of time, so borrowing greatly from primal scream therapy, bioenergetics, and tantric practice he popularised a five-step progression of meditations that let the feisty Occidental pilgrims really shake their sillies out.

In the first stage, meditators are asked to breathe 'chaotically', that is, deeply but without a recognisable rhythm – fast, slow, randomly – a breathing style that apologetically almost induces hyperventilation just by reading about it (sorry). The idea is to 'become dreamy' which is Bhagwan-speak for 'not have enough oxygen', presumably to sharpen the senses while they struggle, on your behalf, to remain conscious.

The second stage, cutely called 'catharsis', is about releasing all those emotions that it might be embarrassing to release in the supermarket, at work, or in the doctor's waiting room. See, according to the Bhagwan, if you don't let your emotions out they get internalised and trapped at a muscular level, which could end up poisoning you, science says so. So this is the stage where you let everything out, loudly, freely, and with abandon, all over the place like a mad lady's custard. This is the bit where everybody shouts, screams, wails, and looks proper bonkers. It's the bit that gets on the news.

Third stage? Literally just jump on the spot for ten minutes. Put your hands in the air! Shout 'HOO!' every time you land! You might feel exhausted, but KEEP JUMPING. Ten minutes of just jumping is a really long time, but you'll discover energy reserves you never knew existed, and you'll find out exactly how many people are willing to jump up and down shouting 'HOO' in the same room as you. The answer is ALL OF THEM, keep GOING.

Then STOP, or as kindergarten teachers across the world are fond of saying: FREEZE. The fourth stage is in contrast to the third stage, and you must be like a dead statue – admittedly an out-of-breath statue dressed in orange. Don't move, and let your mind be quiet. Sure, you've just been jumping up and down for ten minutes, but please stop gasping for breath and concentrate. Honestly the complete and utter exhaustion should make this stage easy. Shhhhh.

The fifth and final stage is dance and celebration, presumably celebrating the fact that your dynamic meditation practice is almost over for another day. Shake your booty if you have any strength left at all, you deserve it. Okay, little secret: you also deserve to keep any money you earn and wear whatever colour you like, but we get it, you're spiritual, go nuts.

Customers – or rather their preferred term 'sannyasins' – lapped this shit up. LOVED it. They kept arriving, kept buying books, kept wearing their necklaces, and even started attending satellite ashrams and retreats that began to pop up in their home countries, with all profits dribbling back to the Bhagwan.

There's absolutely no way of knowing what the Bhagwan's and the Rajneeshees' path would have been without the undeniable and gargantuan influence of Ma Anand Sheela – familiarly just 'Sheela'. Born in India but college-educated in the United States, Sheela became an instant convert to Rajneeshism upon her first meeting of the Bhagwan in the late sixties when she was a teenager. The Rajneeshees without Sheela would certainly have been titanically less interesting, and realistically far less prone to wandering deep into criminal territory. Gurus come and go, and the Bhagwan was an okay guru, but as a figurehead he really could have been any one of a number of people and the story would still be more or less the same as long as Sheela was involved. There has never been, and will likely never be again, a person like Sheela. Thank fuck.

Sheela replaced the considerably less efficient Ma Yoga Laxmi as the Bhagwan's top assistant in 1981, as Laxmi had let the Bhagwan down when he gave her an assignment – to find new places the movement could expand into. Laxmi's father was wealthy and supportive, which made her a usable resource in the ashram's early start-up years, but now that the Bhagwan had established a reasonably steady inward flow of cash, he needed someone with more grit, more organisational ability, and more open-faced malevolence.

Sheela was a driven, uncompromising woman with an unquenchable thirst for attention, unbridled ambition and a superhuman appetite for power. There would simply be no point arguing with Sheela about any topic, and her undiagnosed but certainly existing narcissistic personality disorder means that she feels free to be 100 per cent right about everything without an iota of regret. Empathy is simply not a word that Sheela had time for and, if offered any, she would no doubt tell you to stick it up your arse. If you were to describe Sheela in the mildest terms you could think of, you would still probably use the words 'malicious', 'evil', and 'bitch', with a handful of swear-jar worthy words in ready reserve.

But here's the thing: anybody who wouldn't hire Sheela is an idiot. If you could convince Sheela to be loyal to you, she'd be the best employee you ever had, no question. She'd work tire-lessly, never taking no for an answer. She'd keep going until the job was done, bulldoze over anyone with a roadblock or contra-dictory opinion, and – where necessary and as long as you were still on her side – fiercely protect you from other people, bad press, and tiresome reams of red tape. If you had Sheela's loyalty, she'd walk across hot coals for you, and those hot coals would probably be the burning skulls of your enemies. Say what you like about her bedside manner, but Sheela . . . Got. Shit. Done.

By the late seventies, the Indian government was a bit over the Rajneeshees, and decided enough was enough. They weren't convinced that the obviously thriving business's tax exemption was all that legitimate, and the super-sexy doctrines and unbridled birth control and abortion support of the sort-of religion were not popular with the considerably more conservative larger Indian society. The Bhagwan was anti-marriage and pro-wealth in a country that was not affluent and extremely into traditional marriage. The government was also deaf to the Bhagwan's applications for more land to open additional, larger retreats, as they had enough trouble with the existing one.

In addition to the unwelcome attention and increased restrictions applied by the Indian government, the Pune ashram was running out of room, which was limiting its earning capacity. There were Rajneeshee centres in a number of different countries by this time, and the cash from donations and meditation course fees flowed towards the Bhagwan in a steady river, but the Bhagwan had expensive tastes. The more earning potential and higher accessibility the ashram where you could come face to face with your guru was, the more Rolls-Royces he could own. He already had two Rolls-Royces, but his target number was a nice round 100. He loved having the celebration of capitalism as one of his religion's main tenets, and his ashram even sold souvenir bumper stickers that read 'Jesus Saves. Moses Invests.

Bhagwan Spends'. Regardless of the comical whimsy of your bumper stickers though, being out of favour with the government of a crowded country makes it irritatingly difficult to find and procure large tracts of land for the purposes of cult-building, so all things considered, it was probably time for the Bhagwan to consider his options.

It was also around this time that the guru decided that he could free up a lot of the time that he currently spent doing guru stuff – giving discourses and taking initiation meetings – if he stopped talking. Shutting up would also help him avoid answering tricky questions thrown at him by people from irritating places like the tax department, too. When you're a religious guru and you don't want to answer your critics, you have a unique technique available to you: you can take a vow of silence and tell everyone that it's for religious reasons, which is exactly what the Bhagwan did. He shut his gob one day and it stayed mostly shut for almost four years. Politicians and celebrities who don't want to answer their critics can at best feign laryngitis for a few days, but religion has cute ways of excusing and legitimising all sorts of behaviour, so the Bhagwan just opted out of talking to anybody except Sheela. Luckily for him, Sheela was only too happy to feed her ravenous hunger for attention and step in as spokesperson at every opportunity, including those she created for herself. As all of the Bhagwan's decisions were then being channelled and distributed through Sheela, it's impossible to know how many of the programs and practices she put in place were actually his, and how many bore only the Sheela management seal of authenticity. Sheela was in the rare position where nobody could – and arguably still can't – tell if she was the puppet or the puppeteer.

The Bhagwan was clearly on a winner with his first-world-spiritual-pilgrims-with-spending-money formula, and he didn't want the Indian government crumpling the corners of his golden ticket. He figured – and you can hardly blame him in theory at least – that if people were willing to give him money to be their guru, then he'd be an idiot not to make it as easy as possible for them to do that. If you can get a big bunch of money-spending Westerners to come all the way to India, imagine how many more you could attract if you were actually based in the West. The Pune ashram was somewhere Westerners visited for a while, with a relatively small group wanting to stay for good. The Bhagwan figured the big cash was in making permanent residency in his digs a highly accessible thing for people willing to pay for it.

But where in the West? The answer to that question raises a number of classic cult red flags. It had to be isolated so that they could carry on their religious practices quietly and minimise outside interference. The more remote the location, the more your followers can feel like their compound is the entire world, and the harder it is for non-Rajneeshee concepts and arguments to reach their ears. They needed a lot of room, because more room means more people, and more people means more money and power. They needed enough land to be self-reliant so they could be in contact with, and indebted to, as few outsiders as possible. And they needed a place where the locals would probably be a pushover.

Probably.

The Bhagwan had entrusted Sheela with the task of finding just the right spot, because he knew she'd throw herself at the job until it was done. In 1981 Sheela chose a spot called the Big Muddy Ranch, an area of roughly 64,000 acres running between Currant Creek and Big Muddy Road just southeast of the town of Antelope in Wasco County, Oregon, which is exactly as remote as it sounds. Antelope had a population of just under fifty people, with an average age of sixty years old. That's right. Party town.

Sheela quickly snapped up the ranch for just shy of six million US dollars, knowing it would serve the Bhagwan's purposes perfectly – so quickly that she forgot to check the small print in Oregonian law relating to land laws. Basically, if you want to buy a massive ranch and only use it for farming with a small number of workers, you're all sweet. If you want to buy a massive ranch and use it for a community of a couple of thousand people living as self-sufficiently as possible with lots of buildings though, you have a bit of a problem.

The residents of Antelope looked slightly sideways at what they saw as encroaching hippies at first, but mostly just rolled their eyes. I mean, they didn't get a small group of orange-wearing dingbats of various races planning to start a little farming community in these parts very often, but they could probably live with it as long as the newcomers kept quiet and didn't steal anyone's cooling apple pies from their windowsills. They didn't want to be seen as racist, or as if they, as good Christians, wouldn't welcome a bunch of pagan strangers who talk funny and live in flagrant sin with open arms.

However, the attitude of the locals towards the 'farming community' changed gradually as they realised the scope of the development that was beginning to occur on the land. Sheela, in a fetching yellow hard hat, was sending in the bulldozers, shipping in the wageless workers and laying the foundations, and it soon became apparent that she was building a city. The eyes of the Oregonians began to twitch.

Realising it was time to familiarise herself with local zoning laws, initially Sheela convinced county planners that they were just building accommodation for 150 workers, but gently hinted that there might be thousands of people coming to farm at some time in the future. For such a large, neglected area, it would take a lot of manpower to transform the land to an arable, working farm. Credit where credit is due, though – the transformation the Rajneeshees wrought on the neglected land was astounding. They cleared more than 30,000 acres of it, planted wheat, fruit, and vegetables, and even dammed the creek running through the ranch to form a downright charming reservoir. Officially called Rajneeshpuram but nicknamed 'Rancho Rajneesh', what had formerly been dust, mud, and weeds became a lush, green, organised, arable paradise. Within its first year in Oregon the cult had transformed the land permanently for the better, but the Antelope locals knew they were up to something. Surrounding towns were doing a roaring trade supplying the compound with industrial steel, piping, and building materials, so despite their willingness to accept their business, with that volume of building materials, something was definitely up. Lots and lots of buildings were up.

Rajneeshpuram, now far from being the Big Muddy Ranch, was about to have a massive assembly area, a medical clinic, accommodation houses, a shopping mall, a hotel, a water treatment facility, restaurants, a power station, a school, and a goddamn mini-airport. The locals weren't having it. They gathered together into a loud group full of people with exactly the kind of haircuts you'd expect from late-middle-aged people in the 1980s.

Loyal sannyasins worked their arses off for ridiculous chunks of the day to get food on the table for up to 2000 residents, clean their clothes, tend their crops, maintain their buildings, keep their vehicles in running order, and if they had any energy left whatsoever, have a bit of sex with a few people. In a remarkable stroke of luck, the Bhagwan had already taught them that hard physical labour was a form of meditation, so they toiled gladly and serenely. They'd given up all their money to the Bhagwan, but look what they had in return! Food, accommodation, a purpose, a mild burning sensation whenever they went to the toilet, a lack of autonomy, and no need or invitation to think for themselves. It was sort of paradise, if you looked at it quickly in a dim light and squinted.

The Antelope locals weren't convinced that the rural utopia was legitimate, and they knew for sure it wasn't welcome in these parts. They nagged local and state government to intervene, and people in the offices that count began to look into how the development regulations affecting the compound had been adhered to and the immigration status of its residents. On the other side, it didn't take much for the Rajneeshees to fling a libel suit against anyone who said bad things about them, and there are even stories of counter-intimidation, like Rajneeshees shining bright lights into the windows of Antelopians in the middle of the night, and other kindergarten-level tactics. Things were getting increasingly tense and uptight, and it was really mucking around with everybody's retirement and/or meditation schedule, depending on which side of Rajneeshpuram's fence you lived on.

The Rajneeshees realised that the only way to get around the strict land laws in Oregon that prohibited development of exactly the kind they were planning was to get involved with the local government and subvert the laws, the crafty buggers. They worked smarter, not harder, although admittedly they worked *unbelievably* hard.

Starting small and locally, Rajneeshees started buying up property in Antelope in an attempt to outnumber its existing residents. They also took over the café and general store, which they renamed 'Zorba the Buddha'. The Bhagwan loved the idea of Zorba the Buddha, a mix of Eastern philosophy and Western hedonism. He was also quite partial to the idea of taking over a tiny Oregonian town. Ignoring the grumbling of the locals, in 1982 the Rajneeshee community flourished and petitioned to be incorporated as a city in its own right, a process which was subject to vote. With a blossoming population that easily eclipsed that of the locals the Rajneeshees won the election and – after winning some appeals forced by upset outsiders – became a city. As a city, it was no longer subject to the land laws that stated it could only be a limited agricultural community, so it forged ahead with its own public transport, state–trained police force, and a mayor.

Additionally, enough Rajneeshees moved into Antelope to represent a majority in the town's council elections, so when the long-term residents of Antelope held a vote to disincorporate Antelope as a town to prevent the takeover, they were outnumbered, despite their catchy slogan of 'Better Dead Than Red' – a disappointing waste of banners and t-shirts. Through planning, intimidation, and sheer numbers, the takeover of Antelope and its transformation into the city of Rajneesh was pretty much complete. Residents who remained were now subject to taxes imposed by the Rajneeshees, and had to put up with some of their whimsical digs, such as calling the local waste station The Adolf Hitler Recycling Centre. Oh, Rajneeshees. Such wags.

The Bhagwan remained in silence, meeting with Sheela every evening and slowly amassing more and more Rolls-Royces along with his other addictions: expensive watches, expensive eyewear, Valium, and nitrous oxide. His followers worked and meditated and revelled in their self-sufficiency, loving life in between bouts of STDs and living for their daily glimpse of the Bhagwan. By now their leader owned ninety-three Rolls-Royces, and every day at around 2 pm he would do a slow drive-by along the main road of Rajneeshpuram, where hundreds and hundreds of rapturous followers were waiting to see him and throw flowers at his car. The Bhagwan was flanked by Sheela, other executive-level assistants, and gun-toting bodyguards, because you can never be too careful when you're heading out for a Diet Coke in one of your luxury cars after almost obliterating a tiny local community.

The Bhagwan was aiming for a total of 100 Rolls-Royces – a nice round number – because he figured that nothing displays a commitment to the principle of religious luxury like an utterly obscene number of cars worth millions of dollars. He claimed – through Sheela, of course – that the cars were a symbol of his followers' love for him, purchased as they were with their life savings and vegetarian sweat. An extremely enjoyable side-effect for the Bhagwan – and Sheela, of course, was the media attention that owning ninety-three Rolls-Royces attracted. He became nicknamed 'The Rolls-Royce guru', a far superior nick-name than 'Beardy McSexyPants'.

In November 1984, Wasco county, of which Rajneeshpuram was a part, was preparing for its county court election, and two Rajneeshee members were petitioning to become candidates for positions on the three-person council. Neither candidate managed to get enough signatures to become actual campaigning hopefuls, because county elections are way, way harder to fix than tiny little Antelope town elections. The only thing for it was to try and vote in the non-Rajneeshee candidates that were nonetheless sympathetic to the fledgling movement and try to prevent hostile candidates from being elected.

There are two ways to win an election. The first is to have as many people as possible vote for the candidates you want. The second is to have as few people as possible voting for their opposition. It follows, then, that there are two good ways to rig an election, and if there's one thing that Sheela desperately wanted to do at this point, it was to rig an election. And this particular industrious little go-getter was more than willing to try both ways.

Firstly, Sheela wanted to have as many people as possible voting for the Rajneeshee-friendly guys.

Secondly, Sheela wanted to have as few people as possible voting for the opposition, the Rajneeshee-unfriendly guys.

To achieve the first goal, the cult scoured as many nearby big cities as they could get to for homeless people. Rajneeshpuram had amassed eighty-five school buses to facilitate their own public transport system, so they sprayed themselves out in all directions, well equipped with empty bus seats to fill with easily manipulated people. Rajneeshees would hop off the bus, find suitable needy folk, and offer them three meals a day and a bed in Oregon if they were prepared to come with them. The technique was hugely successful and around 4000 homeless people were transported to Rajneeshpuram.

In addition to the food and accommodation, the new 'recruits' were also offered a couple of plastic cups of beer per day, including a bonus surprise. The bonus surprise was that the beer secretly contained a generous helping of tranquillisers. The homeless people were drugged without their knowledge to keep them calm and complacent, which is the kind of thing that happens when a cult uses human cattle to serve its own purposes. The only thing that was expected of the new arrivals in return for being fed and housed (and drugged) was for them to register to vote and turn up for the Wasco County election. The Rajneeshees enthusiastically promoted their own humanitarian efforts and called the exercise the 'Share-A-Home' program, because the 'Rig-An-Election' program just didn't have the same jaunty tone to it.

Alas, the Oregon Secretary of State twigged to the Rajneeshees' devious game and insisted that any new voters be interviewed before allowing them to register, to determine how serious they were about staying on in Oregon after the election, a requirement for voter registration. Typical bureaucrats, trying to thwart fraud by asking the one question in an interview that would expose fraud. The first plan, of making sure there were enough people to vote the good guys in, was a bust.

To achieve the second goal, of having as few people as possible voting for the opposition, Sheela had a cunning and almost impressively diabolical plan whereby she would poison the county's water supply on election day. Just straight out poison people, without a howdy do or a thank you very much. A couple of sannyasins who worked in the Rajneeshpuram medical centre had been dabbling for a while with cute little strains of salmonella and typhoid, and fiddling around with various strains of the AIDS virus for fun in their spare time, so it wasn't a brand new, surprising addition to the cult's spiritual journey to start intentionally poisoning people. Sheela wanted to poison the town's water supply just before election day to keep everybody at home on the toilet instead of at the polling booths. Sheela, in case you're still in any doubt, was not a nice lady. As so many cults know though, poisoning thousands of people is really hard, so Sheela decided there should be a few practice runs.

First, when three county commissioners visited the ranch for a standard fact-finding go-see, Sheela offered the two commissioners she didn't like glasses of water laced with salmonella, if not for shits and giggles, then certainly at least for shits. Both became ill, one to the point of hospitalisation, because you don't mess with Sheela under any circumstances. The commissioner the Rajneeshees did like downed his untainted glass of water in a few gulps, thanked them very much, and went on his way unscathed.

Next up, Sheela decided to affect the voting community on a larger scale. She and a handful of other high-ranking Rajneeshees tried sprinkling salmonella on produce in a supermarket and smearing it on door handles in the courthouse, but there were no appreciable results. Abandoning attempts to infect people who were buying fresh produce or visiting courthouses, they decided to try some places where they could be sure Wasco County voters would actually go: fast-food joints. Targeting ten restaurants that had salad bars in The Dalles, the largest city in Wasco County and home to its council, sannyasins were despatched to sprinkle salmonella all over the exposed food and into the tubs of salad dressing. They each wandered up to a salad bar, discreetly opened plastic bags full of brown liquid they had concealed in their clothing, and drizzled a light salmonella jus into the vinaigrette or ranch dressing. Shakey's Pizza, Taco Time, Burgerville – no quaintly named restaurant was safe, and soon more than 750 townsfolk were shitting and vomiting their way through mid-to-late September 1984. If you're wondering why you just don't see as many salad bars as you used to, you can thank the Rajneeshees for part of that answer.

Health authorities investigated – albeit inadequately considering their findings – and decided that the cause of the salmonella epidemic was poor food-handling practices. For seven per cent of the population of a town to get sick from poor food handling, the authorities must have thought restaurant staff had dropped their own stools directly into the salad bar. It was only a year later, when they realised that the Rajneeshees were not just a cute and feisty little mob just outside of Antelope but a victory-at-all-costs cult with a biochemistry lab, that authorities linked the poisoning to the actual poisoners.

Even though their poisoning plot wasn't traced back to them until long after the election, Sheela and her in-cahoots compadres were spooked, and abandoned their plan to poison the water supply. Like a petulant toddler, Sheela loudly proclaimed that elections were stupid anyway, and only dumb jerks vote in them.

Canny Wasco County residents knew quite well that the Rajneeshees were keen to have sympathetic representation on the council, so they turned up to the election in droves to make sure they weren't successful. Unsurprisingly, the failure to influence the election pissed Sheela off, and rather than attributing blame to herself and her own failure, she relied on her usual trope of blaming racism and religious bigotry. That's right, Sheela. It's not that people don't like you because you tried to poison a town. It's because you have brown skin and a guru.

Now, the problem with bussing in thousands of homeless people to rig an election is that, after the election, you're left with thousands of homeless people. The new 'recruits' could be grouped into three categories: those who realised that the Rajneeshee lifestyle was exactly what they needed, who adopted its principles and practices with gusto; those who didn't really care about the Rajneeshee lifestyle but quite liked free food and accommodation; and those who were legitimately dangerous and not altogether comfortable around people. The latter category is often homeless and needy because they do not have access to the treatments and care that they need and have mental health conditions that need attention. And for all the communal doctrines Rajneeshpuram supported, mental health assistance for people they were initially just using to win an election was not at all a priority.

Some were ejected from the commune for acts of violence or anti-social behaviour. Some were chastised for minor infractions like leaving their shoes in the wrong place and got fed up enough to want to leave. Many were simply loaded onto buses, driven to nearby towns and dumped. The Salvation Army in the receiving towns was overwhelmed with the workload, suddenly having a town's-worth of people to shelter and relocate. Sheela was happy to source election-rigging bodies from as far afield as possible, but when it came to offloading them, she figured it wasn't worth the petrol to take them back to where they came from, and reneged on her original return-ticket offer – anywhere just around the corner would do. Oddly, people who live in small rural towns in Oregon and their surrounds did not respond well to busloads of mentally ill strangers suddenly appearing in their communities, especially when their communities did not have the resources to cope with the newcomers' needs. The locals' opinion of the Rajneeshees was further soured, if that level of sourness is even imaginable.

Sheela, and arguably the Bhagwan – though his vow of silence trick really had the potential to help him escape the blame for a lot of things – knew that it wouldn't take much for the surrounding locals to morph their rage into further persecution or even violence, so they became fifteen different kinds of paranoid and defensive. The Rajneeshee police force was heavily armed, and a firing range was set up so that regular followers could also learn how to operate the compound's growing collection of guns, sourced from shopping trips to Texas and New Mexico.

Additionally, Sheela was concerned about her own position, and became suspicious and spiteful towards any cult members she felt the Bhagwan was becoming close to or – shudder the thought – preferred. The Bhagwan non-coincidentally picked this time to end his years of silence, so Sheela was no longer the only cult member with access to him, privy to his whims and wishes. The guru had become close to his personal physician and his wife, a rich Californian who Sheela suspected was being groomed to replace her as the Bhagwan's main assistant. She became convinced that his physician was turning the Bhagwan into a drug addict and would either try to kill the guru or help him commit suicide, and, in her power-and-paranoia-induced delusion, decided the Bhagwan needed her protection. She recruited the help of fellow Rajneeshee elite Ma Shanti Bhadra – originally just plain old Catherine Jane Stork from Western Australia – to try to murder the physician by surreptitiously injecting him with adrenalin during a community gathering. It was Big Sheela's Murder Time once again, but this attempt was internal, rather than directed outwards to the cult's perceived intimidators. The attempt failed. Sheela felt like she was losing her grip on the cult.

After a long period of scheming to establish the group, defending the group against real and imagined threats, representing the group as a belligerent and feisty spokesperson, claiming that any detractors were religious or racial bigots, and wearing more and more nun-like, red satin robes, Sheela was done. One morning, the Bhagwan woke up to find Sheela and a small group of her closest associates gone. Convinced they were likely to be arrested, they'd scampered to West Germany to hide.

For years, Sheela had done everything she could to protect the Rajneeshees from the law in order to maintain her position of power. Granted, with poisoning and weapons training, she'd also seemingly done everything she could to *attract* attention from the law, but props are still due for how much hot water she'd prevented the group from being dunked into up until this point.

The protective favour was not returned by the Bhagwan, who now seemed to relish the fact that he was speaking again, taking every opportunity to speak out against Sheela and stretch his creative insult muscles. With Sheela's departing vapour trail still visible in the distance, the Bhagwan invited investigators – long gagging to get inside the ashram – to come in and search the entire compound. His main message to investigators was basically: anything good you find is because we are innocent. Anything bad you find is because Sheela is a criminal. She poisoned people, she attempted murder, she was the greedy one, she was the manipulator, she was the one who antagonised the locals, she stole money from me. The amount of glee and venom that the Bhagwan displayed when he was frenziedly blaming Sheela for stuff was almost admirable. The entire scenario felt to the world like an estranged husband and wife engaged in a slinging match in a divorce lawyer's office. They both accused each other of only being interested in money, power and fame instead of the welfare of their followers. To the untrained observer, it really seems like they were both right.

As investigators swept Rancho Rajneesh with increasing resistance from the initially co-operative remaining Rajneeshees, one of the most unexpected things they found was evidence of the largest wire-tapping operation the state had ever seen. Bugs were found in the Bhagwan's chair, in multiple telephones around the city, in more than thirty of the community's resident and guest rooms, and in its restaurant. The paranoia within the cult meant that its power committee had been secretly listening to its disciples and each other, trying to be a step ahead of any plots to undermine or usurp. Investigators also found a laboratory that looked very much like the kind of place that would develop poisons and other instruments of biological warfare, finally putting two and two together regarding the salad bar poisonings and relieved that it hadn't been the fault of restaurant staff not washing their hands after using the toilet. They realised they now had some crimes worth arresting people for.

Maintaining his own innocence, the Bhagwan and his new merry band of non-Sheela cronies transformed the cult in an attempt to remove any trace of her and the idiosyncrasies the group had adopted while she was around. No more orange or red clothes, he decreed. No more of his own image around people's necks. All of the available copies of the group's spiritual guide-book, *The Book of Rajneeshism*, burned in a massive bonfire along with Sheela's old fancy robes. The ultimate bitch-move in the ultimate bitch-fight: show Sheela that the incredible thing that she'd built from the ground up just didn't exist anymore. Ice cold, Bhagwan. Ice cold.

In another part of the world, having been uncovered as dirty lowdown poisoners, it wasn't long before Sheela and her mates were arrested in Germany and charged with attempted murder, conspiracy to commit murder, and first-degree assault. Extradited to the US, Sheela pleaded guilty and served just twenty-nine months of a twenty-year sentence in California, released for good behaviour, ever the crowd pleaser.

The Bhagwan didn't get off scot-free, either. Authorities found extensive evidence of immigration fraud as, despite his philosophical objection to the idea of marriage, the Bhagwan had encouraged and facilitated multiple weddings between cult members who were citizens of the US and those who were not but liked hanging out at Rajneeshpuram. For a bunch known colloquially as the Orange People, they sure did like green cards.

When he realised that his own imminent arrest was likely, the Bhagwan hoofed it. He *knew* that building an airport in his compound had been a good idea from the outset, and he packed up close to 60,000 US dollars, a massive swag of jewel-encrusted watches and eyeglasses, and his comfy chair, waved his ninety-three Rolls-Royces goodbye, and flew off in his Lear jet. Hey, Bhagwan? The feds *hate* it when people do that. He was stopped when the jet landed in North Carolina for refuelling and promptly charged with immigration fraud. It's quite likely that the arresting officers had never handcuffed a man in such a fancy dress and fluffy hat before.

The Bhagwan was given a suspended sentence, fined US$400,000, and asked extremely impolitely to leave the United States and not return. Like a cranky teenager asked to leave a party, he announced that he was done with America anyway, and this party SUCKS.

Once he'd left the United States, the Bhagwan flew to a number of countries trying to find one that was happy to accommodate a disgraced and globally maligned cult leader, but without having much luck in the area of international diplomacy and having run out of global favours, he found himself back where he started, in Pune.

With their guru gone, the remaining Rajneeshpuram residents didn't see any point hanging around, and eventually ceased operations and left. The Oregon compound is now disincorporated as a city, and is home to the Young Life Washington Family Ranch, a camp retreat for Christian teens who like hiking, swimming, sports, and completely missing the irony that they're celebrating wholesome chastity in what used to be Camp Sexy Time.

The Bhagwan, who called himself Osho in his later years, died of congestive heart failure at the age of fifty-eight. He looked a lot older thanks to the long grey beard and frail manner he had adopted for his entire career as a commercially viable guru. Spending half your life in a grandma-styled armchair is *not* the way to maintain the veneer of youthful exuberance.

The religion itself – also now called Osho – reaps the benefits of the Bhagwan's intellectual property, branding itself globally as a range of meditation schools, relaxation retreats, and corporate stress management seminars. They're everywhere. They're the McDonald's of meditation businesses, available in a city near you. It's funny how once you remove the leaders, some religions look exactly like companies.

After her release from prison, Sheela moved to Switzerland where she started and runs two aged-care homes. Presumably those who send their elderly parents to her for care are either unaware of her history of poisoning people, or they've decided to take a punt regardless. Still, rounding out a career of manipulation, aggressive swearing, flipping the bird, and building a city by helping old people go to the toilet in Switzerland feels like a bit of a fizzer. Couldn't happen to a nicer person.

THE END BIT

or

HOW TO TELL IF YOU'RE IN A CULT

You'll almost never hear anyone say, 'I'm in a cult.'

Most people don't know they're in one until their compound gets raided, or they're arrested for attempted murder, or they've sold all their possessions for an apocalypse that didn't arrive on time.

There's always clues, though. If you're in a group and you have any suspicions at all that you might really be in a cult, see how many times you answer 'yes' to the following questions.

When you joined the group, were they really over-the-top pumped to have you there? If you felt like the people already in the group loved the shit out of you, making your existing friendships and relationships seem lukewarm by comparison, you might be in a cult. Take a long hard look at yourself. You're all right, but those guys are unbelievably excited to see you.

Does the head of your group have an essential role in the group's story? If the main narrative of the group just couldn't either exist or be effectively delivered without the divine gifts or superior expertise of its leader, you might be in a cult. There are lots and lots of people who have claimed to be God's messenger, or at least the holder of life-changing secrets in the past, and the number of those who have turned out to be legitimate is extremely close to zero. What are the odds that you've stumbled across the first one to get it right? Come on. You're not that lucky.

Do you give money to the group, not for goods or services or training, but for access to secrets? Or to help 'spread the message'? If the secret or the message is going to save the world or help humanity progress, then what kind of self-interested, mean-spirited asshole asks for money for that? Sure, people pay for self-improvement books and classes, but you have to remember that if you're not seeing your money's worth of improvement, then it's not worth paying for, and if you have to keep paying for more and more of it, you might be in a cult. If I had an actual solution to the world's problems, it wouldn't be difficult to spread that message. If I had something that sounded vaguely like a solution to the world's problems but was actually just a bunch of empty words, then no amount of your money in my pockets is going to make people listen to it.

Are you being told what not to read? Look, recommending books is great. Recommending only books written by one person is less great. But if you're being told not to read things because they contain dangerous information, you might be in a cult. Cult leaders – and sometimes leaders of dictatorships, let's be fair – don't want their message diluted by irritating facts or differing opinions. If a group's message is threatened by outside voices, the message can't be much chop to begin with.

If you don't do specific things, will something terrible happen? Okay, if you don't look both ways before crossing the street you might get hit by a car, granted. But if you're being told that something very bad will happen if you either do things you've always done before, or don't do things that you've always gotten by not doing before, you might be in a cult. Especially and of most importance: don't let people tell you who you should have sex with, and don't let people tell you that if you don't inflict harm on somebody, bad shit will happen. Those people are bad people.

Are your friends or family suddenly bad people? If you always thought your friends and family were fine, but now you think they might be bad for you even though they haven't really changed, you might be in a cult. You're almost certainly in a cult if your friends and family keep saying, 'You're in a cult, come home.' See, because friends and family are always saying things like that to people who are in cults, while cult leaders try to convince their followers that friends and family are liars and a bad influence on you.

If you've just realised you're in a cult, then you should definitely tell somebody. Today. Tell somebody who isn't in a cult that you're in a cult TODAY.

If you've just realised that your gym *isn't* a cult and you'll have to find some other excuse to never go there, then yeah, sorry. Crunches still suck.

ACKNOWLEDGEMENTS

THANK YOU:

To Mum, Dad, Mike, Shelley, Mitchell, Amelia, and Will, because you're the best, most supportive family and you all help me think my personal projects are worthwhile and that I'm clever, regardless of reality. I love you.

To Tristan, Russ, Kristie Jane, Lorin, Cathrine, Frosty, and Jerry, because you're legitimately excellent friends, patient, unfairly good-looking, and clearly willing to listen to me repeating the same stories over and over again forever. And I mean forever. You're stuck with me, you poor bastards.

To all of the guests who agreed to record episodes of the *Zealot* podcast. Anyone willing to study a cult on their own time and then talk about it with me for no more reward than extremely delicious cheese and usually too many drinks is an excellent human.

To Karen and Georgia, who without knowing it gave me the inspiration to talk about bad stuff in a fun way, and knowingly gave me the opportunity to moonwalk on stage.

To Robert, who let me write this.

And to Charlotte, who always backed me, and who would have loved this.

AUTHOR'S NOTE

MY MATE EDDIE asked me to participate in a 'topic battle' on his community radio show, *Versus*. Basically, he would talk about a topic, I would talk about a topic, and listeners would text in to vote for the winner.

I was going to pick either serial killers or the 1985 teen dance movie *Girls Just Want to Have Fun* as my topic, but then settled on something I thought almost everyone is at least a little bit fascinated with: cults. I figured a couple of hours of research would be plenty to prepare for a fifteen-minute radio chat.

At 2 am on the morning of the radio show, I was still awake, hunched over my computer, gorging on information about every cult I could find. They're terrible. But they're *fascinating*.

Starting a podcast and writing a book were just excuses to keep reading about cults, and I'm not even going to pretend that's not true.

To both tip my hat to my favourite go-to sources for cult information and to tickle any readers' hankering for more, I have to mention where my horrified imagination has been spending much of its time over the past year.

The PBS documentary *Jonestown: The Life and Death of Peoples Temple* is an excellent and balanced introduction to Jim Jones's loathsome trajectory, and Jeff Guinn's book *The Road to Jonestown* is utterly comprehensive. Jones's narcissism means that his last words to his doomed followers were recorded, and they can be found on YouTube if you really insist on listening. Say goodbye to your upbeat mood, though.

If you like to be repulsed on a lighter note, the instructions for the Moonies' three-day sex ritual are spelt out in the publications available on the tparents.org website, one of the Unification Church's own sites. The story of the incredible mass weddings is told by the people participating in them in the Firecracker Films documentary *Married to the Moonies*.

You pretty much can't learn about Australian cult The Family without relying on the work of journalist Chris Johnston and filmmaker Rosie Jones. Their book *The Family* is essential reading, and Rosie's documentary of the same name has footage and voice recordings of Anne Hamilton-Byrne that you want to look away from but absolutely can't.

The utter creepiness of the Children of God cult is copiously recorded in the group's own publications, which have been painstakingly collected and reproduced at both exFamily.org and Xfamily.org. My strong advice should you choose to wade your way through hundreds of David Berg's 'Mo Letters' is to have a bucket nearby to vomit in.

Various *New York Times* journalists and Nicholas Kristof in particular have exhaustively followed and reported on Aum Shinrikyo since the cult released sarin gas on the Tokyo subway, examining Shoko Asahara from his origins to his execution.

While the feature film *Colonia* glosses over some of the more heinous details of Colonia Dignidad and peculiarly adds a romance element, the film's 2015 release triggered some excellent articles about the cult, like the UK *Telegraph*'s 'What happened in Colonia? Inside the terrifying Nazi cult that inspired Emma Watson's new film'.

Heaven's Gate's own website at heavensgate.com provides almost all the information you could ever want about the cult, and makes you feel truly icky about understanding why the members were happy to end their own lives.

Few sources on the Branch Davidians feel as immediate as the *Sinful Messiah* series from the *Waco Tribune-Herald*. The paper had only published the first two parts of a proposed seven-part deep-dive investigation of the cult when the ATF raided the Mount Carmel compound.

Consulting Rael TV – the Raelians' own YouTube channel – for unbiased, objective information about the cult is not advised, but it's unbeatable if you want to lose a few hours trudging through French accents, bad music, dodgy animations and the occasional bit of side-boob.

Finally, you absolutely can't go past the Netflix documentary series *Wild Wild Country* for an astonishing look inside the Rajneeshees in their prime, and *The Oregonian* newspaper also covered the cult in depth while it was in its backyard, occasionally with the kind of hyperbole that fed deputy leader Sheela's hair-trigger wrath.

Go. Read. Watch. Disturb yourselves.

And for the record, I totally won the topic battle on the radio.